Women, Religion, & Space

Space, Place, and Society

John Rennie Short, Series Editor

Women, Religion, & Space...

GLOBAL PERSPECTIVES ON GENDER AND FAITH

Edited by Karen M. Morin and Jeanne Kay Guelke

 SYRACUSE UNIVERSITY PRESS

The paper used in this publication meets the minimum requirements of
American National Standard for Information Sciences—Permanence of
Paper for Printed Library Materials, ANSI Z39.48–1984.∞™

For a listing of books published and distributed by Syracuse University Press,
visit our Web site at SyracuseUniversityPress.syr.edu.

Chapter 3 was originally published in a slightly different form as "Identity Issues and Local Governance:
Women's Everyday Life in the City," *Social Identities* 11 (1): 21–36. Reprinted by permission of
the author and the publisher.

ISBN-13: 978–0–8156–3116–3
ISBN-10: 0–8156–3116–2

Library of Congress Cataloging-in-Publication Data

Women, religion, and space : global perspectives on gender and faith / edited by Karen M. Morin
and Jeanne Kay Guelke.—1st ed.
p. cm.—(Space, place, and society)
Includes bibliographical references and index.
ISBN-13: 978–0–8156–3116–3 (pbk. : alk. paper)
ISBN-10: 0–8156–3116–2 (pbk. : alk. paper)
1. Women and religion. I. Morin, Karen M. II. Guelke, Jeanne Kay.
BL458.W63 2007
200.82—dc22   2007002078

Manufactured in the United States of America

Contents

Illustrations

Contributors

Kathryn Besio is assistant professor of geography at the University of Hawaii at Hilo. She received her Ph.D. in geography from the University of Hawaii at Manoa in 2001. Her research interests are in feminist postcolonial and post-structural theories and travel/tourism and gender, focusing regionally in South Asia and the Pacific. She has published recently in *Area, The Professional Geographer,* and *Gender, Place and Culture.*

Tovi Fenster is a senior lecturer at the Department of Geography and Human Environment at the Tel Aviv University, Israel. She has published articles and book chapters on ethnicity, citizenship, and gender in planning and development. She is the editor of *Gender, Planning and Human Rights* (Routledge: 1999) and author of *The Global City and the Holy City: Narratives on Knowledge, Planning and Diversity* (Pearson: 2004). She is the founder and the first chair (2000–2003) of Bimkom-Planners for Planning Rights in Israel and has been on the board of directors of the Association for Civil Rights in Israel (1994–1999).

Banu Gökarıksel is assistant professor of geography at the University of North Carolina at Chapel Hill. She received her Ph.D. in geography at the University of Washington in 2003. Her research has examined questions of modernity and politics of identity with a focus on the new social spaces of neoliberalism in urban Muslim settings, particularly that of Istanbul. Her current research on the Islamic fashion industry and Islamic women's rights organizations investigates the formation of Muslim identities and spaces within the cultural, economic, and political context of neoliberalism and transnationalism. Her work has been published in *Global Networks* and *Magazine on Architectural Culture*

(Ankara) and in a special issue on cultural studies in *ToplumBilim* (Social Theory) (Istanbul).

Jeanne Kay Guelke is professor of geography at the University of Waterloo, Ontario. She studies how past societies understood and altered their environments, particularly through the lenses of their religious beliefs and ideas about gender. Her recent journal articles appeared in *Environmental Ethics, Journal of Historical Geography,* and *The Canadian Geographer.* Her paper "Concepts of Nature in the Hebrew Bible" first appeared in *Environmental Ethics* and subsequently in three published anthologies.

Leonard Guelke is professor of geography at the University of Waterloo, Ontario. Professor Guelke's research focuses on historical geography, history and philosophy of geography, political geography, comparative frontier settlement, and historical geography of South Africa. Guelke is the author of *Historical Understanding in Geography: An Idealist Approach* (Cambridge University Press: 1982).

Jennifer Kopf is assistant professor of geography in the History and Geography Department at West Texas A&M University. She received her doctoral degree in geography at the University of Kentucky in 2005, where she also completed a certificate in social theory. Research in Berlin archives and libraries for her dissertation on spatial strategies of resistance in Wilheminan German East Africa (Kopf 2005) was partially funded by the German Academic Exchange Service. She conducted additional research in the Tanzanian National Archives and Tanzanian National Museum in Dar es Salaam.

Karen M. Morin is associate professor of geography at Bucknell University in Lewisburg, Pennsylvania. Her research focuses on relationships among nineteenth-century women's travel writing and British and American imperialisms, providing new angles for understanding questions of identity and gender in social geography. In addition to her current interest in women's religious landscapes of North America, she is also working on a study of geographical thought in the United States during the nineteenth century. She has published more than forty research articles, book chapters, and commentaries and serves on a number of editorial boards.

Anna J. Secor is associate professor of geography at the University of Kentucky. She received her Ph.D. from the University of Colorado in Boulder in 2000. She has published articles on gender, political participation, and Islam in Turkey. Her current research project is on the urban geography of civil society and the state in Istanbul. She serves on the editorial board of *Cultural Geographies.*

HaeRan Shin is a lecturer in planning at the Bartlett School of Planning, University College London. Her academic interests include poverty studies, especially women's poverty, planning theory, cultural festivals, urban politics, and immigrant studies. She has focused on the constrained capability and the adaptive preferences of Korean immigrant women in Los Angeles. She completed her Ph.D. in Planning in the School of Policy, Planning, and Development at the University of Southern California in 2006.

Preface

Karen M. Morin

George W. Bush's theocratic U.S. presidency has given many observers a sudden appreciation for the geography of religion. Since his reelection in November 2004, many scholars, public intellectuals, and journalists have recognized the need for a better understanding of the politics of religion in American life (and elsewhere), for example, in understanding the red, blue, and purple maps of the United States that quickly circulated on the Internet[1] after the election and that depicted Republican, Democratic, and mixed regions, respectively. The maps documented election results that Bush's critics perceived as implausible, given that his first four years in office produced two unfinished wars; a record U.S. deficit; and widespread disapproval of the state of social security, environmental protection, and health care. The morning news following the election emphasized that Bush won the day principally by tapping into the "religious morals" of 59 million Americans. The vote culminated what the popular news media described as a gradual American religious turn to the right over the past several decades, and the current Republicans' effective politicization of social conservative issues such as opposition to gay marriage, abortion, and the use of embryos for stem cell research. The Republicans' popularity among Christian Evangelicals and Roman Catholics, especially those in low-populated areas of the South and Midwest, raised new questions about religion's connection to rurality, social conservatism, public space, public discourse, and war, among others.

Of course, what often gets left out of the discussion, and should not, is that there are many Evangelicals and Catholics who are against the war, are anti-death penalty, and are in support of universal health care, environmental stewardship, a just welfare state, and more equitable taxes—and for faith-based reasons. Such beliefs provide opportunities to broaden what we mean by "moral" issues at stake in American politics.

European reaction to President Bush's reelection was illustrated on the front page of London's 4 November 2004, *Daily Mirror,* with a headline that shrieked, "How Can 59 Million Americans Be So Dumb?" The postelection rhetoric of many urbanites in the metropolitan United States expressed the same sentiment of an urgent need to enlighten the ignorant people in those rural, middle states who fundamentally seemed not to understand that a vote for Bush was a vote against themselves. We participated in such discourse ourselves. And yet, as we considered some of our own research on nineteenth-century religious causes (e.g., Morin and Guelke 1998; Morin 2000; Morin and Berg 2001), we realized the extent to which such opinions bore a striking similarity to colonial discourses about the worldviews of "heathen" indigenous peoples in the U.S. interior and colonies. North American and British missionaries, educators, bureaucrats, and others described backward, superstitious, unenlightened people who were in need of the saving power of metropolitan modes of thought, which many of those "formerly ignorant" ultimately adopted.

As numerous postcolonial critics have persuasively argued, however (e.g., Orange 1996), indigenous peoples were not tricked into becoming Christians in those colonial settings; rather, their adoption of Christianity made sense because missionaries (for example) also offered literacy, useful trading networks, a new social status, and protection from enemies in addition to a set of religious beliefs. Thinking about Bush supporters in this context helped us recognize that what is needed is not a liberal dismissal of them or their religious zeal as ignorant or unenlightened, but rather a better understanding of what interests, priorities, and moral frameworks the Christian Right furthered by supporting President Bush.

Contextualizing the role of religion in politics seems especially important in the case of American women voters. Many of President Bush's policies that directly impacted women seemed to undermine funding for the social programs they typically supported. American women had, until this election, favored Democrats who championed issues such as education, health care, child welfare, and reproductive rights; they tended to be suspicious of anything that resembled the 'muscular' foreign and military policies more typical of Republicans. However, in 2004, the gender gap closed sharply as married men and women with children voted virtually the same *(USA Today,* 5 November 2004, "Security Moms Narrowed Gender Gap").

Overall, the 2004 election reminded Americans—as if Americans needed reminding after the 9/11 attacks on the World Trade Center in 2001 and immersion in wars in both Afghanistan and Iraq—that a better understanding of the role of religion in America and abroad was urgently needed. Charges of anti-Muslim bias in government counterterrorism measures (such as the Homeland Security Act) and of Americans' blind spot to the nation's image in the Islamic world highlighted the need for more understanding of religion as a potent social force.

In an 18 November 2004 *New York Times* editorial ("Under the Cover of Islam"), Toronto-based Irshad Manji, author of the controversial *The Trouble with Islam* (2004), argued that there are key differences in public debates about Islam in North America compared with Europe. She explains that people in Europe ask her a question that is never asked in the United States or Canada: "Why would an independent minded woman care about God?" Manji explains that in Europe the entry point for the discussion of Islam is the hijab (the veil or headscarf), whereas the entry point for the discussion in North America is terrorism (where the headscarf "hardly makes a ripple"). Manji asserts that religion itself is not seen as categorically "irrational" or antimodern to many in North America the way it appears to Europeans. Manji herself is a religious Muslim because it

> supplies a set of values, including discipline, that serve as a counterweight to the materialism of life in the West. I could have become a runaway materialist, a robotic mall rat who resorts to retail therapy in pursuit of fulfillment. I didn't. That's because religion introduces competing claims. It injects a tension that compels me to think and allows me to avoid fundamentalisms of my own. (A29)

Manji's insights into the needs and desires satisfied through religion are instructive. Tragically, and contrary to what she also argues, women carrying visible signs of Islam do come under direct suspicion and attack in the United States and Canada in addition to Europe, as Alvi, Hoodfar, and McDonough (2003) amply document. Their cases raise questions about the geographies of the veil as well as how American First Amendment rights to religious freedom affect men and women differently.

The imagined threats posed by the Muslim woman's hijab stand in stark contrast to the provocative translation of veiling by hip-hop artist Lil' Kim. Kim's performance of the "bikini bourka" on the front cover of the December/January 2003 issue of Russell Simmons's *One World* magazine forces us to think through the nexus between Islam and women's liberation (after Chan 2004). The image of Kim wearing an Afghani-like bourka over her face and shoulders while exposing her breasts and much of the rest of her body was roundly condemned by right-leaning Islamist groups in the West who argued that the image was an attack on both Islam and women. Did Lil' Kim's image expose a clash of civilizations? East and West are not comfortably wedded in this photo; rather, they seem to grate against one another. Or does posing such a question in the first instance make unsupportable Orientalist assumptions about Islamic cultures in the East versus the West (Said 1978)? And in what sense can the question be filtered through Black American culture that has a long association with the Nation of Islam? We think the image forces geographers in particular to question the meaning of the bourka and bikini in various spatial contexts and what each might offer—or deny—women in those contexts. Although non-Muslims carry many suppositions about what the bourka offers or denies, they might very well question in what sense the bikini represents liberation politics for women.

Such an understanding is not inconsequential. On the same day that George Bush was reelected U.S. president, the Dutch filmmaker Theo Van Gogh was stabbed and shot to death in Amsterdam, presumably as retribution for his film *Submission,* which depicts violence against women in Islamic societies. Like Lil' Kim, Van Gogh triggered outcry from right-leaning Muslims.

The preceding examples of issues involving women in contemporary American culture demonstrate that geography matters a great deal in efforts to make sense of religious tension or conflict, but also of taken-for-granted norms of religious belief and practice. The red, blue, and purple maps became popular precisely because they illustrated spatial differences, although such maps have a tendency to elide differences among men and women with regard to morality, religious practices, and experiences. Highly educated American women in the Northeast were more likely to vote Democratic in 2004, but this

1. Lil' Kim's "Bikini Bourka." From One World, *December–January 2003. Photograph by Alexei Hay, courtesy of Icon International. Reproduced with permission.*

point only reifies the religious and regional cleavages between them and women who are Southern born-again Christians and who viewed "family values" as more important than liberal causes. Fundamentalist Islam and the status of Muslim women have radically different meanings to people, depending in part on *where* they encounter the hijab. Hip-hop grew out of a particular American inner-city subculture, and Lil' Kim's photo would probably be as antithetical to the American Christian Right as it was to devout Muslims, less on account of the photo's confrontation with Islam than because their own Christian-derived family values include female modesty—except in perhaps certain *spaces* such as the bedroom or the beach.

In this book we provide a forum for thinking through issues of gender, religion, and geography. We bring a geographical sensitivity to the norms, ideologies, behaviors, and everyday worlds of women embedded in the three principal monotheistic religions—Christianity, Judaism, and Islam—across cultural and historical contexts. The papers and discussions collected here were first presented in two sessions of the 2004 Association of American Geographers annual conference in Philadelphia. They are organized by three distinct yet linked themes: women in colonial regimes, religion and women's mobility, and new spaces for religious women. We would like to thank all the participants in those sessions, including Rachel Daack (2004) for her presentation and Anne Godlewska for her wonderfully provocative commentary. We would also like to thank Bucknell University for covering some subvention fees, as well as Mary Selden Evans and her reviewers and staff at Syracuse University Press who enthusiastically supported and graciously guided the project to publication.

Introduction

Women, Religion, and Space—Making the Connections

Karen M. Morin and Jeanne Kay Guelke

Most of the theology and practices of Christianity, Islam, and Judaism were developed by men at times and places when women's inferior social (if not metaphysical) status seemed self-evident and where men placed premiums on women's sexual virtue. Reading patriarchal foundational texts for information on gender and geography reveals ideological frameworks and related practices that (re)produce a corollary of women's spaces of inclusion, exclusion, and containment, regulating women in particular ways both discursively and materially.

Women's and men's religious experiences may differ significantly because religions often promote segregation in ritual practices, congregation attendance, ordination, religious life, and religious identities. Such differences have geographical expressions within faith communities and outside of them as well. They define religious women's experiences in diaspora communities and shape women's access to experiences of so-called public spaces. Religious practice often requires a spatial separation of men and women that comes with associated power differentials. A worship service, for example, may be highly spatialized, as men typically officiate and have control and access to exclusive sites of power (and "the sacred") within a religious building. The Roman Catholic Church, for example, prohibits women from administering sacraments and maintains separate communities for men and women joining religious orders. In most of the major Christian denominations until only recently, only men could hold pulpits in congregations or senior administrative positions within their central hierarchies. In Orthodox Judaism, women remain prohibited from the altar and have separate seating from men in religious services and rituals. Spatial practice in the mosque in traditional Islam similarly separates worshippers.

Perhaps to offset such exclusionary practices some faiths segregate religious women into specific career opportunities and lifestyles, such as orders of Roman Catholic nuns who teach in parochial schools or work in hospitals. Many Western denominations also sanction separate women's auxiliary organizations for charitable purposes. Yet, traditionally, most of the monotheistic traditions have located women's primary arena for religious practice not in the public house of worship or church-sanctioned organization but in the private home. Traditional Judaism restricts women's time-bound religious duties, such as lighting Sabbath candles, to the household. In the New Testament St. Paul forbids female preachers and advises that women attain redemption through their duties as wife and mother (Ephesians 5: 21–33). Taking their cue from St. Paul, Christian clergymen historically taught women to be obedient to their husbands. There is a great deal of spatiality to such religious precepts, because they principally reinforce women's "proper" location in the home. This is not specifically true for men, who can be "good Christians," for example, while also being soldiers or traveling salesmen.

Historians of religious women identify strategies used by female preachers, women's benevolent societies, nonconformist denominations, Roman Catholic convents, and Protestant female seminaries to subvert the spatial restrictions of conventional domesticity (Brekus 1998; Ginzberg 1990; Eason 2003; Braude 1989; Coburn and Smith 1999; Porterfield 1997). Indeed, a religious calling seemed to be the most important way in which "respectable" nineteenth-century women could leave the traditional household while maintaining their moral capital, such as by becoming missionary teachers or by taking holy orders. Within the "patriarchal bargain" (Kandiyoti 1988) religious women negotiated and generated alternative spaces for preeminence or autonomy, regardless of their obvious and fundamental goal of spreading their faith. The Roman Catholic convent, for example, may regulate religious women and place them under the Vatican's authority, but it is also a female space of administration, economic subsistence, intellectual advancement, and sometimes retreat. In their benevolent work, such female societies also often owned significant financial assets and real estate. This concept provides an important supplement to feminist observations of the legal restrictions placed upon single or married women in the eighteenth and nineteenth centuries, when statutes seriously limited women's ability to own or inherit property in their own right. As chartered or quasi corporations, religious women's organizations could own and manage their own property such as the convent, but also the YWCA hotel and maternity hospital (Ginzberg 1990).

Some Christian women in the United States, even within the more restrictive norms of the nineteenth century, also deployed their faith's own proof texts and concepts of morality to negotiate with churchmen in support of enlarged spheres for women. These women used New Testament verses beyond Paul's mandates in Ephesians to underscore their faith's goal for the entire world as a land converted to their vision of Christianity (Hackett 1995; Hill 1985; Robert 1996; Wiesner-Hanks 2000). For example, it was difficult for patriarchal Christian men to refute determined and devout women's arguments that Jesus's mandate of global conversion required women to become more proficient in Bible reading and better educated as teachers so that they could more effectively bring the gospel to their own children or young pupils (Lindley 1996; Hitchcock 1858).

Although many feminists such as Fessenden (2000) have argued for the need to consider religion as another source of women's differences, and although much has been written about how religion regulates women's sexuality (Webster 1995; Wiesner-Hanks 2000), scholars of women and religion seldom focus on the spatial implications of such differences. *Women, Religion, and Space* draws out the geographical dimensions and spatial implications of the study of religion and women that have been neglected both within "women and religion" studies as well as within geography. Few have asked, for example, how religious women created and supervised female-managed spaces or how they negotiated and contested male-controlled religious spaces in order to pursue their own personal goals. The purpose of this volume is therefore to reveal more explicitly the connections between women's studies, religion, and geography.

With a few exceptions (such as Kay 1997; Dwyer 1999a, 1999b; Secor 2003; Spain 1992) little attention has been paid to the question of women and religion in geography, and particularly within the geography of religion subfield, women (and gender) are seldom investigated (cf. Park 1994; Stump 2000; Kong

2001). This may be due largely to the gender blindness inherent in typical geographies of religion, which are undertaken at the scale of the culture group or
of competing ideologies. Many geographers of religion would see their research as inclusive of both women and men, rather than male oriented. Examples include textbook chapters devoted to mapping religious affiliations in
different regions (Norton 1998; Fellman, Getis, and Getis 2001), studies of
geopolitical religious conflict (such as between Israel and Palestine), and discussions of sacred places as well as historical geographies of particular religious
groups (Hervieu-Léger 2002; Holloway and Valins 2002; Ben-Arieh and Kark
1989–1997; Olsen and Guelke 2004; Brace, Bailey, and Harvey 2006).

As indicated in our opening paragraphs, however, political geographies can
have obvious implications for gender- and women-sensitive studies. Human
geographers who are beginning to look more closely at religion as another
identity marker (like age, ethnicity or race, nationality, physical ability, and sexual orientation) and who are considering religion as a source of difference with
associated spatial patterns must also consider that religion is not simply another way of studying social difference. Religion is more than "difference" or
"identity politics" in that it has its own epistemologies and metaphysics that
can, nonetheless, produce multiple ways of being in the world, because religious beliefs are embedded within larger webs of historically situated social
formations and relations of power. And yet, as religion entails the internalization of particular modes of moral conduct, a particular idea of the self, and
particular relationships to secular and religious laws, it operates to many believers as a foundational mode of development of self-identity and spatial behaviors. Thus, the aim of this volume is to cast some needed light on how the
religious imagination works through other axes of social difference to shape
and order space.

In that sense, our project builds on the important work begun in the recent
volume edited by Falah and Nagel (2005), which we view as a significant and
complementary project to our own, albeit with a narrower focus. Falah and
Nagel's collection brings issues of space and place to the forefront of accounts
of Muslim women's lived experience by investigating development processes
mediated by Islamic practices and discourses, through study of migration and
mobility, and through analysis of media and other representations of Muslim
women. Our project builds upon this work by including additional groups

(Christian and Jewish as well as Muslim), by considering colonial or historical contexts, and by examining religion as more than an identity marker. In addition, many of our authors write from personal experiences as transnational subjects negotiating religion and space.

Like Falah and Nagel (2005), we take as a premise that the discipline of geography offers many important insights into the study of women and religion. We want to make explicit the extent to which religion regulates women spatially and to explore how religious women negotiate and define spaces and their sense of themselves within them. We hope to clarify, moreover, that different women uphold, negotiate, or contest such divisions and that they are never complete, as many of the authors in this volume demonstrate. Such divisions also rely on a set of gender ideologies that are implicit or explicit in religious belief systems, embodied through particular men and women. Thus, although our primary focus on women rather than gender in the volume may seem like an outdated feminist approach, we emphasize that each of our authors simultaneously considers the dynamics of gender difference as crucial to those women's experiences (as are other axes of social difference, race, and class in particular).

Triangulating Women, Religion, and Space

What, then, might be some contributions of studies of religious women, or of secular women confronting religion, to human geography today? What theories might inform our volume's themes of women in colonial regimes, religion and women's mobility, and new spaces for religious women? In order to delve a bit deeper into the fertile field of investigation offered by our triangulation among women, religion, and space, we offer the following vignettes for consideration.

• Medieval Roman Catholic nuns routinely worked outside of their convents within their communities and served as missionaries to overseas colonies, enjoying considerable freedom in their personal mobility. But in 1662 clergymen at the Council of Trent sought to confine European nuns to their cloisters (Strasser 2001).

• More than 150 years later, the powerful Queen Kaahumanu of Hawaii graciously granted to a small band of American Protestant missionaries some land for their compound. A missionary wife nevertheless recorded her consternation one Sunday in 1825 that their benefactor seated herself in the chapel at the same level as the minister and facing the congregation (Grimshaw 1989).

• During the 1970s, Hindu women in northern India protested their loss of access to government-managed forest reserves, prompting scholars to debate the influence of Hindu goddess beliefs and gender roles in the now-famous Chipko environmental movement (Shiva 1988; Agarwal 1998).

• Today in Western nations, public and scholarly debate finds a flash point in the veil worn by Muslim women (Alvi, Hoodfar, and McDonough 2003; Dwyer 1999a, 1999b). Can the veil be understood as a symbol of a Muslim woman's oppression? Does it confirm her right to legitimately and modestly occupy public space? Is it to be understood primarily as a symbol of religious affiliation? Or something else?

Geographers would immediately recognize in the above examples their familiar themes of land management and tenure, access to public land, imperialism, migration, human ecology, spatial behavior, and contested space. With a little more probing, we would find further food for geographical thought. For instance, how do particular religious or gendered identities depend upon specific places? The identity of missionary applies only in "heathen" or "gentile" locations; a veiled Muslim girl attracts attention today in France's public schools but not in Islamic contexts where the veil is common. To ask further why religious authorities in both seventeenth-century Europe and in many Islamic communities today regulate women's mobility in public places, or why the nineteenth-century missionary wife interpreted the actions of the Hawaiian ruler as *out of place* in the Protestant chapel, is to delve into the underlying theme of the production and representation of *space*.

Geographers today debate the definition of *space* but we use it here in the sense of categories of places in the collective or abstract, such as "the city," "at school," or "in public." Geographers often use the adjective *spatial* to discuss peoples' movements at different scales of analysis, ranging from the daily activity paths of an individual Iranian woman donning a headscarf before shopping in her local market to large refugee movements of Albanian Muslim women in the former Yugoslavia fleeing paramilitary assaults.

To geographers, particular places or types of space (such as the missionaries' church in Hawaii or "the convent") are not merely neutral backdrops to human actions but are imbued with culturally inscribed meanings and power relations. Both individuals and groups of people may control, contest, or negotiate their access to kinds of spaces (such as nuns' cloisters or Muslim girls in Paris protesting the headscarf ban in public schools) or specific places (such as Hindu women insisting upon their access to a forest reserve in northern India). People also contest space on a more ideological level, in terms of who has the power to ascribe dominant or normative meanings to a sacred site. Disputes may occur between or within faith communities (fundamentalists versus feminists) as well as across religious versus secular divides. Although their work does not focus on either women or religion, readers familiar with the "production of space" and "rights to the city" concepts sketched above and articulated by Henri Lefebvre (1991b) and Don Mitchell (2003) can infer their utility in understanding such women, religion, and space issues.

In between commonly accepted, taken-for-granted meanings of places versus highly contested aggressive territorial conflict, people often debate the proper uses of space, because to determine the meanings and appropriate symbolism pertaining to space is to dominate the battle for hegemonic control over it. For instance, in what way does the Muslim girl's veil worn in a public school classroom confront the ideology of France as a secular nation? How did the Hindu women's traditional environmental beliefs challenge secular managers' Western-derived policies about public access to forest reserves? In the Hawaiian example cited above, Queen Kaahumanu did cede her place at the head of the congregation at the clergyman's request, which the American missionary community promptly interpreted as a moral victory that leveraged their control over her subjects (Grimshaw 1989). Cresswell (1996) noted that a society's belief that an action or person is "in place" or "out of place" is more than metaphorical but has real political and material consequences.

Space that is *encoded* (represented, interpreted) through popular religious beliefs or by religious authorities is often simultaneously gendered in the eyes of a particular society, in part because the religious regulation of women's sexuality often has a spatial dimension and because religious practices tend to differentiate between spaces allocated to men and women (although again, such allocations never go uncontested). Orthodox Judaism's exclusion of women from the altar of the synagogue due to menstrual prohibitions and sex-segregated Roman Catholic cloisters exemplify such interactions between religion and gendered space. Religious faiths often interpret space in highly symbolic ways, just as women's mobility may have serious ramifications for concepts of family honor (Peleman 2003). Similarly, secular authorities may seek to regulate their subjects' religious and gendered activities in order to support their concepts of cultural superiority and rational governance. The U.S. federal government's efforts to abolish Mormon plural marriage before 1890 would be one such instance. In the Chipko example cited above, one can infer a contest over traditional female common property rights versus male-dominated government agency control simultaneously with a clash between traditional local religious beliefs about forests versus secular management objectives.

When religion is invoked in the contest to define space or place, therefore, competing parties may draw lines between what they define as modern versus premodern or antimodern sensibilities. Religious authorities may seek to regulate women's access to their sacred sites regardless of whether the women are members of their own faith, just as secular authorities may constrain both secular and religious women's behavior such as in marriage and childbearing customs.

Spatial contests also occur at various *scales,* ranging from an individual's personal space (body) to the residence to the urban neighborhood to the nation or supranational level. Different interpretations of space and appropriate spatial conduct occur—and are contested—at these various scales as well (Marston 2000; Purcell 2003b). For example, the "local" Chipko movement in India gained international attention, which brought considerable pressure to bear on Indian foresters. When Queen Kaahumanu yielded her seat in the Hawaiian chapel in 1825, the American missionary community present interpreted this "local" act as having regional significance. In seeking careers as overseas missionary teachers, nineteenth-century American women to a degree subverted the Victorian "angel in the house" ideology of woman firmly planted in the (local) home. Religion, then, has the potential to restrict women to household and local scales as well as to enlarge their sphere of activity to international levels. Religion is of particular interest in the politics of scale by including a cosmic scale beyond the globe in its beliefs of afterlife, heaven, and divinity and in its ecclesiastical districts (parish, diocese, mission field), which vary from discussions of scale based on traditional political jurisdictional boundaries (municipal, provincial, national).

The links between identity, scale, and place are particularly intriguing for missionary women who traveled and worked in areas remote from their homes with the support of their religious denominations, at a time when those same denominations situated the typical Christian woman's domain as restricted to the domestic sphere. Indeed, the female objects of evangelical movements sometimes found that the more "advanced" societies in fact applied far more restrictions to women's mobility than they had experienced under their traditional and supposedly less-enlightened mores (Grimshaw 1989).

Contents of the Volume

Although *Women, Religion, and Space* is organized into the three themes mentioned earlier, other links among the chapters occur through such issues as contested space (chapters 1 through 5), women's empowerment in the margins (chapters 1, 6, and 7), immigration (chapters 2 and 7), interstitial public and private spaces (chapters 5 and 7), state formation (chapters 1, 2, and 4), and religion's relation to modernity versus traditionalism (chapters 4 and 5). Each chapter offers a case study of particular women and religious issues in situ that illustrate in more depth how women, religion, and space interact in specific locations.

Our goal in producing an inclusive volume that touches upon women of different cultures, faiths, and periods recommends attention to the impacts of colonial regimes upon colonized people as well as colonized peoples' experiences, agency, and contributions to the emergence of new places and societies. Chapter 1 on colonial Tanzania reveals efforts by German authorities to suppress two potentially subversive Muslim women's religious movements by restricting their access to sites where the women's practices flourished. Jennifer Kopf's work, based on research in the German and Tanzanian National Archives, looks at the repression by the German colonial government of two movements within Islam in colonial Tanganyika that involved changes in the ways women practiced Islam and challenged the established colonial regime: the call for women to build mosques and pray like men and the spread of Dervish circles.

In chapter 2, Leonard Guelke describes the tensions in seventeenth-century South Africa between European racism and the conversion of women of color to Christianity, with attendant church-sanctioned intermarriage. These tensions ruptured into the beginnings of apartheid with the subsequent immigration of white women to the colony and interpretation of Christianity as a specifically European heritage. For the Dutch colonial regime, categorizing women by race/ethnicity and religion was absolutely fundamental to the apartheid project because of the centrality of marriage and baptism in the Dutch Reformed Church. Religion and race had numerous repercussions for women's and children's legal entitlements, such as landholding. Apartheid also varied spatially, with more interracial marriages in the Cape Town core than on the colonial margins.

Women's rights or entitlements to public spaces, how they negotiate space in their day-to-day lives, and the role that religion plays in their activity patterns are all important geographical considerations. Human geographers are aware that ideologies of women's "proper place" vary across religious groups in different locations and are aware of the degree to which different groups of women uphold, negotiate, or contest the normalized spatial patterns of behavior (cf. Kay 1997; Dwyer 1999a, 1999b; Secor 2002, 2003; Falah and Nagel 2005). But such patterns are dynamic. We must also ask what happens to spatial concepts affecting women in a society undergoing major changes in its religious and gender norms, such as under the impress of immigration to a new country, modernity, or conversion to a new faith (McMichael 2002; Fenster 1999a).

Thus, the ideological basis of the gendered division of space and women's negotiation of space in their day-to-day lives constitute the second important theme for this volume, religion and women's mobility. Urban space may be considered in various ways, such as the contrast between the parochial space of the neighborhood where women feel free to socialize with neighbors and friends versus the spaces of strangers or the contrast between moral and immoral landscapes for women as religious authorities define them (Lofland 1998). Beyond the limits of these typologies, it is clear that most societies have different expectations for women and men in their access to space outside the home and that these expectations vary by ethnic identity, socioeconomic class, and other variables, often in highly personal and nuanced ways. Of course most urban public spaces today are not neatly demarcated as strictly male or female but are encoded with far more complex and subtle variables relating to individuals' religion, ethnicity, notions of modernity, and other social markers as well as to the morphology of the city itself (Spain 1992; Ruddick 1996; Bondi 1998).

Within this context, in chapter 3 Tovi Fenster examines contemporary ultraorthodox Jewish neighborhoods in Jerusalem compared with those of New York and London. She shows how the construction of these neighborhoods as patriarchal religious spaces that prescribe women's proper attire in public depends upon government policy and the religious minority or majority status of the communities. Her chapter highlights the links between cultural and religious gendered constructions of public spaces and urban planning and management. Looking at other ultraorthodox neighborhoods in other cities reveals that such constructions of patriarchal religious spaces do not exist where the role and power of local communities is less significant within the nation-state political context.

In chapter 4, Banu Gökarıksel considers the ongoing conflict between modern secularism and traditional Islam in Istanbul and its impact on female consumers who must navigate between these competing identities when out in public space. Gökarıksel's ethnographic study of shopping malls reveals that the construction of urban Muslim middle-class identities involves the weaving together of discourses of neoliberalism, modernity, and Islam. Within the secularist framework of state modernity in Istanbul, these practices challenge the republican definition of secularism in public space, thus underlining the significance of geographic theory to gender and religion and revealing the place-specific formulations of secularism and modernity. Her discussion interrogates both the potential and the limits of "consumer-citizenship" and highlights the gendered and political nature of secular and religious spaces and the paradoxes of neoliberal Islamism.

Valentine (1989) was one of the first geographers to note that urban women today experience a complex set of decisions, routes, feelings of confidence, and fears when walking on city streets, notably at night. Fear of assault or harassment out-of-doors indeed confines many urban women to their homes at particular times or discourages them from taking the notion of public space too inclusively (Macey 1999; Peleman 2003). This is not necessarily the case for men out-of-doors. In part to negate unwanted harassment of women, Orthodox Jews, many Islamic societies, and the Christian Amish (among others) prescribe particular modest apparel for women outside the home, but differently interpreted and enforced in different subcultures (Secor 2002; Alvi, Hoodfar and McDonough 2003; Mazumdar and Mazumdar 2001; Herrera 2001).

Religious and gendered representations of urban space can also affect non-religious women and women of different faiths, particularly in the realm of clothing restrictions and prescriptions for the use of public transportation. Western women tourists to some Asian countries, for example, are warned not to wear scanty summer clothing when entering religious buildings or neighborhoods of conservative adherents in the Near East. To understand such codes of behavior and their role in constructing religious space, in chapter 5 Kathryn Besio examines contemporary tourism guide books and their discussion of religious sites and gender-appropriate conduct for female tourists in Pakistan, an area where she has conducted extensive fieldwork. Women travelers often visit religious sites such as cathedrals and mosques, gazing upon religious landscapes from their positions as secular and modern subjects. However, in some Muslim countries such as Pakistan, travelers are compelled to experience the religious landscape in a much more embodied manner, through adoption of local clothing, norms of bodily comportment, and sex-based segregation in public places. Besio's chapter shows how these religiously based prescriptions and practices produce women travelers' embodied knowledge of a gendered self as secular and modern and, at the same time, supports the notion that neo-colonialism today clearly affects local religious beliefs and gender ideologies (Dahles and Bras 1999; Aitchison 2001).

The figure of the Western Christian woman missionary is another example of the intersection of gender, religion, and space, at times an agent of the colonial government or at least a promoter of its supposedly superior level of civilization but also a moral critic of that occupying power (Robert 1996; Morin 2000; Morin and Berg 2001) or even an agent of such feminist goals as improved women's health care and literacy. In the third part of the book, which focuses on new spaces for religious women, Jeanne Kay Guelke and Karen M. Morin argue in chapter 6 that the religious and personal goals of nineteenth-century Christian missionary women were achieved through communitarian organizations, female-only residences, education, and missionary work that basically deployed Christian precepts through shifting the scale of women's proper sphere. We explore alternative and more complex models of pious Christian women's spaces based upon human geography's recent concerns with the production of space and the politics of scale, arguing that religious women's autonomy and increasing spheres of action reflected their ability to marshal community-level resources and to align with their church's global evangelical project, notwithstanding prevalent ideologies that positioned women within the household.

In chapter 7, HaeRan Shin examines the experiences of Korean immigrant women to Los Angeles and the new religious spaces offered by that process. Shin conducted in-depth interviews with forty-two Korean-born Christian women who immigrated to Los Angeles. Traditional restrictions on women's behavior carried readily from Confucianism to evangelical Christianity, which, together with the dislocating, marginalizing aspects of their immigrant status, served to confine many of her older subjects to their homes, apart from the economic mainstream. Shin argues that Christianity plays an essential role in forming Korean immigrant Christian women's identities and provides a social network. Religion helps these women adjust emotionally to a new place, but does so in ways that limit their ultimate mainstreaming into society.

Anna Secor concludes the volume in an afterword that offers some reflections and suggestions for further research at the interface between gender, religion, and space. Together with Secor our hope is to provide some directions in which such new research might proceed. Political analysts in the United States realized for some decades that women formed an important voting block, but the unexpected shift by female voters in 2004 to moral values and homeland security policies with religious foundations suggest one such direction. More vital to this volume are the continuing need to grapple with the legacy of colonialism for women's personal autonomy; to question women's complicity with various political-religious regimes that limit their access to and mobility within public spaces; and to understand more fully and support women's agency in creating new spheres of influence via their encounters with religious systems.

Part One ... Women in Colonial Regimes

1

Repression of Muslim Women's Movements in Colonial East Africa

Jennifer Kopf

In what ways can changes in women's religious expression challenge the state?[1] To answer this question, this chapter examines two developments in Islam as described by the German colonial governor's office in Dar es Salaam, Tanzania, from 1908 through 1913.[2] Investigation and prosecution of both developments dominate files of the Tanzanian National Archives (TNA) of the period. Both were seen as women's movements and as political threats to the colonial state. Both were investigated thoroughly and put down fiercely by the colonial government.

The first development was the distribution of a "Mekkabrief" (Mecca letter) that came to the attention of officials in the southeastern part of the colony in 1908. The letter—thought to have fallen from heaven in Mecca—reportedly contained instructions for women to pray as well as men and had purportedly led to the planning of a mosque for women in the city of Lindi. From the text of the letter it is difficult to see any connection to the status of women per se. The letter requires believers who read it to make copies of it and send them to other cities. Copies of the letter in the archive do not mention women, mosque building, or gender differences, yet discussion in the same files refers repeatedly to building mosques by and for women and to the use of women by the "schemers" hoping to undermine the colonial state who were ultimately responsible for the letter.

The second event is the spread of Dervish circles. This was the focus of another circular from the governor to district officers on 15 February 1909, less than one year after the Mecca letter. Dervish worship practices involve ecstatic movement and chanting. This Sufi Islamic order is organized by brotherhoods. The governor claimed that the Dervishes' "leaders' goals could not be united with the calm and security of the protectorate" (TNA G 9/48).

In this chapter I ask how women came to be perceived as central to these movements and why these movements presented such a threat to the colonial government. It is rare for women's movements to be understood as representing a nation. Descriptions of both the Mecca letter and Dervish circles in the archives refer to the danger presented by changes in women's religious practices; they risk rebellion by the entire population, not only by women. In a colonial discourse that frequently refers to a people "and their women," this concern about women's movements is unusual, to say the least. The conclusion ultimately reached by the colonial administrators was, in both cases, that male strategizers had planned the movements as challenges to the colonial state. The scant attention that is paid to these movements in subsequent histories, anthropologies, and religious studies of Islam echoes this explanation, dealing with them as minor parts of broader changes in a masculinist Islam during the colonial period (for example, see Becker 1968; Martin 1969).

I propose that the force with which these changes in religious practice were put down can be explained by increases in women's control over their own mobility more fully than by the official explanations given in the files suggest. Domosh and Seager's (2001, 115) assertion that *"gendered differences in mobility and access to transportation are among the more ubiquitous—and 'ordinary' of spatial controls"* implies that women's increased capacity for mobility can lead to intense reaction against those changes. I suggest that reactions against the Mecca letter and Dervish movements were related to contemporary shifts in gendered structures of power in Germany and to changes in gender roles around the Maji-Maji rebellion in 1905 and 1906. The chapter therefore briefly discusses turn-of-the-century German racialized gender roles and the Maji-Maji rebellion as background to understanding the reactions of German male administrators to reported changes in the ways women in German East Africa practiced Islam. Additionally, this increased control of their own mobility came at a time when European governments used "bio-power" (Foucault 1984) to bring subjects into the state's economic and cultural systems. By directing their energy to Dervish circles, women denied the colonial government the opportunity to co-opt this power for its projects. In the context of these shifting power relationships, individuals in the colonial government understood the changes in women's mobility brought by the Mecca letter and by Dervish circles as challenges to the state.

The term "German East Africa" signals a place and a time: the place is Tanganyika, now mainland Tanzania and parts of Uganda, Rwanda, and Burundi; the time begins with the German conquest in 1888 and ends with the end of World War I, when the Versailles Treaty required Germany to relinquish all colonial possessions. In the millennium prior to the "scramble for Africa," Muslim Swahili culture flourished on the East African coast from Somalia to present-day Mozambique. Indian, Arab, and internal and coastal African groups shared in Swahili culture while maintaining their distinct ethnic identities (Middleton 1994) and practicing various types of Islam. In the mid-nineteenth century, Zanzibar's economic networks reached inland to the Congo Basin, from whence slaves and goods were sent to Zanzibar. This trade brought a Muslim presence to the interior (Kwamena-Poh et al. 1982) and brought central Africans to the coast.

The German Empire was forged through a series of nineteenth-century tax and trade agreements and wars of annexation. Dominated by Prussia, fractured by "culture wars" between Catholics and Protestants, and shocked by rapid industrialization and urbanization, Germany sought a national identity. The colonies provided the peoples against whom this identity could be shaped (Friedrichsmeyer, Lennox, and Zantop 1998). The German colonial empire is one articulation of modernity as are the colonialisms of other European powers.[3] With Protestant and Catholic sects hostile toward each other in the aftermath of the culture wars, missionaries fought one another over colonial territory, and specific Christian belief systems influenced policies only indirectly. In the absence of a clear religious tradition, scientists, social scientists, bureaucrats, the press, and others explored cultural, racial, and other explanations for difference and conflict between Germany and its colonial subjects.

The German colony in East Africa was founded in 1881 and was run by a charter company until the German government appointed its first governor there in 1891 (National Archives of Tanzania 1973). Although East Africa was extremely cosmopolitan and had links to peoples and places around the Indian Ocean for a millennium prior to colonization, German colonial discourse categorized people according to their ancestry and even considered families that had been in Africa for generations as "foreign." The few German settlers were concentrated in plantations in the mountains in the northeast portion of the colony and in Dar es Salaam, the German administrative center and port (Koponen 1994). German colonial supporters were keenly aware of Zanzibar's historical, cultural, economic, and political influence on East Africa. Despite the attacks by Christian sects on each other within the German Empire, Germans identified Germany as a Christian nation battling against Islam for cultural as well as political and economic reasons. Numerous policies were directed at undercutting Islam as a source of power because of its connection to Zanzibar and because of the potential for Islam to unite the peoples of German East Africa. Islam and Muslims are demonized in the administrative files on which this chapter is based.[4] Throughout the German files, cosmopolitan Swahili culture, formed centuries before German exploration of the region, is discussed as "African" with "foreign" Arab and Indian intruders.[5] The files do not indicate the ethnicity of the majority of participants in either case but suggest that outsiders manipulated gullible black Africans in both incidents. The Mecca letter affair ended in the arrest of several Arabs, and Dervishes were traced back to interests on the Somali coast.

Multiple categories of difference including the condition of coloniality, gender roles, and discourses of religion and "race" interacted in complex, ambivalent ways to lead to the repression of the Mecca letter and Dervish circles. The relationship of gender to location and race gives one example of the ambivalence of these interactions. German colonial officials suppressed changes in African women's religious practices precisely because the German nation existed via its relationship with race, gender, and religion. Greater freedom for European colonial women may be inversely related to African women's freedom (see chapter 2), yet here, too, such an inversion is an ambivalent one. Because I also see a direct relationship between German and East African women's conditions within the colonial context, I turn next to an overview of these, before continuing with an analysis of the Mecca letter and Dervish circles and the threats they posed to German colonialism.

Nineteenth-Century Changes in Black and White Gender Roles

At the turn of the twentieth century, gender roles in Germany and in German East Africa underwent considerable change. Limits on the rights of (European) women in Germany were under attack, from proletarian and bourgeois women's movements to the feminist radical nationalism of the colonial author Frieda Freiin von Bülow. German women's movements began in earnest at the 1865 *Frauenkonferenz* in Leipzig, at which the *Allgemeinen Deutschen Frauen-verein* (General German Women's Association) was founded. Such movements sought women's suffrage, among other goals. The Imperial Law of Association (*Vereinsgesetz*), which forbade women to gather for political reasons or take part in public meetings of a political nature, severely limited women's political participation in Germany. It was lifted in 1908 (Evans 1976, Frederiksen 1981).

Industrialization had changed family relations in the Reich by removing production from the domestic sphere. The effects of this change on proletarian and bourgeois women differed. Proletarian women sought social assistance, such as child care, to help them in their double responsibilities of paid employment and the family. Bourgeois women insisted on greater attention to the role of the mother as the centerpiece of civilized society and sought a strengthening of the nuclear family (*Kleinfamilie*) and increased responsibility for women within the family (Frederiksen 1981).

Although black women's sexuality was at the margins of European art at the beginning of the nineteenth century, by its end African women were featured centrally in European high art and popular culture as exciting sexual beings, at once dangerous and enticing (Pieterse 1992). In European social sciences, descriptions of Africans correspond with descriptions of animals, criminals, and prostitutes. African women were represented as pathologically sexual. European racisms called for the civilization (i.e., Westernization) of other peoples in various ways: "Arab women were to be 'civilized' by being undressed (unveiled), while sub-Saharan women were to be civilized by being dressed (in clean, white, British cotton)" (McClintock 1995, 31). The coastal women involved in the Mecca letter and whirling Dervishes were likely Swahili, an ambivalent (from the German perspective) position between African and Arab. In contrast to representations of African women as sexualized and dangerous, European women were represented as so civilized that their presence could both "uplift" Africans and prevent European men from the dangers of "going native."

The tensions between race, gender, and power are central to Frieda von Bülow's novels. For von Bülow, the colony was a space in which German women could grow to be liberated and independent, Germany could overcome

Prussia's humiliation in the 1800s, and the difficulties of life there could make real men to lead the German nation. Her protagonists ultimately achieve independence from men and prove their moral as well as racial superiority over African women. The European heroines generally begin as strong-willed, stubborn women, seeking power and moral meaning in life, and are ultimately "tamed," thereby finding fulfillment. Occasionally, this "taming" takes the form of giving up their independence for their husbands' authority; more often it is the circumstances of the women's lives that teach them not to rely on weak men and to escape romantic ideals. At the novels' conclusions, they are most often independent, frequently run farms in Africa, and are happy in their role of aiding others (Wildenthal 2001).

The European women in von Bülow's novels rarely interact with Africans in more than passing roles as house servants. This discursive strategy simultaneously erases the African presence from East Africa and furthers the "intimate tyranny" (Achille Mbembe; quoted in Eigler 1998, 72) of everyday life depicted in the colony. Calm interaction with Africans and Arabs in the early pages of the novels sets the stage for later scenes of violence, in which Germans lash out to defend themselves against violence by their "inferiors." Readers are thus prepared to accept violence as a necessary part of the colonizing project. African women are portrayed as brutish, lacking in self-restraint, and sexually free in opposition to middle-class German women, who are depicted as self-disciplined and prevented by their role as moral paragons from enacting their desires (Eigler 1998). This racialization of sexuality is used to discipline gender norms more generally:

> White men used racial difference to discipline women of their own race and class by constructing racialized sexual identities in which white women represent chastity and women of color, promiscuity. These representations operate to ensure the sexual control of white women while justifying the sexual exploitation of women of color by white men. (Smith 1998)

Non-European women's gender roles were thus important in establishing and maintaining both racial hierarchy in the colony and gender roles in Germany. Racism and sexuality interacted differently in various models of male colonial domination. Wildenthal (2001) describes the "imperial patriarchs" and the "liberal nationalists." Both could demonstrate their strength by controlling black women, either through personal force or through regulation.

The imperial patriarchs were the German men who first took colonial lands in East Africa. They generally spoke a local lingua franca and used local agricultural methods. Their dream was of colonial space unencumbered by the bureaucracy of modern Germany, a space where a European man could build his fortune by using his talents and connections as he alone saw fit. These men frequently viewed taking an African wife or concubine as yet another way of expressing their superiority in a hierarchy that was simultaneously racial and political and as a way to cement relationships with influential families. This was expressed by a German colonizer in Cameroon, who wrote:

> The eternal feminine, also under dark skin, is an excellent charm against low spirits, to which one is so vulnerable in the solitude of Africa. Apart from these values for the soul, there are also practical advantages of personal safety. Having an intimate black girlfriend protects one from various dangers. (Buchner 1887; quoted in Wildenthal 2001, 81)

The brutality through which these relationships with African women were enforced raised the question in observers' minds of whether colonialism was a civilizing mission or whether German men were liable to succumb to less-than-civilized behavior in these "unruly" places (Wildenthal 2001).

The liberal nationalists arrived in Africa later, and relied on the state, not personal connections, to provide them with access to African land and labor. They sought to build an idealized homeland overseas, an egalitarian society in which deserving colonists could be upwardly mobile. Their colonial dream was of a perfectly regulated space, one in which a man could be assured that following the rules would be rewarded. Governor Albrecht von Rechenberg and Colonial Secretary Bernard Dernberg belonged to this group. For the liberal nationalists, European men's sexual relations with African women could not be a simply personal choice; these relationships were "race mixing," a danger to the foundations of this new society (Wildenthal 2001).

Colonial Wars

No primary or secondary source in the archive conclusively links either the Mecca letter or whirling Dervishes to any plot to overthrow the state, but the incidents are dealt with strictly in the narrow sense of a security threat. This can be explained by German militarism and the German assessment of Africans as militants. Two relevant events in the military history of German colonialism are the Nama and Herero Wars in German Southwest Africa and the Maji-Maji rebellion in the southern part of German East Africa in 1905 and 1906. Historians have recently reexamined both of these conflicts, connecting them to imperial discourses on race, gender, and sexuality.

German Southwest Africa

The 1907 elections in Germany have been referred to as the Hottentot elections. In 1904, a German general had ordered the extermination of the Herero people in Southwest Africa (Friedrichsmeyer, Lennox, and Zantop 1998, 12–14). Leading up to the election, the German public became aware of this military campaign and the German parliament extensively debated colonial policy. Speakers from across the political spectrum described the order to drive southwest African peoples into the desert to die of hunger or thirst as cruel, yet they did not see this as a crime against *humanity* because they viewed Africans as lacking in essential humanity. This logic could also be applied in debates on miscegenation. If Africans, as a race, were not fully human, then antimiscegenation laws could be based on the requirement that all parties in a marriage must be of age and neither insane nor mentally retarded (Smith 1998). The determination that black Africans were not entitled to full legal personhood did not carry over to Arabs, whom Germans gauged as perhaps being capable of eventually approaching European levels of culture.

The Maji-Maji Uprising

The Maji-Maji uprising features prominently in the history of Tanzanian independence. President Nyerere referred to it as "the national epic of Tanzania" (Gwassa and Iliffe 1967, 1). It involved numerous African peoples over a wide region with varying topographies and climates. Unable to combat their military opponents directly, German forces retaliated against the civilian population, burning villages and stationing troops at "strategic food-producing locations" (Kjekshus 1977, 150). This brutal repression was designed to bring on famine and to make the southern third of the colony into a wasteland (Iliffe 1969). The majority of African casualties in the Maji-Maji conflict were probably noncombatants who died of starvation (Kjekshus 1977, 187). Histories at the scale of the state (Crosse-Upcott 1960, Stollowsy 1988, Iliffe 1967, Wright 1968, Redmond 1975, Hassing 1970, Bald 1976) consider Maji-Maji to be "Tanzania's most spectacular manifestation of the rejection of colonial rule" (Redmond 1975, 407). These proto-nationalist accounts emphasize the unity of African peoples in the struggle and give a central role to an elixir, or "Maji," that would make wearers impervious to bullets.

More recently, Sunseri's (1997) reevaluation of available documents shows how this dominant interpretation is a continuation of colonial explanations of the rebellion, combining "economic grievance" views of colonial reformers with "witchdoctor conspiracy" views of pro-settler factions. Sunseri finds that changes in gender relations at the household level brought about by communal labor projects preceded Maji-Maji and continued after its repression. Men were called to work in communal cotton fields while other colonial laws endangered traditional methods of dealing with drought, plagues, and other agricultural difficulties. Women increased their use of medicines of protection and also assumed traditionally male roles in agricultural production, leading to a renegotiation of household spheres of power. These medicines became the center of historiography that transferred them to male warriors and described their transmission by a spiritual healer and his disciples. Sunseri concludes:

> Men working away from home often returned home with novel ideological bases of power which superseded previously established local practices. Foremost among them was Islam, which provided radical norms for reckoning descent, landholding, inheritance, community power and marriage contracts, usually at the expense of women. (Sunseri 1997, 60)

Although Sunseri states that Islam "usually" operated "at expense of women," Islam—like any world religion—is fluid, responding to local changes in conditions. The Mecca letter and spread of Dervish circles for women are examples of the adaptation of Islam to changing gender roles.

The Mecca Letter

In late 1906, as repression and retaliation against the Maji-Maji rebellion were nearing their close, a new governor arrived in German East Africa, Baron Albrecht von Rechenberg, a specialist in Eastern Europe. During Rechenberg's governorship, the German Colonial Secretary Bernhard Dernberg instituted reforms in colonial policy designed to stimulate African peasants' participation in the colonial economy as smallholders, trading on European markets. These reforms moved the colony closer to the liberal nationalists' dream of a perfectly regulated space, undercutting the power relationships through which planters had established themselves and the colony. Planters questioned Rechenberg's knowledge of Africa while Rechenberg believed that enacting the planters' model of African laborers on European-owned plantations would lead to a landless proletariat (Iliffe 1969).

On 7 July 1908, Governor Rechenberg received a telegram from district officer Wendt, in the southern port city of Lindi, alerting him to "written orders of a greater Islamic tendency" in a letter that contained "strongly aggressive plans against Europeans and missionaries," which had apparently been sent to settlements all along the coast, giving the population "strong fantasies through speeches in mosques" (TNA G 9/46). The text[6] of this Mecca letter does not appear to be threatening to Europeans but, as Rechenberg explained in a letter to the Colonial Office (TNA G 9/46), it was usually accompanied by an exegesis that spelled out the threat clearly. This second document explained that the sinners to be avoided were Europeans and that the approaching apocalypse and golden era of Islam referred to an overthrow of colonial rule; when the end of the world approached, according to this preaching, only Islam would remain. Rechenberg reported that this exegesis was not always sent along with the letter, and when it was sent, it was often destroyed upon receipt. Furthermore, he claimed that the letter itself was full of analogies and parallels, such that its meaning could not be understood without this explanation. Even this explanation of the dangers that colonial officers saw in the letter does not explain how it involved women's mosques and prayer rituals not included in the text of the letter.

Unable to determine the letter's source, the governor requested all station chiefs to investigate whether the letter had reached their stations and what the reaction had been. Although the initial discussion of the letter referred to the danger of a potential Arab resurgence, one immediate harm caused by the letter, according to responses by district officers, was that women who had been in relationships with European men sought to be released, and many servants ran away and were not turned in by the police, even if they stayed in town. This was an affront to both the imperial patriarch and liberal nationalist models of colonial domination. For the imperial patriarchs, the "waywardness" of these women constituted a disruption of the power relationships at the basis of the colony. For the liberal nationalists, servants—whatever the terms of their servitude—who broke out of their roles as servants disrupted the smooth operation of the colony. The inability of the police to deal with this unruliness constituted a breakdown of the regulatory structure central to the liberal nationalist dream.

The documents are not explicit, but the phrase "in relationship with European men" signals a sexual relationship, and the request to be released strongly suggests that women may not have been in these relationships entirely of their own free will. The complaint of sexual assault was not new. In his discussion of the conquest of the coast, Jackson (1970) repeatedly quotes primary sources which mention German sexual abuse of African women as one cause of resentment against the German invasion. As discussed above, the imperial patriarch colonial system dominant in the first decade of German colonization and cultural representations of colonialism permitted sexual relations between colonizing men and colonized women—and brutality from the men to the women—as a necessary part of colonization. Arguing "as if the world were divided in two" (T. Mitchell 1988), Governor Leist in Cameroon and Carl Peters in German East Africa both excused their own violent behavior toward African women—inexcusable in metropolitan space—as acceptable in the colony because, they claimed, it was part of the normal African sexual order. African protests against their behavior make it clear that this was not the norm. Wildenthal (2001, 74) writes that "the scandals publicized the uncomfortable fact that German colonial rule rested not only on superior firepower, economic domination, and strategic diplomacy, but also on the sexual coercion of African women." A call for women to separate themselves from these relationships could be read as a protest both against sexual violence against African women and against the governing system of which it was a part. The responses of station chiefs to Governor Rechenberg's queries about the Mecca letter make it clear that it was received as just such a call.

The ability of these women to move freely in town constituted an assault on colonial control of mobility on two scales: first, individual women reclaimed control over their own bodies, and second, men who had held them found they could not rely on other men—the police—to return "their" women to them.[7] At the scale of the city or region, the women's freedom to walk the streets without being reported signified a deep absence of colonial social control. Mosque construction would add the edifice of "women's spaces" to the city, but would not change the character of the street; women's actions within closed buildings would remain out of view.

Mindful of the extensive Maji-Maji rebellion in the same region just two years earlier, the governor sent a military attaché to investigate. Within a month, ringleaders were rounded up, interviewed, and publicly displayed. Rechenberg analyzed the reasons behind the letter in a report to the colonial office, quoting the full text of Wendt's telegram and longer follow-up communication (TNA G 9/46). Rechenberg believed the letter was counterfeit. It lacked a signature, had no date, and was not written in pure Mekka dialect; it gave the impression of having been written by someone whose native language was not Arabic. Furthermore, the letter had arrived by a much more circuitous route than those normally sent from Mecca on holy days every two or three years. Another reason to doubt that the origin of the Mecca letter could be Islamic, he wrote, was that Muslims had learned since the initial uprising when the colony was taken twenty years earlier that the Germans were quite tolerant of their religion; Muslims would therefore have no reason to call for the end of the German administration. Rechenberg suggested that the purpose behind the letter was not to call Muslims back to their faith, but to use Islam as a base from which to stage a rebellion. Rechenberg states that the significance of calling women to prayer and building a mosque for women was that through women the seditious message could be spread through the ranks of the Askari (African soldiers in the German military), even those who had remained loyal during Maji-Maji. Quoting Wendt, the District Officer in Lindi, Rechenberg reported:

> The entire cleverness of the Orientals here now comes to daylight, in that they attempt to move accompanying phenomena to the fore and thereby to darken the act itself. As a consequence of the coercion pressuring the women to pray, there have certainly been cases in which husbands acting in good faith have been deceived. (TNA G 9/46)

Comments in the archives bring women into the discussion of the Mecca letter, and this analysis takes them out again. The Mecca letter originated from (presumably male) "Orientals" and was directed at "husbands acting in good faith." Women carried the danger, but merely as vessels of a plot to motivate men to overthrow the colonial state. Many well-meaning individuals were pulled into the affair by the command for women to attend Koran lessons, which were used by some teachers for immoral purposes, according to Rechenberg. It is unclear from the text of his letter whether this is the "deception" of "husbands acting in good faith" or what the "immoral purposes" were. Women are portrayed as implements for men's actions. Women's participation in or offense at "immoral purposes" is not mentioned in Rechenberg's letter.

The events in Lindi gave Rechenberg clear evidence of the intention to use Islam to weaken the Askari's loyalty. He was surprised at the letter's response, with hundreds of people pressing into mosques in Lindi and Kilwa that normally only had congregations of twenty or thirty. Nevertheless, he found government tolerance vis-à-vis Islam to be the correct position, and stated that because people knew the government was not anti-Islamic, they were open to explanations that the letter was false and should be ignored. In order to highlight the government's tolerance, Rechenberg suggested having the protectorate declared "Dar el Islam," a land in which believers are not called to holy warfare. Because most Muslims in the colony recognized the Khalif in Constantinople, he suggested that the ambassador there could prevail upon the Sultan to have such a declaration made. This possibility was investigated and then rejected because of the possibility that this designation might lead to attempts to overthrow the colonial regime, because it was not Islamic (TNA G 9/46).

The district officer at Lindi who first reported the letter drew a connection between the Mecca letter and Maji-Maji. His report stated that colored people of high and low standing referred to the Mecca letter affair as another Maji-Maji, indicating the desire to do away with European rule. He found that many Wamwera people who had obeyed orders from the coast and gone along with Maji-Maji had declared their unwillingness to take part in a second uprising ordered by people on the coast. Agitation based on the Mecca letter was largely undertaken by pseudo-Mwalimu (teachers of Islam), who he said claimed to study and teach Islam but who were actually barely literate. He wrote that he had been unable to take any action against them on his tour of the district, because they carried out their agitation in secret. Furthermore, he sought to avoid giving any appearance of intolerance. He had, however, prosecuted some of them for fraud, because they led schools in which nothing was taught—they did not know enough to teach, in his judgment—but the parents nonetheless were charged twenty or thirty rupees, fees that ordinarily were paid with goods.

After these prosecutions, many of the other so-called pseudo-Mwalimu had gone to the coast to avoid the same fate. These connections, he believed, were the basis for the control the coast had over the interior even when people in the interior continued in their old ways and, further, that the call to prayer, even for non-Muslims, was constant from Maji-Maji to the Mecca letter. He felt that the desire to be rid of European government was present in all colored peoples although they had disparate ideas of how to do this. The different camps, he said, included true Muslims who followed the letter of the Koran, such as Kadi Omari, the prayer leader at Lindi, who were interested in European education and technical knowledge, in order to do away with the great advantage of the Europeans. The opposite group, which he called "Boys, Drinkers, and Travelers," sought to bring about a revolution. The difference between these positions, he thought, explained the conflicts against some Muslims in the Maji-Maji rebellion (TNA G 9/46).

By encouraging women to pray in their own mosques and to leave their employers, particularly if they were in sexual relationships, the Mecca letter challenged colonial security systems as well as racialized gender roles at the foundation of the colonizing relationship. In response, the German colonial military lashed out violently to defend the state.

Whirling Dervish, Howling Mob?

As noted above, Islam was one of the ties connecting the East African coast to other locations around the Indian Ocean for centuries prior to German exploration and colonization. The majority of Muslims in Tanganyika and Zanzibar in the early twentieth century were Sunni of various sects, with an Indian Ismaili minority (Martin 1969, 482). Dervish brotherhoods had long been present there and in other parts of Africa, connecting those regions to Islamic brotherhoods elsewhere. In some regions, they played a major part in anticolonial opposition (Amiji 1971; Martin 1969, 471). After the Mecca letter reprisals, German officials became concerned that Dervishes also threatened the colony's security.

Dervish practices are described in the German administrative files as involving the repetition of religious formulas during the repeated performance of a certain physical movement, eventually bringing on a highly contagious state of euphoria, in which masses can be moved to take senseless actions. Certain women were supposedly susceptible to this euphoria, hence the call for women to participate in prayers.[8] Once the contagion was spread to women's bodies, it could be sent out by centrifugal force to transform masses into unthinking, dangerous mobs, ready to act at the signal of the clever mind that had planned the frenzy in advance. The solution was for the state to control the spaces in which this "dangerous material" could be used. Believing again that agitators from outside the colony were using Islam for the advancement of a political agenda—this time they were from the Barawa coast in southern Somalia—Rechenberg addressed the background of Dervish leaders:

> As far as Barawa (Dervish) influences are at work, the religious moment, the fanatical, anti-European Islam is at play. The Islam of the protectorate, on the other hand, is known to be not aggressive, but completely patient. It has no reason to change, as long as our absolute tolerance permits unencumbered belief practices. (TNA G 9/48)

In this contrast of Islamic practices within the colonies with the Dervishes' foreign influence, Rechenberg represents women's religious expression (under the influence of outsiders) as inherently dangerous, irrational, and aggressive. This image departs from highly sexualized constructions but still maintains that African women are dangerous and must be controlled.

Rechenberg felt that careful administrative politics (outlined below) were a better strategy against Islam than legal measures would be. He did, however, restrict the spaces in which these practices could be followed: Dervish circles were not restricted in mosques, but required permission from the local police outside of mosques, in other buildings or in private courtyards, and were forbidden in public places or streets. Rechenberg's fear was that Islam would unite populous tribes to fight European culture. To prevent this type of religiously based political movement from overtaking the colony, Rechenberg found it necessary to stem the influence of Islam on various fronts. He delineated three different groups that would have to be dealt with to prevent an insurrection based in Islam: "Mohammedans" as a religious group, "native rulers," and "Negro tribes." Rechenberg believed that it would be easier to enforce measures against individuals than against entire groups, so Negro tribes had to be kept from conversion to Islam. This strategy would require governance following the motto, "just and benevolent, but if necessary also decisive and strict" (TNA G 9/48).

To ensure the loyalty of native rulers, district officers could use all measures they deemed appropriate to raise the rulers' honor and standing. This might include allowing jumbes (African "chiefs")[9] and sultans to keep larger portions of the taxes they collected. If Rechenberg considered the results of possibly supporting despotic, corrupt local leaders, there is no sign of it in his reports. Rechenberg found that religious Muslims were hostile to the intrigues of Dervish leaders. He favored policy designed to drive a wedge between Muslims who sought to overthrow the government and those devout believers who were loyal to the Europeans. This was necessary both to keep them from joining forces and because if they did join together, the flow of information on the movement would be stopped. Referring to the above-mentioned three groups, Rechenberg's report states that "these circles must absolutely be protected in their religious feelings and must also be raised up in their feelings of their own importance." Rechenberg suggests that wise district officers would, for example, consult with native leaders about decisions.

Furthermore, Rechenberg found it imperative that everyone involved with the government of the territory be familiar with Islamic beliefs and customs, because Islam-Arabic culture had held sway in the region for centuries prior to the arrival of the Europeans. Besides making frequent use of the resource books available to them, local officials were to carefully choose advisors in Islamic issues.

Muslim women participating in Dervish circles used their bodies and space in ways not anticipated by German Orientalists. Foucault's "bio-power" can be useful in understanding the response to Dervishes. Bio-power involves "the body as a machine: its disciplining, the optimization of its capabilities, the extortion of its forces, the parallel increase of its usefulness and its docility, its integration into systems of efficient and economic controls" (Foucault 1984, 261). The application of bio-power consists of detailed requirements for many minute actions that tie subjects in to state economic systems. Foucault's studies of bio-power involve institutions explicitly established and controlled by the state—prisons, schools, and mental institutions—in order to direct the activities of its subjects to support the state.

Colonial governments attempted to control the body movements of subjects in an attempt to gain control over the population. Timothy Mitchell's *Colonising Egypt* (1988) examines the use of these techniques of power by British colonizers in Egyptian schools, model villages, and the military. In these situations, as in the sites Foucault analyzed, specific actions were required in order to support economic production and to bring about "implicit obedience" (T. Mitchell 1988, 175). In regulating Dervish practices, the governor similarly attempted to control the movement of bodies in order to bring subjects into line with colonial policies. The designation of places where one is permitted to whirl or is prohibited from whirling can be aptly described as "anatomo-politics of the human body" (Foucault 1984, 262). The regulation of whirling Dervishes could also be viewed as "an investment in life" (ibid.), but because they proscribe rather than prescribe certain actions, they are much less specific than the regulations of bio-power. It might be more appropriate to consider Dervishes a sort of "anti-bio-power" in which the body's capabilities and forces are used to break out of the docility called for by systems of efficient and economic controls. The anatomo-politics of Dervishes lays claim to precisely the forces of life that the colonial state hoped to harness. By participating in Dervish circles, black African women once again clearly took control of their own bodies at multiple scales. A body engaged in ecstatic whirling, "susceptible to senseless actions" (TNA G 9/48), is not available for rationally planned programs of economic production. (They also were not sexually available to colonizing men seeking a way to concretize relations with important families, a "charm against low spirits," or protection from danger.) Fellowship with Dervishes from West Africa to Southern Arabia, to Turkey, to Indonesia connected women with potential political opposition. (Recall that women in Germany were permitted to attend meetings of a political nature beginning only in 1908.) This was destabilizing to the hierarchy on which the Empire was built.

Conclusion

This rereading of colonial files on the Mecca letter and whirling Dervishes in German East Africa suggests that German colonial officials' responses to these Islamic movements derived from European men's desire to control African women's mobility at various scales. In contrast to pressure for continued changes in gender relations in Germany, the colony was a space in which men dreamt of "correct" power relations, whether that referred to power relations in which individual men created their own destinies, or power relations in which men established a self-justifying rational hierarchy. New uses of space in Islamic practice transgressed against ideas that were foundational to the colonial state. European discourses on gender and sexuality, on African and Arab peoples, on Islam, and on the relationship between "home" and "colony" overlapped and interacted in the German understandings of and reactions to these movements. In both cases, women's movements were assumed to be the result of male planning, directed at overthrowing the state. Both reactions are based in fear that changing roles for women in Islam would lead to women changing their position in society and that, ultimately, changed relations would challenge the social order and German national identity upon which the colony was predicated.

Black Muslim women, represented as vessels of a treacherous message in the Mecca letter incident, were seen as likely to spill out a dangerous message to a broad audience made senseless by participation in chanting and whirling. The administrative files on which this study is based do not contain information on how many women were involved in these movements, individual women's names, or any comment by women. The only words of non-Europeans included in the files cited here are testimony in court cases following the Mecca letter, as recorded by court scribes. The intentions of women participants in these movements cannot be clearly read from their actions (especially not from their actions as seen through the lens of colonial administrators). We can, however, observe that they chose to depart from European expectations that they were essentially sexually licentious or trapped by a static Islamic practice. I believe we can also safely assume that their involvement in these movements was the result of their own decision making, at least at some level, not the result of having been pressured or fooled by racial and gender superiors.

In response to the Mecca letter, women reclaimed control over their own bodies, a disruption of power relations forged by early colonizers. However, these relationships had already begun to lose their value to African social groups engaged in them, as regulation replaced relationship as the center of power in the colony. The new regulatory framework did not recognize the power networks formed by imperial patriarchs' relations with African women and their families. The positions of Europeans at the top of the regulatory hierarchy instituted by liberal nationalists required discourses on colonized peoples that upheld the racialized, gendered social structure of the colonial empire. By walking away from the positions assigned to them in this hierarchy, women also disrupted this network of colonial power. In response to women's participation in the whirling Dervishes movement, women's spirituality, heightened by the whirling ritual, was represented as a danger to the colony. This move equated women with dangerous forms of Islam, rationalizing a regulatory system in which both Islam and women were controlled by others. Regulating the practice of Dervish circles was a double move, which permitted discourse on "women as irrational" to continue, while also limiting the whirling activity, freeing up the energy otherwise spent on ecstasy for use in furthering the colonial economy.

2

Conversion of Native and Slave Women in Dutch Colonial South Africa

From Assimilation to Apartheid

Leonard Guelke

Religion, identity, place, and gender are important themes in the formation of Dutch colonial society in South Africa from 1652 to 1795. The theology of Calvinism in part defined the character of seventeenth- and eighteenth-century colonial society in Dutch South Africa and developed two different expressions in urban areas such as Cape Town versus in the colonial interior. Religious conversion, baptism, and church marriage of slave women and their children initially facilitated the incorporation of Asian and African women into the European-oriented society of Cape Town, which was controlled by the Dutch East India Company (Vereinigde Ostindische Compagnie, abbreviated here as "the Company") and also legitimized the offspring of multiracial marriages. In the central place of Cape Town the Company supported a program of converting slaves to Christianity. In the early decades of colonial rule European male colonists often married freed slave women. The mixed-race children of such unions were initially absorbed within the white community.[1] Toward the close of the seventeenth century most became part of small but growing free communities of Christians and Muslims of Afro-Asian and mixed-race persons. With the subsequent hardening of racial attitudes among the whites, these communities came to inhabit an intermediate social status between Europeans and slaves and were the founders of today's Cape Coloured community.

The Calvinist principles of the Dutch Reformed Church in the rural interior, in contrast, fostered a rigid apartheid regime at the beginning of white settlement, because its members attached significance to being born of Christian parents. Their interpretation of church principles meant that the only road to conversion lay in being educated in Church doctrine, which was not possible for autochthonous people of color in the absence of teachers and missionaries. The settlers of the interior envisioned and then perpetrated a world in which Christianity was a European monopoly. In both its urban and rural forms Calvinist theology ultimately discouraged the amalgamation of peoples of different races and cultures.

In this chapter I first discuss how interrelationships of race, religious conversion, the status of women, and marriage fields were constituted differently in the capital and in the interior, in large part due to different European populations in positions of authority. The power of the Dutch East India Company's official integration policies did not extend spatially to an alienated white settler society living beyond its surveillance and management. Both Cape Town and rural societies were nevertheless dominated by patriarchal men. I consequently show how women's various racialized identities became essential to the dominant calculus and how the racialized grounds upon which patriarchal authorities included or excluded women as wives, partners, or mothers was crucial to the subsequent development of apartheid society in South Africa.

The racial issues relating to the conversion and marriage of women of color have received much scholarly attention from historians of early Colonial South Africa, but few have convincingly explained how apparent religious equality of Christians of various heritages, cultures, and "races" transformed itself into blatant apartheid and white supremacy. The explanation presented here is that the apparent religious and racial equality of the early Cape had less substance than many had hitherto thought and was easily reversible, when social conditions changed to favor a European racism that had never been abandoned. Jonathan Gerstner's (1991) analysis of the gate-keeping aspects of Calvinism regarding baptism and hence marriage fields is a critical contribution to this problem, because it goes beyond the references to the "elect of God" tropes of the nineteenth century Afrikaner nationalism to probe the principles on which membership in the Dutch Reformed Church was defined. Gerstner thus permits more sense to be made of the paradox of assimilation and apartheid on the basis of baptism and marriage. In this chapter I take up Gerstner's findings to explore the different ways the Dutch Reform religion could be used to create both societies of inclusion and exclusion depending upon the specific social, economic, and geographical circumstances.

Race, Christianity, and Colonialism in Dutch South Africa

By the mid-seventeenth century the Dutch East India Company had colonized strategic areas of present-day Indonesia and established a thriving spice trade. The strong commercial, entrepreneurial, and bourgeois elements of Dutch society were concentrated in the autocratic men who ran the Company. Their conviction in their own military and cultural superiority manifested itself in their belief that the Dutch Reformed faith was the only true religion, and in their overseas ventures the Company established the Dutch Reformed Church as the only official religion (Boxer 1965; Scammel 1980, 415). The Dutch Reformed Church was based on strict Calvinist principles that emphasized the importance of individual salvation at the same time it proclaimed a theology of predestination. A successful life was interpreted as indicative of God's favor, and successful people considered themselves to be God's elect. These Dutch colonizers reduced non-Christians to the status of "heathens," whom the Dutch thereby rendered as suitable subjects for subjugation and enslavement.

Because the Company's Dutch workforce was almost entirely male, the unbalanced sex ratio in the Dutch areas of Indonesia began to create difficulties for the Dutch authorities as they sought to create an ordered and well-run colonial society. They sought to solve the problem of unruly single males (following the Portuguese precedent) by permitting European employees to marry local women who converted to the Dutch Reformed faith, with an eye toward stabilizing their male workforce and creating a Dutch-speaking hybrid class of children who would grow up to become loyal and useful colonial subjects (Furnivall 1944, 465). Yet the racism of Dutch society at the time became evident when the Asian wives and biracial children of the Dutch colonists were forbidden to settle in the Netherlands (Boxer 1965, 217). Dutch settlers and Company officials returning home had to sell their slaves and say good-bye to their colonial-born wives and children. The Dutch strategy was effectively to create two worlds: the home nation, to be governed by home rules that prohibited slavery and excluded people of color; and the colonies, governed by colonial rules in which slavery was a vital institution and racial mingling was tolerated, provided racially mixed couples did not aspire to make their homes in the Netherlands. The permanent colonial population was initially to comprise its original inhabitants, imported slaves, colonial officials, and a generally lower class of Dutch "free burghers," some of whom married former slave women.

The idea of establishing a small Dutch East India Company post at the tip of South Africa around 1650 was strictly a pragmatic business decision. The Company had difficulty in maintaining crews for its ships on the long return voyage from Indonesia to the Netherlands because of the death toll from scurvy. The directors believed that a "halfway house" in South Africa would enable Company fleets to take on fresh provisions and provide a place for sick crew members to rest and recover. The favorable report of two Company men who had been shipwrecked at the Cape for several months influenced the choice of Table Valley at the Cape of Good Hope. Their report described the valuable resources of this area and emphasized that the indigenous people were not as hostile to Europeans as they were reputed to be (Moodie 1960, 4). The indigenous Khoikhoi and San, known collectively as Khoisan by modern scholars, secured a livelihood as pastoralists and hunter-gathers, respectively (Barnard 1992, 16–36). They were often away from the Cape in search of better forage or food resources, perhaps giving the colonial-minded Dutch the prerequisite notion that the land was "empty."

The Dutch religious perspective on colonial peoples around 1650 subsequently applied to South Africa when the Dutch East India Company sent Jan Van Riebeeck to found a small settlement at the Cape of Good Hope, and he became its first governor. Van Riebeeck had a clear agenda for how colonial society should be structured, based on his experiences in Indonesia. The Company's initial task force was overwhelmingly male, but in keeping with contemporary practice a few Dutch wives accompanied senior Company officials. Van Riebeck shortly requested his Company superiors to send slaves to the thinly populated Cape to help in the task of developing the settlement, thus firmly linking the place to the larger world of colonialism. Most of the slaves came from India, Indonesia, Madagascar, and other parts of Africa (Shell 1994, 41), because a vigorous slave trade was already in existence in these areas to supply the Company's Asian colonies. The Company provided slave children with a Christian education, encouraged baptism in the Dutch Reformed

Church, and enabled some slaves to achieve free status. Some slave women not only became familiar with Dutch culture, but on the Indonesian model, married male colonists upon achieving freedom and converting to the Dutch Reformed Church. Conversion often preceded freedom but was not a requirement for such status.

The Dutch East India Company's decision to found a small settlement at the Cape in 1652, however, did not include a program to Christianize the Khoikhoi as had been suggested by the authors of the report proposing a Company colony at the Cape. Instead, the Company sought simply to capitalize on the Khoikhoi's cattle wealth and fresh meat supply by treating them as autonomous or free people and aspiring for mutually beneficial trading relations. The Company instructed van Riebeeck to maintain good relations with the Khoikhoi people and to avoid any actions that might harm peaceful interactions with them (Moodie 1960, 7–8). Although this policy implied that the Khoikhoi would be treated with consideration and respect, the Europeans charged with carrying it out regarded the Khoikhoi as savages or wild people. Van Riebeeck himself would have enslaved the Khoikhoi at a moment's notice had not his instructions absolutely forbidden such action (Thom 1954). The Company directors wanted to avoid any actions that might provoke the Khoikhoi and upset the fragile peace in the belief that peace would produce better, and cheaper, results than war.

As a good Company servant van Riebeeck did what he could to foster the good relations his superiors demanded. To this end, he hired a young Khoikhoi woman as a servant in his household with a view to teaching her Dutch. This experiment was so successful that this woman, known to the Dutch as Eva, became a valuable interpreter for the Company. She converted to the Dutch Reformed Church and eventually married a prominent European colonist in a ceremony attended by the governor (MacCrone 1965, 43; Moodie 1960, 280). This union, however, was the only solemnized church marriage between a European and Khoikhoi that occurred during the entire period of Company rule, from 1652 to 1795.

The pronounced differences in the way the Company constructed its religious obligations toward the Khoikhoi versus slaves hinged on whether they were seen as part of, or separate from, colonial society. The Company treated the Khoikhoi as independent and autonomous people who retained responsibility for their own affairs. In contrast, slaves were in the colony because of the Company and were considered to be part of colonial society with the potential of becoming free members of it. Company officials took the responsibility of providing religious instruction for its own slaves seriously, but showed little interest in the Khoikhoi. The handful of Khoikhoi who became Christian converts did so in exceptional circumstances and were not representative of the Khoikhoi as a whole. The Company attitude to the Khoikhoi was also extended to privately owned, non-Company slaves, whose religious education was considered to be the responsibility of their owners.

The role of the Dutch Reformed Church was subordinated to the interests of the Dutch East India Company. In theory the Dutch Reformed Church was an independent organization, whose authority emanated from the classis, or governing council, in Amsterdam. In practice the Company decided what its role should be in its colonial possessions. That role was largely one of ministering to European colonists and providing instruction for Company slaves. With a handful of exceptions Dutch Reformed ministers were happy to follow the Company's lead as to where they should focus their energies and showed little interest in missionary activity among the indigenous people.

The Company also created, in the early years of its Cape outpost, a class of independent European Protestant colonists or free burghers, invited to become independent businessmen and entrepreneurs to supply the Company with the produce and services it needed (Böeseken 1984, 28–29). The Company encouraged the free burghers to make the Cape Colony their home, and it made provisions for wives in the Netherlands to join their settler husbands in South Africa. Some bachelor free burghers married former slave women who converted to the Dutch Reformed Church, following the long established colonial practice in Indonesia (Böeseken 1977, 78).

The freed female slaves who became eligible marriage partners for European settlers had characteristics that differentiated them from most Khoikhoi women. Such women usually spent many years imbedded within Dutch colonial society, were familiar with its culture, and spoke fluent Dutch. In contrast, the Khoikhoi women for many decades following the founding of a Dutch colony at the Cape retained a strong measure of their tribal culture and had limited knowledge of European ways. European colonists were not inclined to see Khoikhoi women (with the notable exception of the partly Europeanized

Eva) as potential marriage partners, and Khoikhoi women were evidently happy to live in their communities. This situation changed in the eighteenth century, as Khoikhoi tribal society disintegrated, forcing many Khoikhoi to seek closer ties with European setters for their economic survival.

The interracial marriages, which were a regular occurrence in the first decades of colonial society in South Africa, have often been pointed to as evidence of racial tolerance in the early period of Dutch colonial rule (e.g., Böeseken 1977, 79–83). Many children of such marriages were integrated as full members of Dutch colonial society and as adults married European partners (De Villiers 1996). These indications of "racial tolerance," however, need to be evaluated in a colonial context in which the Dutch applied different rules to their colonies and to the Netherlands.

Jonathan Gerstner (1991, 259) has shown that these overt discriminatory practices as they applied to Christian women of color were underpinned by a Calvinist theology that did not accord the same value to converts as it did to people who were born into the Dutch Reformed religion, especially if those converts were non-European. The unequal status of non-European converts to the Dutch Reformed Church is well illustrated in the case of Eva. After several years of respectable marriage and motherhood, Eva lost her husband to a colonial war. As a widow she was accused of leading a dissolute life that included alcoholism and having children with different partners. When she died the Company gave her a Christian burial, but her obituary condemned her and her people as being congenitally unsuited to Christianity (Gerstner 1991, 248; Elphick 1977, 203):

> Brought to the Christian faith, and being made from a female Hottentot almost into a Netherland [sic] woman . . . she returned, and for the rest led such an irregular life, that for a long while the desire would have existed of getting rid of her, had it not been for the hope of the conversion of this brutal aboriginal which was always hovering in between. She, like a dog, always returned to her vomit, so that finally she quenched the fire of her sensuality by death, affording a manifest example that nature, however closely and firmly muzzled by imprinted principles, nevertheless at its own time triumphing over all precepts, again rushes back to its unborn qualities.

This harsh judgment on Eva was somewhat self-serving in that it helped justify the Company's feeble efforts at converting Khoikhoi people in general. If the Khoikhoi converts were likely to follow Eva's path there was no point in bringing them to a Christian way of life that their savagery would overwhelm. Paradoxically, the Company had a more positive view of its slaves, who were considered to be more suitable candidates for Christianity than the autochthonous people.

In allowing if not encouraging interracial marriages the Dutch East India Company adopted a pragmatic policy which had much to do with the benefits of a population of Dutch speaking colonial-born subjects who would become loyal and useful Company employees, at home in the colonial environments in which they were raised. MacCrone (1965) and Fredrickson (1981), in seeing religion as a mechanism of assimilation that transcended race, failed to emphasize that the power of religion also depended upon social circumstances in bridging European racial prejudices. Conversion provided the basis of legal marriages between people of different races, but most Company officials and settlers did not view a convert as having the same social status as a born Christian. How a converted woman and her children fared and whether the Dutch encouraged conversion depended upon social mores that worked in tandem with a theology biased against giving converts equality with established Christians. In the early Cape (and in Indonesia) a small number of male settlers found marriage partners from among local women, who did not in this early period have many European women with whom they had to compete for social status. But subsequently the status of women of color and their children significantly deteriorated.

Race and Gender in a Settler Colony

The status of South Africans of color began to deteriorate in 1679 when the Dutch East India Company initiated an expansion of its Cape settlement, which to that point had served principally as a transit stop for Company ships in the East Indies trade but had as yet to sustain itself on its own food production. During the next twenty-five years a rapidly growing Dutch population of free settlers expanded onto rich agricultural lands that had formerly supported many Khoikhoi pastoralists (Guelke 1989b, 73–74). Many of this second wave of European settlers were already married and immigrated in family groups; others subsequently married single European women who came to the Cape under the sponsorship of the Company. Although the settler population after 1679 was still largely male, the increasing number of white women enabled a predominantly white settler community to become viable. This number was tiny by modern standards, and the total white population of free adult settlers still numbered less than a thousand by 1705. The newer settlers intermarried with the older ones, and many children of the earlier interracial marriages were absorbed into the emerging European-oriented society.

Although the Dutch East India Company officials created an appearance of racial equality, it was not at the same time committed to an ideal in which all races were of equal value. The racial sensitivities of Company officialdom were incorporated in the thinking of Adrian Van Reede, a high-ranking commissioner who was charged with reporting on the Cape settlement in 1685. In that year the Cape was in the midst of expansion and reform under an energetic governor who had been given a mandate to expand colonial agriculture using Dutch settlers and slaves (Böeseken 1977, 79–83). The commissioner was impressed with the vitality of the European settlement but also shocked by the number of visibly mixed-race children (Elphick and Shell 1989, 127).

Van Reede introduced a series of new laws relating to slavery and marriage that were of critical importance in defining the future character of the colony. He made it easier for well-conducted Christian slaves to gain their freedom after thirty or forty years of service and stipulated that male and female slaves with part-European ancestry (numbering about one-quarter of the slave population at the time) were to be freed at ages twenty-five and twenty-two, respectively. Van Reede prohibited marriages between Europeans and slaves of "full color." His measures were specifically designed to assimilate the part-European Christians into the predominantly European free population, while ensuring that freed African and Asian slave women would no longer become wives for white settlers, with the objective of maintaining the long-term European character of the settler population. Van Reede intended that the growing settler population of the Cape become a segregated Christian Reformed community of increasingly European extraction.

Van Reede also evidently believed that the growing white settler population of the Cape was a sufficiently viable, self-reproducing Dutch community to no longer necessitate interracial marriages that had characterized Indonesia and the early years of South African settlement (Boxer 1965, 217). Van Reede clearly thought that the Cape merited a home standard rather than a colonial standard in matters of race and revealed the fundamental racism that undermined Dutch official attitudes. The Van Reede directives coincided with a hardening of racial attitudes in the rural areas of the colony. The free Blacks, who had been pioneer settlers of the Stellenbosch region, no longer felt welcome and departed for the more tolerant environment of Cape Town (Elphick and Shell 1989, 221).

The expansion of the colony beyond the Cape peninsula established both a spatial and social division between the residents of Cape Town and its immediate vicinity and the emerging rural societies of the interior. In Cape Town, the Company, notwithstanding Van Reede's directives, continued to support an open policy with respect to interracial marriage, and it conscientiously promoted baptism of the large work force of Asian and non-Khoikhoi African slaves whom it controlled (Elphick and Shell 1989, 127). Although racial prejudices present from the colony's beginning remained a factor in Europeans' perceptions of people of color, intermarriages across the color spectrum continued to occur. A racially stratified society emerged with people of mostly European descent claiming the highest social status, followed by more visibly mixed-race individuals and freed slaves, occupying an intermediate social stratum. Asian and African slaves were at the base. The boundaries between these recently defined classes were still permeable rather than rigid barriers, as many slaves subsequently obtained their freedom and a few free Blacks acquired land and slaves.

The Company screened its white colonists from the Netherlands, Germany, and the French Huguenot population on the basis of their intended commitment to the orthodox Calvinistic brand of Protestantism that characterized the Dutch Reformed Church. No other denomination was permitted in the Cape Colony. Their main period of immigration was from 1679 to 1707. Beyond the Cape Town environs, the white settler society that emerged in rural areas was sharply divided on the basis of class and race. Free colonists were either overwhelmingly white or were so considered, whereas slaves and indentured workers were of predominantly Asian and African descent. Unlike in Cape Town, no intermediate class of free Blacks emerged in the rural interior, and the early free Black farmers living beyond the Cape Flats migrated out of the region (Elphick and Shell 1989, 221). In this racialized climate the early multiracial character of the first free settlements did not endure. The rural white settlers also owned non-Khoikhoi slaves but rarely baptized them, an apparently race-based notion that developed well before the emergence of the widely held economic argument that baptized slaves might have to be freed (Shell 1994, 330–50).

At the beginning of the eighteenth century, the rural white settler community retained a distinctively "frontier" character (Guelke 1988, 460–68). Males greatly outnumbered females, although the ratio was more balanced than it was in earlier decades. As a result, many male settlers either never married or waited until middle age in order to become sufficiently established to make an attractive proposal to a European woman. The typical first marriage ages of Cape women were in the teens, often to older men, many of the previous generation. Widows also were in demand for remarriage, particularly where they inherited significant property from their deceased husband's estate (Guelke and Shell 1983, 279–80). Widows under Dutch law had full control of their own affairs, but on remarriage forfeited this independence to their new husband. It is interesting to note that about half the older widows did not remarry, evidently preferring to manage their own affairs than to relinquish their independence in a new marriage. Few young women remained single, and once married, white women bore an average of eight children (Guelke 1988, 467). In their role as colonial housewives they relied upon the labor of slaves or Khoikhoi domestic servants.

In the early eighteenth century, the free farmers gained a stronger sense of community in a successful dispute with Governor Adrian van der Stel, who had used his privileged position to establish himself as a major agricultural producer in competition with the colonists. This dispute (which led to the governor's recall) also provided an early indication that colonists were beginning to incorporate their Christian religion as part of their colonial identity and were reluctant to share it with the Khoikhoi and their slaves. They strongly supported their local Dutch Reformed minister who attacked the efforts of another clergyman, the Rev. Petros Kalden, who sought to convert Khoikhoi to Christianity. Kalden's association with the governor did not help him with the colonists, but there is no evidence that his religious efforts were anything more than a personal commitment (tolerated but not encouraged by the Company). Kalden's critic, Rev. Le Boucq, argued that the Khoikhoi were not properly prepared for conversion (cited in Gerstner 1991, 232):

> Holy Baptism is so shamefully abused here that it is an abomination. It is performed on everyone, without distinction, not determining if the mothers or fathers be Christians, or without passing appropriate acts of adoption. Indeed one has good reason to believe that if the Governor sent a sheep in human clothing to the ministers, that they would have baptized it.

Even assuming that this attack had pastoral care rather than racist motives, it clearly condemned policies that would have enabled the Khoikhoi to be baptized. It also found widespread support among the European settlers, who were aghast at the prospect of unlettered Khoikhoi becoming members of their church. Le Boucq was the first pastor in South Africa to become "a hero among the farmers" (Gerstner 1991, 233).

In the eighteenth century, the European community experienced rapid natural increase, and a growing number of settlers acquired ranch land in the interior, where they made a living raising cattle and sheep. The pastoral frontier was made possible by Dutch East India Company land policy that permitted settlers to acquire frontier land for nominal rents, but the frontier society that emerged was largely isolated from Company rule. In this process vast areas of South Africa became incorporated into the Dutch colony at the expense of the indigenous Khoikhoi and San, who lost their former grazing and hunting lands to the invaders. The survivors of frontier expansion often became clients or serfs on European lands (Guelke and Shell 1992, 803–24). Although the Company remained in nominal control of newly settled lands, the geographical isolation of frontier regions gave settlers considerable autonomy in managing their affairs. They used this autonomy to establish harsh rule over the Khoisan peoples, who were subject to much violence and cruel punishments.

Within this context of dislocation, violence, and isolation, the European settlers used religion to justify their privileged status. In effect, they claimed Christian parentage as the basis for entrance into the emerging and increasingly white South African landed society. The Christian religion served the agenda of the white community and gave them an ideology with which to dominate heathen (i.e., nonwhite) people (Gerstner 1991, 258–62). The word "Christian" indeed became a synonym for the white colonists: they referred to each others as Christians and were so identified by other groups.

In this world of Christian exclusiveness, in which slave or Khoikhoi blood quantum became the basis for ineligibility for baptism, it became virtually impossible for non-Europeans to become Christians. Thus, racist selective requirements for Christian identity became the ideological foundation, rather than race directly, on which an apartheid society was established and maintained. The Khoikhoi and eventually other people of color were naturalized as congenital, permanent heathens, for whom baptism could never eradicate their heathen roots, and who consequently could be subjected to routine violence (Newton-King 1999, 37–62; Viljoen 2001, 28–51). This rationale was used to justify a genocidal war against the San, as they resisted settler encroachments on their lands (Newton-King 1999, 37–62). As heathens in the path of God's chosen people, they could expect no Christian mercy.

Khoikhoi-White Relationships in the Colonial Interior

The devastating smallpox epidemic of 1713 produced a situation in which many autonomous Khoikhoi communities disintegrated, leaving many Khoikhoi women who survived the smallpox outbreak in greater numbers than the men. In Khoikhoi society women traditionally milked the cattle and probably acquired some immunity through their exposure to cowpox. When these Khoikhoi women formed unions with Christian slave men (of Asian, other African, or hybrid descent) and bore children, the white settlers petitioned the authorities to make such children indentured workers to the whites (Elphick and Malherbe 1989, 32), rather than regarding them as free people of color. The smallpox epidemic hastened a process that was already under way and would continue for the rest of the century. Yet the Khoikhoi remained technically free, although they no longer had viable tribal societies to look after their physical and spiritual well-being.

The vigorous commitment of orthodox settlers in the colonial interior to the Dutch Reformed Church did not prevent white men and Khoikhoi women from forming partnerships, but in so doing they cut themselves off from both their faith community and institutional protection. Throughout the eighteenth century, white men outnumbered white women by about two to one (Guelke 1988, 461). This unbalanced sex ratio of the interior fostered sexual unions between white males and Khoikhoi women, but their children had no claim to legitimacy as defined by the church or government. They formed a separate frontier community, whom the whites simply called "Bastards" or "Bastard Hottentots" (Elphick and Shell 1988, 202). These children of white-Khoikhoi parents were by definition half-white and would, under the Cape Town policy as it applied to slave children, have had rights to baptism and consequently entrance into the European Christian community. This policy was ignored in remote areas. In contrast, the Dutch Reformed settlers emphasized the Khoikhoi blood of these biracial children and by extension, their heathen ancestry.

The difficulties involved in interracial partnerships under frontier conditions are illustrated in Viljoen's (1995, 13–31) study of a European settler, Hendrik Eksteen, and his Khoikhoi partner, Griet. This couple lived together, in the eastern interior, for twenty years in the mid-eighteenth century and had five children together. Griet clearly saw their relationship as one of husband and wife. When Hendrick began having affairs with other Khoikhoi women, Griet was outraged and eventually murdered him. After Hendrick's death, which was deemed initially to be an accident, Griet took over the running of the Eksteen farms, as any European widow would have done. This action made the orthodox community uneasy. When further violence and murder occurred on Griet's farms the neighboring settlers armed themselves in the belief that a "volksopstand" or insurrection of Khoikhoi and slaves was imminent. Although no uprising occurred, Griet subsequently was taken into custody and tried for the two murders.

Griet's treatment indicates the limits that applied to Khoikhoi women in the South African interior. They could indeed continue a long-term relationship with a male settler, but it existed outside the law and involved no European property rights. White colonists in the interior essentially decided that any ancestry on the "heathen" (Khoikhoi) side of the racial divide was sufficient grounds for exclusion and unequal treatment (Guelke 1989, 93–100).

Baptism, Racial Segregation, and Migration

The colonists' legacy of frontier expansion in the face of ethnic conflict under-pinned their emerging Afrikaner identity, through the ideology of what be-came known as the "Voortrekkers" embarking upon the "Great Trek." Anna Steenkamp, sister of Voortrekker leader Piet Retief, famously explained the rea-sons for withdrawal from the Cape Colony and their expansion into Khoikhoi and San homelands, as a result of their opposition to the more liberal baptism and marriage policies in force in Cape Town (quoted in Bird 1885, 1: 459):

> Our slaves . . . being placed on an equal footing with Christians, contrary to the laws of God and the natural distinction of race and religion . . . it was impossi-ble for any Christian to bear down beneath such a yoke; wherefore we rather withdrew in order thus to preserve our doctrines in purity.

The settler attitudes on religion, marriage, and race that entrenched themselves on the eighteenth-century South African Dutch colonies became the basis of Afrikaner identity and resistance to British rule during the nineteenth century. Ideas on women, religion, and space that crystallized on the Cape Colony's in-terior became the foundation upon which the Boer republics of the Orange Free State and the Transvaal were established, as well as twentieth-century apartheid politics (Thompson 1969, 405–46). This tie between racism and identity ill-prepared the rural Afrikaners for the abolition of slavery in the nineteenth century, let alone for a world in which all people shared equal rights before the law (Templin 1984, 99–181).

Discussion

What were the origins of South African apartheid? Modern scholars of Dutch South Africa generally discount religion as a formative factor in the shaping of colonial society or else suggest that the case for religion had yet to be made. A key issue is assessing the role of Calvinism in the Dutch Reformed Church as it informed the racial attitudes of the European settlers. An early attack on Mac-Crone's (1965) religious explanation of such racial attitudes came from Legas-sick (1980, 68), who argued that racism was stronger, if anything, in Cape Town and that relatively fluid race relations existed in the rural interior. The evidence in support of his thesis, however, is open to alternative interpretations. Legassick did not recognize the rigid divide between the orthodox community and the Khoikhoi and hybrid populations. He argued that fluid race relations characterized society in the rural interior, in which chief-subject or patron-client relationships predominated over the more rigid racial order of master and slave that typified Cape Town and vicinity (Legassick 1980, 68). Yet Legassick overlooks the lack of mechanisms in the interior for Khoikhoi clients or serfs to become part of the free community, in contrast to Cape Town where slaves routinely gained freedom, and with their freedom, the legal rights of colonial burghers.

Elphick and Giliomee (1989a, 526–27) focus their interpretation of early South African race relations on the legal status of groups created by the Dutch East India Company. They express several reservations about the impact of Calvinism, arguing that the clergy did not discourage intermarriage, that scholars had yet to define religion adequately in the South African context, and that its influence on South African society had not been properly documented.

Du Toit (1983) argued further that there is no persuasive evidence that the eighteenth-century Voortrekkers saw themselves as a "chosen people," a religiously inspired identity modeled on the book of Exodus. If "chosen" is seen as a brand of group nationalism in which a people as a whole enacts a God-given destiny, then it is fair enough to note that this concept of Afrikaner identity and nationalism did not emerge until the nineteenth century. If, however, "chosen" status accrues to Christians more generally, then I argue that it was a basis upon which the rural colonists distinguished themselves from people of color.

Ross (1993, 74–81) argues that religion was not an important element in the rural interior until the late eighteenth century. He points to the non-Calvinist origins of many settlers and cites a well-known traveler who commented on low rates of church attendance in Cape Town, surmising that attendance would be lower in rural areas, which he did not visit. Although early evidence on church participation is sketchy, stronger evidence of religiosity survives for the second half of the eighteenth century, when more travelers described the frontier. Ross (1993, 74–81) attributes it, however, to a "religious revival" with little evidence in support.

Giliomee (2003, 41–45) adopts Gerstner's (1997, 16–30) view that South

African settlers believed that they had a monopoly on Christianity on account of their descent, but he discounts the importance of religion until the late eighteenth century. Like Ross (1993, 74–81), he posits, with little evidence, a religious awakening to account for more frequent reports of the Afrikaners' beliefs. His evidence on the lack of religion in rural settler South Africa fails to differentiate between members of the orthodox Dutch Reformed community and other Europeans who lived with the Khoikhoi and who were definitely not religious by European standards.

I have argued in this chapter that the rigid theology of the orthodox settler community inevitably produced different social realities. The Christian community of orthodox believers considered themselves to have a special relationship with the Almighty that was their exclusive birthright. In their eyes the non-Christian rural settler community was composed of everyone else—from heathen pastoralists and hunter-gatherers to lapsed European settlers who had, by associating with indigenous people, lost their status as members in good standing of the settler community.

It is a truism of much social geography research today that space and power relations are mutually constituted, an argument with considerable force in colonial South Africa. Race relations, religious conversion, the status of women, and marriage fields were constituted differently in the capital and in the interior, in large part because of different colonial populations in control: the Dutch East India Company with its official integration (though nevertheless racist) policies versus an alienated white settler society living beyond its day-to-day reach. With both societies dominated by patriarchal men, women's racial identities paradoxically became crucial to their calculus, and which women were included or excluded as wives, partners, or mothers was a cornerstone of the subsequent development of apartheid society in South Africa.

Part Two ... Religion & Women's Mobility

3

Gender, Religion, and Urban Management

Women's Bodies and Everyday Lives in Jerusalem

Tovi Fenster

The idea of exploring the links between gender relations, religious identities, and urban management by focusing on cultural constructions of women's bodies came up while I conducted fieldwork in which I talked to residents of Jerusalem and London about their everyday experiences in these cities.[1] This analysis is based on research carried out between 1999 and 2002 in which residents of London and Jerusalem were interviewed regarding their everyday experiences as related to three concepts: comfort, belonging, and commitment regarding the various categories of their environment including home, building, street, neighborhood, city center, city, and urban parks (Fenster 2004). People told their stories about their lives in the city related to these categories, and from their daily experiences I drew out an understanding of the gendered aspects of comfort, belonging, and commitment in the city. The people interviewed represent both the "majority" hegemonic, that is, the Jewish secular population in Jerusalem and the white middle class English in London, and also the "minority," the "other" whether Bangladeshi immigrants in London or Palestinians in Jerusalem. This wide range of cultural expressions and ethnicities revealed the multilayered expressions of belonging both in their formal structures as citizenship definitions and in their personal, intimate, private expressions in daily practices in the city.

This chapter extends research (Fenster 2004) that explores women's mobility in the context of their "rights to the city," defined by Lefebvre (1991a) and D. Mitchell (2003) as individuals' fundamental freedom to occupy urban space. It does so by looking at the notion of women's bodies as sites of honor and modesty or shame and disgrace and the role of clothing as mechanisms of normal-ization and acceptance. I initially focus on the Jerusalem neighborhood of Mea Shearim, because my interviews indicate that it is a place whose occupants de-fine "rights to the city" in exclusionary and religiously orthodox ways. Jewish orthodoxy, for example, requires women to dress modestly in public by cover-ing their bodies and heads. Mea Shearim occupants seek to apply these reli-gious dress codes to all women who enter their neighborhood, whether they are orthodox Jews or not. Mea Shearim, described in detail below, was specifically established as a place where ultraorthodox Jews could live completely accord-ing to their religious regulations, making it a kind of sacred space.

Most women I interviewed in Jerusalem, secular Jewish and Palestinians, mentioned the ultraorthodox Mea Shearim neighborhood as an area they asso-ciated with bodily discomfort and tensions, an area they therefore avoid walk-ing through because of the sense of threat there:

> It is very uncomfortable for me to go to Mea Shearim; it is hard for me to accept the authority of somebody who is extremist and rejects me from humanity. "They" will not accept me in all of the clothes that I wear and I have to force my-self to adopt their own identity and it is not comfortable for me. The same in churches or mosques. (Sarit, Fenster interview, 22 April 2000)

> Mea Shearim is a less comfortable place for me. I can't dress the way I like. . . . I like to walk there but. . . . (Suzana, Fenster interview, 13 July 2000)

> Mea Shearim is a place I avoid visiting. I don't dare because I feel that it is not only that I don't belong but it is like a gated place only to ultraorthodox [peo-ple] and only for Jews so I never went there and even didn't think of going. (Magda, Fenster interview, 25 March 2001)

These narratives clearly express how the women's bodies become sites of polit-ical and municipal struggle based on religious norms and values of modesty, honor or shame, and disgrace. Indeed women's bodies are necessarily cultural forms and whatever role anatomy and biology play they always interact with culture (Bordo 1997) but in certain occasions (such as those described above) culture and more so religion have a "direct grip" on women's bodies through various mechanisms such as the practices of clothing. These practices have sometimes problematic effects on women's right to the city.

The Body and the Right to the City

Women's bodies, dress, and daily practices become key issues in the construction of spaces as "public" and thus "permitted" or "privatized" in the name of religious conduct of the body (see also chapter 4). Their daily experiences emphasize how "bodies and spaces construct each other in complex and nuanced ways" (Longhurst 2005, 93). Moreover, their experiences reflect the extent to which women's bodies, embodiment, clothing, and representation become a trigger to the violation of citizenship rights, especially the right to the city and the right to dress how one wishes in public spaces. It is therefore another illustration of what has been termed by Charlotte Bunch (1968) as "personal politics" (in Longhurst 2005). The "body" is perceived as the personal "container" of identities and therefore the site for everyday spatial negotiations. This is so especially for women whose lives are largely centered on the body either on its beautification and the reproduction, care, and maintenance bodies of others, or as contested site of cultural and religious norms (Bordo 1997). In this respect the "politics of the body" have their direct connection to the discourse around the right to the city.

The right to the city as Lefebvre defines it (1991a, 1991b), asserts a normative rather than a juridical right based on inhabitance. Those who inhabit the city have a right to the city. It is earned by living in the city, and it is shared between the urban dweller, the one who uses the city without living in it, and the city citizen, the one who lives in the city. This means that both those who live in the city permanently and those who use it temporarily have the right to take part in the urban creation—urban everyday life in the city. This concept of right to the city includes within it two main rights (Purcell 2003a). It is the right to appropriate urban space in the sense of the right to use, the right of inhabitants to "full and complete use" of urban space in their everyday lives. It is the right to live in, play in, work in, represent, characterize, and occupy urban space in a particular city—the right to be an author of urban space. It is a creative product of and context for the everyday life of its inhabitants. The second component of the right to the city is the right to participation. It includes the rights of inhabitants to take a central role in decision making surrounding the production of urban space at any scale, within the state, capital, or any other entity that takes part in the production of urban space. As Dikec (2001) points out, this entails the involvement of inhabitants in forms of institutionalized control over urban life, which include, among others, participation in political life and taking an active role in management and administration of the city (ibid.).

It is interesting that secular women living in Jerusalem, regardless of their nationality, ethnicity, or religious identity, mentioned certain neighborhoods as a cause for bodily discomfort and tension because of their dress. Women in London, by comparison, did not talk about such experiences in their everyday lives although they lived in a city that is also a home for multiple ethnic, cultural, and religious communities. Obviously, tensions within multireligious communities exist in many other cities (Naylor and Ryan 1998), and sometimes these tensions have effects on women's movement in urban spaces (Secor 2002). However, Mea Shearim represents a more complicated situation; while such sacralization of space denies *individual* rights of secular women to the city it reflects the *group* right to difference claimed by the ultraorthodox. The right to the city as Lefebvre interprets it is never absolute. In many world cities, for example, corporate workplaces, high-tech offices, and office buildings in general become "privatized" and thus "forbidden" beyond the reception desks, and entrances to "strangers" are always under surveillance and controlled with video cameras. This is especially so since the 9/11 events in the United States, after which many public spaces became privatized or exclusionary through additional security measures.

The cultural construction of the body and its implications in the "right to dress" in public spaces is also challenged in certain circumstances. Women and men might be arrested if they walk naked or in what is termed "improper" clothing in certain public spaces. In certain American states such as Utah, there are debates about whether nursing mothers have the right to breast-feed their babies in public because of the association of women's breasts with immodesty.[2] There is also a large body of work that shows that women sometimes voluntarily limit their mobility and movement in public spaces because of fear of sexual harassment or assault (Valentine 1989; Madge 1997; Pain 1991).

These growing limitations to "the right to the city" in the name of security, fear, religion, and cultural norms make it more and more important to discuss the tensions between these powers (religious groups, high-tech "security" actors, or patriarchal norms in general) and *individual* rights to the city, which include the right to one's own body and dress. I have chosen to focus my discussion on one specific example—the tensions between what might be termed a group's right to *difference,* such as a religious minority's right to maintain their religious and cultural norms even if this includes the prerogative to police appropriate access to their urban neighborhood, and *individual* rights to the city of other residents or visitors, in this case of secular women expressed in their "right to the body cover" or the choice of their dress. I also want to highlight the effects of these tensions between the different sets of rights on local governance.

The discussion of ultraorthodox right to difference vis-à-vis individual rights of nonorthodox women to the city in Jerusalem is incorporated within the wider context of Israel as a declared Jewish state, which faces constant conflicts in its social, cultural, and political identity and allows issues of women's bodies and dress to become spatial constraints. The Mea Shearim neighborhood's monitoring of women's attire is only one of the many tensions between secular and ultraorthodox communities in Jerusalem, which notably include disagreements on what public activities are allowed on the Sabbath—the resting day for the Jews. (Jewish law entails the halt of public transportation, the closure of shops, cinemas, theater, and other public activities in Sabbath.) Although the ultraorthodox perceive the Sabbath as a holy day and demand the prohibition of profane public activities in much more extreme ways than in the Diaspora because of the holiness of the land of Israel, the secular demand their freedom to use public spaces and public activities. Such tensions are expressed in violent fights and stone throwing on cars passing through ultraorthodox neighborhoods on the Sabbath, road blocking by ultraorthodox men near their neighborhoods, or demonstrations against cultural activities on the Sabbath.

Hasson (1996, 2002), Hasson and Gonen (1997), and Shilav 1997) discuss these religious-cultural tensions between secular and ultraorthodox Jews in Jerusalem, particularly exploring the dynamics of "spaces of conflicts" that were constructed between ultraorthodox and secular Jewish people and the various strategies each side adopts to meet its goals. My focus, by contrast, is on contradictory expressions of the right to the city, focusing on women's bodies and dress as major aspects of these conflicts and missing in current research. I next elaborate on the historical background and the daily practices of the sacralization of public spaces in Jerusalem.

Public Spaces as Sacred in Mea Shearim

Historical and Political Background

Foucault is probably one of the most well-known theorists of the body today (Grosz 1997). In his work he makes connections among pleasure/pain/sensation/knowledge and power and relies on a belief that power functions directly on bodies by means of disciplinary practices. Mea Shearim (Hebrew for "one hundred gates") can be perceived as such a site of (religious) power that functions directly on women's bodies by means of disciplinary practices expressed in women's dress.

Its segregated character was determined in 1874 when the neighborhood was established as one of the first neighborhoods built in west Jerusalem outside the walls of the old city. Its founders, members of the ultraorthodox community, set up clear rules to maintain its religious identity and homogeneity. For example, they decided that residents would not sell or rent their flats to non-ultraorthodox Jews, let alone to non-Jewish people (Ben Arie 1979). This means that the neighborhood has been characterized from the outset as a "ghettoized space," a reflection of the strong religious identities of its residents, which among other things dictate strict rules of body and clothing. Its site allocation, distant from what was then the city center (in the old city) and distant from any means of public transportation, is another "ghettoized expression" of the neighborhood, meant to keep its religious identity and maintain its distinctive lifestyle (ibid.).

It is important to emphasize this historical background as it highlights the distinctive character of this group within the ultraorthodox community. The residents of Mea Shearim represent more conservative and extremist viewpoints than other ultraorthodox communities, perceiving secular lifestyles, especially in the holy land of Israel, as illegitimate according to their interpretations of Jewish traditions and norms, including that of the body and clothing. Moreover, the ultraorthodox community in Mea Shearim does not accept the sovereignty of the state of Israel and does not perceive itself as part of the citizenship discourse, which entails specific duties to the state. (For example, men do not serve in the Israeli army although military duty is compulsory in Israel.) Furthermore, within the framework of their religious way of life there is no room for individualism let alone principles of democracy, equality, and participation in civil secular activities. It is a highly hierarchical and patriarchal society in which authority and power are determined according to family connections and degree of knowledge of the Jewish holy books. Its power and hierarchy operate by means of strict disciplinary practices.

But this declared denial from citizenship duties does not prevent Mea Shearim residents from taking a very active role in local politics. The religious leaders of the community are especially involved in negotiations with the municipality over their local interests. Their leaders also acknowledge the importance of their votes both for the government and the municipality and make sure that all their members do realize their right to vote,[3] and thereby gain significant power in the city council government coalitions.

However, this custom of spatial segregation and political participation exists in many other ultraorthodox Jewish neighborhoods in different cities around the world. Even today, ultraorthodox communities usually choose distant sites as their preferred locations. For example, Kiryat Joel, a Satmar town in New York State, was established in the 1970s at a distance of about 44 miles (70 km) from the New York city center to protect the residents from "external influences" and to allow the children to grow up free from the influences of drugs and crime (Mintz 1994).[4] This geographical isolation created the "shtetl type" of life free from immorality and profanity of secular urban life (Valins 2003).

Using Young's (1998) terminology of the "ideal city life" these communities actually practice the principle of "living together as strangers," meaning living as part of modern life but as a separate group. They are becoming what Kymlicka (1998) terms religious sects, such as the Amish or Hutterites in the United States and Canada. These groups have been granted exemption from the usual requirements and duties of citizenship such as military service during wartime or compulsory education for children beyond the eighth grade. Likewise, the ultraorthodox can be seen as a religious sect in their exemption from the duty of serving in the Israeli army, which is also an important means of socializing young adults into mainstream Israeli society. At the same time, the ultraorthodox communities in Israel and in the Diaspora run their own cultural and educational systems and conduct their own educational curricula, which do not include much study of citizenship, mathematics, secular history, and other areas of education that are compulsory in the general education system in Israel. What does distinguish between ultraorthodox communities around the world and Mea Shearim is that Mea Shearim is located in the heart of Jerusalem and the Jewish state, whereas most of the others are isolated within large non-Jewish nations. However, in spite of the proximity of Mea Shearim to a municipality based upon principles of religious tolerance, certain areas of Mea Shearim are still managed by its residents as isolated, ghettoized, and sacred space, especially in their treatment of women (Shilav 1997; Braun 2004).

Modesty Walls

Mea Shearim's gendered ghettoized character has a clear visual and spatial expression. Large signs hang at the two main entrances to the neighborhood on Mea Shearim Street—the main street of the neighborhood—and also at the entrances to the small alleys and shops located within the neighborhood. These signs pose a clear request in Hebrew and English. Sometimes the message in Hebrew and English is similar, sometimes it is slightly different (see Fig. 2).

> Please do not pass through our neighborhood in immodest clothes.

This request regarding modest clothing refers to women's bodies only as it is specified in the Hebrew language. Hebrew is a gendered language that uses feminine and masculine pronouns and verbs so that the gender of the object of a request or command is always clear. The signs also specify the exact reflections of bodily honor and modesty according to Jewish law and practice (see Fig. 2).

> Modest clothes include: closed blouse, with long sleeves, long skirt, no trousers, no tight-fitting clothes.

These specifications in fact clarify the Jewish religious construction of women's bodies as sites of modesty and honor or shame and disgrace. The rather de-

2. A main entrance to Mea Shearim (Jerusalem). Photograph by Tovi Fenster.

tailed conditions of modesty do not leave any space for individual interpretations as to its meaning. These very detailed specifications related to the appropriate ways to cover all parts of women's bodies is a visual expression of Foucault's account that power functions directly on bodies by means of disciplinary practices (Grosz 1997) that are specified in these signs. Another expression of this account appears at the bottom of this sign where there is a specific request using again the feminine gender in Hebrew. In English it says:

> Please do not disturb our children's education and our way of life as Jews committed to God and his Torah.

The Hebrew version of this sign emphasizes the sacredness of the neighborhood:

> Please do not disrupt the sacredness of our neighborhood and our way of life as Jews dedicated to God and his Torah.[5]

The signs in Hebrew are more explicit about the sacredness of the place probably because power has to be more explicit internally, that is, among Jewish groups, rather than with people from outside Israel such as tourists. The sign ends with mentioning "the neighborhood residents" as those who signed this request. Lately, similar signs in Hebrew only have begun to appear in shop entrances as well and again ask women (see Fig. 3):

Please enter my shop with modest clothes only.

Here, too, the specifications of modest clothes are mentioned and the request for women not to destroy the sacredness of the neighborhood is mentioned as well. This recent practice to install signs on shop entrances signifies the extremist tendencies to maintain modesty in the streets of Mea Shearim by people who live in the neighborhood but also by shopkeepers who are not necessarily members of the community but who put up these signs to show the local residents that they follow the strict rules of modesty. They thus legitimate their space as appropriate for local residents.

Although these signs can be perceived according to Foucault as symbols of internal relations of power and knowledge that are expressed in disciplinary practices, the religious declared reasons for putting these signs in the streets and shop entrances have to do with the sacredness of the Land of Israel as the promised Biblical land in the eyes of the ultraorthodox. This holiness necessitates practices of modesty and dress not only by ultraorthodox women but by secular women as well because women's modesty is a very basic rule in the religious Jewish lifestyle (Yosef Shilav, personal communication, 2004). These practices can be seen as symbolic "border guards" that help to identify people as members or nonmembers of the community. Here again, women's bodies and dress are often the major signifiers of such border constructions (Yuval-Davis 2000). Women's bodies and dress, Muslim or Jewish, indicate that the body and its covering are expressions of dominant ideologies and representations either of "Muslim women" (Dwyer 1997) or "Jewish women" and also as sites of contested cultural representations. In addition to the dress code for observant Jewish women indicated above, orthodox Jewish women in public will also cover their heads in some fashion, such as with a hat, headscarf, or wig. Though less visible than the Muslim bourka, the head coverings of orthodox Jewish women equally signify religious identities.

Other sets of disciplinary practices in Mea Shearim are targeted toward mixed groups passing through the neighborhood. Because of its unique reli-

3. *Entrance to small shop in Mea Shearim (Jerusalem). Photograph*
by Tovi Fenster.

gious and spatial character, the neighborhood has become a popular place for
visitors and tourists partly because tourists are interested in the explicit cultural symbols of its seclusion. The practice of tour groups walking around the
neighborhood in mixed gendered groups also destroys the religious norms of
Mea Shearim as sacred space for its occupants. In orthodox synagogues, for example, men and women sit in separate spaces, a practice that ensures that there
is no male contact with women's impurity during menstruation. Ultraorthodox Jews extend such gender segregation to many aspects of daily life so that
gender-mixed groups beyond the family level are a rare occurrence. Thus, tour
groups of men and women pose a difficulty for Mea Shearim beyond the imposition of the mass tourist gaze.

GROUPS passing through our neighborhood severely offend the residents.
PLEASE STOP THIS.

These signs show the gated nature of the neighborhood with its "modesty
gates" or, as its residents phrase it, "modesty walls." These walls construct the
bodily boundaries of the religious and cultural identities of its residents and
transform its main streets into sacred spaces that exclude women of other be-

liefs who do not follow the strict rules of modest dress along with mixed-gendered groups who disobey practices of gender segregation. However, such signs can also be interpreted as part of the politics of identity of the community, which struggles against "intolerance of difference" in modernity (Kong 2001). Moreover, these signs may express the "right to difference" of ultra-orthodox women's bodies who feel more comfortable in such a gated space, in which their own modest dress is a norm rather than the exception it would be in other secular public spaces in Jerusalem (Fenster 2004).

As such, these signs serve as a defense against "inappropriate" dress and lifestyles, which contradict the group's norms and standards of behavior. Such a construction of public spaces as sacred is contested in any case (Kong 2001), mainly because sacred is a contested category as it represents "hierarchical power relations of domination and subordination, inclusion and exclusion, appropriation and dispossession" (Chidester and Linenthal 1995, 17; quoted in Kong 2001). A sacred place is constructed by appropriation of a property, through the politics of exclusion, by maintaining boundaries, and by distancing the inside from the outside (Kong 2001). As Sibley mentions (1995, 1998), forms and norms of exclusion are not only the practices of the majority against the minority but also the practices of the minority against the majority, as in the case of Mea Shearim.

Control and surveillance of public spaces through women's bodies demonstrate the tight links between bodies and cities: "The city in its particular geographical, architectural, spatializing, municipal arrangements is one particular ingredient in the social constitution of the body" (Grosz 1992, 248; quoted in Longhurst 2005). In this example, the social constitution of the body and the determination of clear boundaries of forbidden and permitted serve as a means to maintain the sacredness of a space and to keep its disciplinary practices. This is not new. It is as old as ancient Judaism and it goes back to the spatialized institution of the Second Temple and the structuring of private and public space at the individual day-to-day level (Valins 2000).

The spatial boundaries of the forbidden and the permitted also relate to norms and orders of the acts prohibited on the Sabbath. In addition to permitted and prohibited public activities, Sabbath regulations also prohibit the transfer of heavy objects between different private and public spaces because carrying them is considered work, which is forbidden on the Sabbath. Such institutionalization of religious and social order exists in ultraorthodox neighborhoods today in many cities around the world, as expressed in the construction of a neighborhood boundary called the *eruv* or *erub* (Hebrew for mixture) (Valins 2000; Schecher and Friedlander n.d.). Under Jewish law, Jews may circumvent the proscription against carrying anything into an open public space on the Sabbath by establishing a fence or some other type of artificial boundary around their neighborhood that essentially redefines it as community space. I elaborate on this point in the final section. Here I wish to present the argument that even if such boundaries reflect norms and identity constructs of the ultraorthodox people and their right to (group) difference, they might contradict the (individual) rights of women and men of other religious identities to the city.

The Right to the City and the Right to Difference

The previous section illustrates the conflicts between Lefebvre's (1991a, 1991b) terminology of the right to the city and a distinctive group's right to define mobility and accessibility within their neighborhood, as claimed by residents of Mea Shearim (Young 1998). This discussion takes several directions: first, the right to the city and the right to difference; second, individual rights versus group rights; and third, the extent to which such discourses can be incorporated in local governance's policies and politics.

Many academic works have incorporated the notion of the right to the city in their analysis of urban everyday life (Kofman 1995; Kofman and Labas 1996; Yacobi 2003; Fenster 2004; Purcell 2003a; Dikec 2001; Cuthbert 1995; D. Mitchell 2003). This analysis is usually integrated in the discussion of new forms of citizenship that challenge the traditional, hegemonic nation-state. These new forms of citizenship refer not only to the legal status of citizens provided them by the state but also to membership and belonging within a community and the tactics and practices to claim citizen rights. Citizenship is viewed as continuously negotiated through everyday practices (Secor 2004).

These new forms of citizenship challenge capitalist power relations and their increased control over social life (Purcell 2003a). They also challenge the static "top-down" analysis of citizenship and present an approach to citizenship as a spatial strategy that includes certain definitions of belonging, identity, and rights (Secor 2004). As Purcell (2003a) indicates, these processes entail rescaling, reterritorializing, and reorienting of both the economy and forms of citizenship. This means that the economy and citizenship are not so much dependent on state legislation and action (rescaling), but refer to different "territories" such as cities and regions more than the state (reterritorializing) and reflect their reorientation (for an elaboration, see Purcell 2003a). In this context of political and economic restructuring the Lefebvrian construction and meaning of "the right to the city" can be interpreted as a form of resistance to traditional structures of citizenship, which means that the traditional top-down forms of citizenship are challenged by bottom up daily practices of "using" the city. This rather radical understanding of citizenship begins with the belief that the right to the city is based on inhabitance in the city as opposed to other forms of membership that are determined by nation-state citizenship. The right to the city or the right to urban life, which is based on inhabitance, entails two main rights: "the right to appropriate" urban space or "the right to use" urban space; and "the right to participate" in the production of urban space, which means the right to take active part in creation of urban life and urban spirit (Purcell 2003a). These normative rights encompass not only rights to resources but the right to be the author of urban space, the right to belong in the city and contribute to it.

Alongside these sets of rights, Lefebvre indicates the individual "right to difference" or the right to be different, which involves the right of individuals not to be classified into categories by the homogenizing powers but to maintain their own difference (Dikec 2001). Moving the discussion to group identity and rights, can we discuss the right to difference of the ultraorthodox as a group right and the practices of modesty walls as its expression? In other words, is the group unit rather than the individual a valid component in the discussion of the right to difference? Young (1998) assures the political importance of the concept "social group" as the unit, which motivates and mobilizes social movements such as the women's movement, gay movement, or elders' movements more than those of exclusively class or economic interests. However, she asserts that group identity should be understood in relational terms, and although social processes of affinity and separation define groups, they do not always give groups a substantive identity because each of the group members possess multiple identities besides the group identity: "There is no common nature that members of a group have," she asserts (273). However, she also argues that the inclusion and participation of everyone in social and political institutions sometimes requires the articulation of "special rights" that meet the needs of a group's difference. Here, she mainly refers to "oppressed groups" such as women, gay communities, elderly people, or other groups who suffer from exploitation, marginalization, powerlessness, cultural imperialism, and violence and harassment.

Can such conditions be related to the position of the ultraorthodox in Jerusalem? Perhaps so in their eyes; but arguably these conditions apply better to secular women. Kymlicka's (1998) definition of religious sects as groups, which demand exemption from civil society because its norms contradict some of the group's religious practices, can be useful in this discussion. He argues that sometimes these demands for exemption are indeed a form of withdrawal from the larger society, but that some of them show a desire for integration. For example, Kimlicka states that orthodox Jews who wanted to join the U.S. military needed an exemption from the usual regulations so that they could wear their yarmulkes. This practice can be seen as an example of a group right to difference, which expresses a will to integrate in civil life and duties. Following this line of thinking, can we then interpret the modesty walls as an expression of the ultraorthodox's desire to integrate in the sense that these "walls" are more symbolic than physical and are condoned by the larger metropolitan area? Or does the Mea Shearim example represent a struggle against intolerance of the modernized secular polity, with women's modesty practices as the price paid for this struggle?

One can also challenge the municipality's role in this struggle. That is, do municipalities adopt the Lefebvreian standpoint of the individual's right to the city and then prohibit practices of modesty walls in the city, as they deny nonorthodox women's "right to use" the city; or are Mea Shearim's practices part of a group identity and right to difference in privatizing public spaces as sacred that should be respected, especially in an era when the Lefebvrian right to the city is denied in the name of security, for example?

Relating to this matter, Benvenisti (1998) argues that the claim for religious autonomy or the sacralization of space is justified only if it does not contradict fundamental norms and state legislation. As he argues, the formulation of such a "religious ghetto" is acceptable as long as it is based on cultural and religious heritage preservation principles. Benvenisti argues that this is the case of the ultraorthodox as much as the claims of the Aboriginals in Australia, the First Nations in Canada, and the Sami in Scandinavia to maintain their traditional lives. The only problem Benvenisti sees is that such norms, which create exclusion, can harm women's rights. The solution Benvenisti suggests is to allow these communities to express autonomy so long as they respect the rights of the majority. His solution introduces the concept of "gendered rights to the city." Where minority groups place serious restrictions upon women, gender complicates this "group right–individual right" tension dramatically.

Elsewhere I discuss similar debates (Fenster 1999a, 1999b) regarding planning procedures for ethnic groups such as the Bedouin in the Negev. There, the particularistic cultural-religious identity of the male Bedouin perpetuates women's subordination by dictating norms of modesty and seclusion. Modernist, professional planning that is intolerant of such identity-related issues actually designs Bedouin towns in such a way that women will not use public spaces because of the danger of abusing their modesty in the eyes of the males. For example, modernist planning assumes high population density, the construction of one main urban center to the town, and zoning regulations that separate residential and economic areas. These planning practices force Bedouin women to work outside their tribal affiliated neighborhood and enhance the chances of unwanted meetings between women and men of different tribes, which threaten women's modesty in Bedouin beliefs (ibid.). An "intolerance of difference" is actually expressed in modernist planning when the design of Bedouin towns is made according to a universalist modernist approach that in fact worsens the already subordinated situation of Bedouin women by putting more restrictions on their daily freedom of movement in the town, including going to work.

If we look back at women's narratives presented at the beginning of the chapter they emphasized that they found their treatment to be offensive regarding their right to the city and their "right to the body," which was violated by the patriarchal power of the modesty walls. How do the politics and policies of the municipality deal with the conflict between the right to difference of a group and the right of use of individuals? And does this right to difference, which entails the construction of privatized spaces as sacred, occur in other cities? The next section tackles these debates.

Women's Bodies and City Governance

Dealing with conflicts between individual gendered rights to the city and group rights to difference I first wanted to understand the municipality standpoint regarding the modesty signs. I talked to the chief of the City Enforcement Department at the Jerusalem Municipality, a department that deals with enforcing municipal bylaws, including those concerning licensing for street signs and businesses. I asked him about the legality of the signs in the streets of Mea Shearim. He affirmed that in general the municipality is very rigid in enforcing municipal bylaws by imposing licensing for street signs and businesses. But in Mea Shearim, he said, it is different.

Although the signs there are illegal because they were not approved and licensed by the municipality, the municipality's workers cannot enforce the law. The chief of the City Enforcement Department defined this area as "outside the law and outside enforcing the law" (interview, 20 July 2003). He explained the difficulty of enforcing this bylaw in Mea Shearim due to lack of enough labor power: "Even if we take down these signs they will put them up again." This admission in fact reflects the struggle of the ultraorthodox group to establish its politics of identity and community by challenging the sovereignty of the municipality and perhaps its "intolerance to difference." It also expresses the Mea Shearim's group lack of recognition of the municipality's sovereignty. But this is probably also an expression of the municipality's implicit politics (meaning policies that are not clear and public) not to interfere with Mea Shearim's practices because of local politics and power relations within the municipality's council. The chief of City Enforcement Department admits that if such signs restricting movement appeared in secular neighborhoods, the municipality would have reacted forcefully against this practice. Thus, in spite of their illegitimate status these signs still hang in public spaces, transforming the neighborhood into a gated one.

Does this practice of sacralization of public urban spaces also reflect the group identity and the right to difference of ultraorthodox in other cities in Israel and abroad? In other cities in Israel such as Tel Aviv, certain neighborhoods are populated by ultraorthodox communities but with no explicit exclusionary signs. There are similar signs in the city of Benei Brak, for example, a city with a majority of religious residents, but these signs are less offensive and perhaps less exclusionary.[6] Shilav (1997) analyzes the management of ultraorthodox cities in Israel relating to the extent to which the ultraorthodox communities themselves are flexible or tolerant of people with less-rigid religious practices living within them. For example, in Beitar Ilit, one of the ultraorthodox cities in Israel,[7] the municipal authority is not tolerant toward nonreligious members of the community itself, in this case rebellious youth.[8]

Practices of sacralization of public spaces are also not known in cities outside Israel where ultraorthodox communities live, such as in the United States, Canada, and Britain. This is perhaps because some live in isolated areas where there is no need to protect themselves from outside "negative" influence. Moreover, in New York where there is a concentration of ultraorthodox communities in Brooklyn and in Kiryat Joel, those communities are very active politically and make sure they benefit from "affirmative policies" of the federal government. They claim to experience discrimination on economic bases because their religious beliefs do not permit them to work on Saturdays. They use human rights legislation to argue that they are a protected class under cultural as well as religious identities. This means that the ultraorthodox in the United States gain their rights to difference within American legal frameworks (Shilav 1997).

The ultraorthodox communities in Britain represent another example of how their right to difference is practiced within legal frameworks and with no violation of women's right of use in the city. These communities live mainly in Manchester and London. In Manchester they include 90 percent of the city's Jewish community. There, they express their needs for segregation and the marking of clear boundaries between themselves and the rest of the world (Valins 2003). However, their practices do not include control of women's bodies and clothing but of living in homogeneous communities as an act of security. Another spatial religious practice of the Jewish community in Britain is the construction of an artificial boundary (*eruv* or *erub*), within which Jews are permitted to carry items in public spaces on the Sabbath. Congregations in modern cities may construct an *eruv* by stringing up overhead wires to create a sort of boundary around their neighborhood, often with the consent of the local utility company, "a complex device consisting of posts and wires, which is able to change the classification of space (from public to private)" (Valins 2000, 576; see also Schechter and Friedlander n.d.).

The erection of an *eruv* in fact eases Sabbath restrictions on carrying articles outside one's private property, especially for the elderly, infirm, and parents with young children.[9] Valins (2003) argues that the construction of such boundaries, although not so visible, within the context of modern or postmodern urban spaces and the surrounding secular population makes the determination of such practices politically and religiously fraught. This is especially so among the secular Jews, who fear that such boundaries would create a Jewish ghetto similar to the Jewish ghettos before World War II. Nevertheless, the community members practice this spatial difference within the legal framework of the nation-state or the municipality requirements, and they submitted a request for a planning permit. They obeyed civil and municipal bylaws and asked for legal permission to establish spatial changes that resulted from their own religious identity of difference. By doing that they did not deny anyone else the right of use in the city and its public spaces.

Conclusion

This chapter posits the debate between the individual right to use public urban spaces, the right to the body and the group right to difference within the framework of ethno-religious communities' constructions of urban spaces as sacred and women's bodies and dress as a practice of such constructions. I challenge the power of municipal authorities in Jerusalem to accept or prohibit gendered exclusionary constructions of space and present an alternative to such practices in the analysis of the multilayered meanings of citizenship. The case of Mea Shearim represents an extreme example of a site of power that functions directly on women's bodies. An ultraorthodox community, which because of its desire to maintain "pure" and "sacred" ghettoized spaces, acts illegally by constructing symbolic gates at the entrances of the neighborhood, which defines disciplinary practices on women's bodies.

The basic dilemma posed by this chapter is whether such a situation, which denies secular women's rights to some public parts of the city because of the religious construction of the body as a contested site of modesty, can be simultaneously accepted as an expression of daily religious practices of a distinct community that struggles to maintain its difference. The chapter does not provide a clear-cut solution but rather exposes the multiple implications of such situations. Feminists' first reaction to such exclusionary practices in the city might be negative, but the different meanings and implications of such situations reveal contradictory meanings of the right to the city and the contrast inherent between them, a situation that becomes more and more apparent in multiethnicized, multisacralized, and multinationalized global urban spaces. Such dilemmas will be part of city governance's daily occupation as diversity becomes an increasingly important issue in new global spaces. One of the major challenges of city governance is how to respect both individual and

4

A Feminist Geography of Veiling

Gender, Class, and Religion in the Making
of Modern Subjects and Public Spaces in Istanbul

Banu Gökarıksel

On 29 June 2004 the European Court of Human Rights (ECHR) announced its judgment on the case of *Leyla Şahin versus Turkey* in favor of the latter, finding the existing ban on "Islamic headscarves" at universities as a necessary measure to protect the republic, pluralism on campus, and the "secular Muslim majority" (ECHR 2004).[1] Veiling has been a persistent topic of intense political debate in Turkey. This debate has only heightened since the 1980s with the imposition of regulations that restrict headscarves in public institutions (although variably implemented), the electoral success of Islamist political parties, and increasingly visible forms of social mobilization for or against veiling (Göle 1996; Özdalga 1998; Secor 2002, 2005). After the ECHR decision, veiling debates erupted once again over definitions of laicism, liberalism, and democracy in Turkey and in Europe (Gökarıksel and Mitchell 2005).[2] By mid-July, these debates escalated into an argument over the boundary and meaning of public space.

The head of the secularist Council of Higher Education—a state institution established after the 1980 military coup to oversee the administration of all universities—put forth a state-centered understanding of public space as a space that is determined by the presence of state officials and the requirements of state regulation and control (Radikal 2004). In contrast, the so-called Muslim democrat prime minister defined public space on the basis of civil liberties and pluralism, underlining the significance of tolerance and respect for difference (Yalçınkaya 2004; Zaman 2004). This widely reported exchange generated numerous articles and opinion pieces in Turkey about different conceptions of public space, citizenship, and the modern state. Overall, this was a rare and crucial occasion for exposing the centrality of space to competing understandings of secularism and modernity. These debates highlighted the significance of space for constructing secular modern subjects, "the public," and states. Yet this focus on public space interestingly did not include the ultimate target of headscarf bans, the bodies and practices of Muslim women (headscarf-wearing or not), and the gendered construction of (secular) public space. Also missing from these discussions was the cultural battle over the stigma that the headscarf and new styles of veiling carry in Turkey, not only as a threat to secularism but also as a marker of low-class status, provinciality, and backwardness. The class and migrant associations of the veil underline the specificity of the historical and geographical context that has shaped the Turkish experience of modernity.

Recent works in geography have emphasized that space is not merely an expression of ideology. Instead, space is central to the operation and reproduction of an ideology as well as to acts of transgression and resistance that may change and potentially overthrow that ideology (Cresswell 1996; Lefebvre 1991b; D. Mitchell 2000). The foci of geographers writing in this vein have been diverse, including analyses of the spatiality of capitalism (Harvey 1989) and the ideologies of class, gender, and sexuality (Bell and Valentine 1995; Domosh and Seager 2001; Sibley 1995; Valentine 1996). The ideology of secularism and its geographies have drawn comparatively little attention. Just like any other political ideology, secularism operates through the construction, organization, and encoding of spaces that represent, embody, and sometimes enforce "secular" values, norms, and practices.[3] These spaces include an interlinked network of scales from the body to that of the nation and the globe.[4] Women's bodies, dress, and practices are key to the construction of each space as secular, modern, or religious (see chapter 3). Moreover, as the description above from the head of the Council of Higher Education illustrates, from a secularist perspective, public space is broadly defined as the primary site of secularism and is guarded by state institutions.[5]

From the same perspective, the religious is limited not only to the realm of the private/personal and the official sacred spaces (e.g., mosques) but is also closely monitored by the state. However, the mobile bodies of women (marked as secular, religious, or modern) push the definitive and disciplinary limits of public space. The imposition of boundaries that delineate public versus private and secular versus religious on everyday spaces is central to the secular state's strategy of sustaining this political ideology and of cultivating "modern" subjects. Yet, it is also these boundaries that are challenged and are used to construct subjectivities that are critical of the specific terms of secularism and modernity imposed on them. How are secular and religious spaces constructed? How is this spatial division of the secular and the religious contested? This chapter focuses on the space of shopping malls in Istanbul to examine these questions.

Studies of religion, including geographical approaches, mostly focus on "officially sacred" (Leiris 1988; as cited in Kong 2001) spaces and practices. Lily Kong (2001) argues for new geographies of religion that expand beyond the officially sacred. Along this line, this chapter supports a new feminist geography of veiling and religion that highlights the gendering of the normative geographies of the everyday and "in place/out of place" bodies and practices.[6] I analyze a seemingly unlikely space for studying religion—shopping malls—and the daily, seemingly mundane activities that take place in malls such as shopping, socializing, or "killing time."[7] Only through such an analysis does it become possible to see the pervasiveness of both the secular and the religious in the everyday spaces and practices of urbanites. This examination reveals that often the secular/religious division is more fluid and blurry than rigid. Yet, this division still informs the meanings and reference points in relation to which subjectivities are constituted. My argument is that within the specific context of Istanbul, shopping malls have become one of the key spaces where what it means to be modern, secular, and Muslim is not only reproduced but also contested. This contestation occurs in gendered terms and practices that both constitute and challenge the normative geographies of urban space in Istanbul.

The constitution of the contemporary spaces of shopping malls and certain women's bodies as modern and secular is shaped by the historical construction of modernity in Turkey. If we take modernity as Ong (1997, 171) suggests, "as an evolving process of imagination and practice in particular historically situated formations," then it becomes important to question the specific ways in which modernity as a vision is defined and redefined and as a project is revised and materialized across shifting temporalities. Inflecting Ong's emphasis on historical context through geographical specificity enables the critical examination of changing and contested understandings of secularism, social distinction, and gender across space. My approach to modernity follows Ong's view of modernity as a vision, as a set of ideals and ideas that inform the design and implementation of cultural, socioeconomic, and spatial projects.

This chapter draws largely from ethnographic data collected in Istanbul from 1996 to 2004 in the space of shopping malls and department stores that carry veiling fashions.[8] I have conducted more than 100 semi-structured interviews with mall-goers, mall and department store management, sales personnel, and urban planning officials.[9] Additionally, I have analyzed advertisements, bulletins, magazines, Web sites, maps, and government publications. Participants in my research included women and men whom I contacted using my personal networks and others whom I did not know beforehand and approached at malls and department stores. For the purposes of this chapter, I focus mostly on a selection of interviews with mall-goers whose views represent different sides of the wider public debates about gender, religion, and modernity in Istanbul. I present an analysis of their narratives within the context of the larger projects of modernity of the secularist state and Islamist movements in Turkey.

Secularism and Modernity in the Republic

Both shopping malls and the veiling fashions that are the focus of public debates are fairly new in Turkey; both have emerged and found salience since the 1980s within the new context of neoliberalism and of desired integration into the European Union and the global economy (Gökarıksel 2003). Their primary locations are urban centers. Shopping malls are mostly built in the midst of inner city neighborhoods and some as components of large-scale mixed-use developments.[10] In this way, malls in Istanbul resemble more the recent urban development projects across the United States than their suburban predecessors.[11] Within this context, malls are heralded widely by the public and the media as the culmination of the republican tradition of modernization and are welcomed as the symbol of Turkish modernity in the global era.[12] In contrast, the public is deeply divided about whether headscarf-wearing Muslim women are part of this modernity or not. The novelty of many veiling fashions and the socioeconomic characteristics of their wearers are often overlooked in public discussions because headscarves are simply taken as a sign of religious "re-vival" among rural, working-class migrants who "fail" to adapt to urban modernity (Göle 1996; Gülalp 2003; Secor 2002). Veiling fashions are recognized only when the headscarf is referred to as *türban,* a term loaded with political signification meaning a "refusal" to modernize and tied to the growing threat of "Islamic fundamentalism." Both of these views posit the headscarf as outside of modernity and "out of place" at shopping malls. These designations and divisions can only be understood within the historical context of Turkish modernity.

In Turkey, the ideology of the early years of the republic often referred to as Kemalism, after its founder and first president Mustafa Kemal Atatürk, set the terms of the state's vision of Western-oriented modernity. The equation of the modern with the secular began in this period. Following the establishment of the republic in 1923, a series of drastic reforms was carried out that aimed at nothing less than transforming the everyday life of its citizens. French-influenced political ideology of laicism was a cornerstone of these reforms that served the distancing of the new republic from the Ottoman Islamic past, the building of the nation-state, and the cultivation of new citizens. Laicism in the Turkish context meant not the complete separation of the state and the mosque but restricting the role of Islam in public life on one hand and bringing the institutions and funds for Islamic training and practices under state control on the other (Davison 2003; Göle 1997a).[13]

The new republic radically extended the early modernization projects of the nineteenth and early twentieth century by abolishing the Islamic Caliphate and Islamic law, banning religious orders, dissolving religious courts and schools, and revising legal and educational systems according to various Western European models (Zührer 1993, 64–66, 125–27). It was in the same period that the State Directorate of Religious Affairs was founded to oversee the administration of mosques and the training and activities of religious clerks who had become state employees. Through these reforms the state attempted to restrict and to monitor cultural and political forms of Islam and to suppress those interpretations and practices of Islam that were seen as a threat to the republic (Yavuz and Esposito 2003). Kemalism has found support in considerably large segments of the populace and has remained influential and even definitive into the 2000s.[14] Since the 1980s, the secularist definition of the "modern" has been increasingly challenged by competing constructions of modernity that incorporate Islamic values and identities.[15]

Secular Spaces

Spatial transformation and the encoding and decoding of spaces at multiple scales were central to the state's project of secular modernity and Westernization. Public spaces as well as private spaces, including the most private and "closest in" geography of the body (Rich 1986, 212; as cited in Valentine 2001, 15), were to be reconstructed according to the new principles of the republic. From the very start, modernization has targeted public *and* private spheres, including the spaces, patterns, and habits of living, work, and leisure in urban and rural areas, albeit the application of these projects was significantly uneven, favoring urban and town centers at the expense of rural areas. The new architectural styles of the buildings, monuments, boulevards, parks, etc., of this period embodied the ideals of the republic and in turn, shaped the transformation of the entire fabric of Turkish society through the lifestyles, social practices, and values they enabled and promoted (Bozdoğan 2001). Spatial changes were key to "living modern" in the new cubic houses and apartments decorated according to European and American styles, in the new offices and industrial buildings, and in the new spaces of leisure and entertainment such as music and dance halls.

Shopping malls in Turkey started to open in the late 1980s in a context of neoliberal economic policies that departed significantly from the early state-centered policies of the republic. Nevertheless, the shopping mall became one of the iconic representations of modern life in Istanbul (and in the rest of Turkey). State and city governments (despite changes in political orientation, see Bora 1999), numerous newspapers and magazines, television news programs, and advertisements of the malls have reinforced and disseminated this view about shopping malls. Likewise, my interviewees have consistently defined malls as "modern" spaces where "modern" people go.

The engineer of Turkey's neoliberal restructuring, Turgut Özal, prime minister and then president throughout much of the 1980s, was instrumental in envisioning and promoting the building of the first mall in Istanbul (özdemir 1999; cited in Öktem 2003, 151). Özal personally inaugurated Galleria in 1988.

Galleria was presented as the symbol of Turkish modernity in the 1980s (and of the success of Özal's policies). Many of my research participants also described Galleria with a sense of national pride; it indicated that Istanbul was on a par with the modern world. Most described their feelings of awe and fascination on their first trip to Galleria. Galleria's management similarly presents Galleria as putting an end to the Turkish envy of the West, underlining a persistent theme of Turkish occidentalism.[16] Other malls followed rapidly the example of Galleria, and in 2004 there were seventeen shopping malls in Istanbul alone.

In 1999, after a necessary "facelift," Galleria was described as "Europe without a passport" by a retail consultant in Istanbul.[17] This slogan was coined much earlier by Akmerkez shopping mall in its full-page advertisements to celebrate its first anniversary. Akmerkez opened in 1993 at the intersection of three middle- and upper-class neighborhoods with its glass-covered towers of offices and condos on top of a luxurious shopping mall. One of the most popular national news channels, ATV, took the towers of Akmerkez shopping mall complex as the symbol of "the city" soon after its opening.

The space of shopping malls has been constituted as modern and by extension secular in the wider cultural context of modernity in Istanbul. Malls designed entertainment activities and celebrations on national religious holidays along with special events for national holidays and New Year's Day. The activities held on religious holidays were only remotely religious, if at all (Gökarıksel 1998). They mostly gestured toward reinventing "traditions," such as Ottoman court music concerts and Ottoman-style candy for kids, that could easily and safely become part of "secular" Muslim lives. In the mid-1990s, during a period of "crisis" following the first success of the Islamist Welfare Party in local elections in Istanbul, Akmerkez mall took the equation of modern and secular a step further and stated openly its secular identity (Gökarıksel 2003; Navaro-Yashin 2002a, 2002b). To do so, Akmerkez resorted to the republican practice of placing Mustafa Kemal Atatürk's pictures inside and outside the mall to align itself with the secularist modernity of Kemalism. Since then, the display on the first floor has expanded and become permanent with the addition of Atatürk's infamous "Speech to the Turkish Youth."[18]

The statues of Mustafa Kemal Atatürk, who symbolizes the process of modernization and the new republic in his person, have decorated public squares, parks, boulevards, and school yards in Istanbul and elsewhere in Turkey. His

4. Akmerkez shopping mall decorated with elaborate lights for New Year's (December 2004). Photograph by Banu Gökarıksel.

pictures have adorned the walls of state institutions, classrooms, offices, and even living rooms. In a sense, following the ideals of the early republic has become something of a "cult" of Kemalism (Navaro-Yashin 2002a). The placement of Atatürk statues and pictures has served to mark a space as secular and to represent devotion to the state project of modernity. Atatürk's presence in public and private spaces continues to remind onlookers of the past threats and struggles (including the "dark" Islamic Ottoman past and the War of Independence fought against European occupiers following World War I) and of the need to claim the modern, secular republic and to constantly guard it against old and new threats, especially that of Islamic fundamentalism. Akmerkez mall's placement of Atatürk pictures has warned the public of "rising" Islam and asserted once again that modernity is secular.

The secularity of malls is also confirmed by the absence of stores that sell new styles of veiling fashion. The Turkish veiling industry has flourished in the past decade, producing new models, colors, and styles of tesettür[19] clothing and even tesettür tennis clothes, swimming suits, and other expressions of haute couture.[20] The design of these stores is sleek, combining metal, glass, and bright

5. *Atatürk's picture and speech to the Turkish Youth on display on the first floor of Akmerkez shopping mall (December 2004). Photograph by Banu Gökarıksel.*

lights like that of the shopping malls. Yet, as of 2004, none of the shopping malls in Istanbul (including those located in more conservative areas where women's headscarf-wearing is very common or the norm) had any shops that specialize in veiling fashions. Veiling fashions are present in malls only on women shoppers' bodies that carry the latest styles of *tesettür*. This presence causes uneasiness about the perceived contradiction between veiling and being at a mall in my secularist research participants. Their perceptions stem from the historical construction of modern bodies and dress in Turkey.

Embodying Modernity

Michel Foucault's work has shown the centrality of the corporeal to the control of populations and its connection to the operation of modernity in Western Europe (Foucault 1977, 1979). In Turkey, too, the state project of modernity has involved "bio-power" through corporeal transformations to establish new structures of governmentality (Secor 2005). A new secularist, modernist moral conduct and worldview were to be cultivated in the new Turkish citizen (see

Scott 1998, 90). The physical body was also to be transformed through activities of "modern" sports and dance and the adoption of "modern" mannerisms and demeanor. The display of the republican youth's healthy and athletic bodies has been a significant performance at celebrations of national holidays.[21] Within this framework, dress was also to be changed as part of "deculturation" and "reculturation" according to the new vision of modernity (Bourdieu 1977). As Göle (1996) contends, the reforms of this period aimed at transforming the habitus of citizens and dress was an agent in the transformation of values, behavior, relationships, and lifestyles away from tradition and religion.[22]

Changes in dress and the body were directed toward both men and women. For example, the *fez* and all other religious headgear of men were outlawed in 1925, and Atatürk personally advocated for the brimmed hat or homburg as the symbol of the modern male subject. But the most prominent and controversial embodiment of modernization was the female subject. Women's bodies and practices have been bound up in the complex web of social, cultural, and national values such as morality and honor. In Göle's words, "within the emerging Kemalist paradigm, women became bearers of Westernization and carriers of secularism, and actresses . . . gave testimony to the dramatic shift of civilization" (Göle 1996, 14). An ideal republican woman was constructed to represent modern Turkey. The Kemalist woman is an "enlightened" subject in and outside of home; she is educated and professionally, socially, and politically active (Arat 1997; Durakbaşa 1998; Kandiyoti 1998). Spatially, this vision was to culminate in the end of gender segregation and the encouragement of women's presence in public spaces of work, education, and social activities. Yet, this ideal woman was still defined primarily within the bounds of the modernized home (Bozdoğan 2001), and her public presence was legitimate as long as she was fully devoted to the nation's progress and was asexualized and defeminized (Kadıoğlu 1998).

As a secular, modern woman, the republican ideal woman did not wear a veil. The veil has been seen to bind women with traditional and religious ties and to prevent them from becoming "civilized human beings" (Göle 1996, 13). It has also been perceived to invoke the religious demarcation of bodies and to instigate gendered divisions of space. Accordingly, it was women's *unveiling* that was presented as the necessary condition, vehicle, and symbol of the republic's modernity. Although this attitude did not lead to banning the veil in the early republic, female bodies in Islamic attire were cast as marked by tradition and religion and, therefore, not modern.

As Göle points out, modernization has not been independent of "class relations of power" and "Western taste as a social indicator of distinction established new social divisions, creating new social status groups (in the Weberian sense referring to lifestyles) and thus changed the terms of social stratification" (Göle 1997a, 70).[23] In this sense, the veil defined "Other" women and started to be associated with provinciality and a low-class status (Secor 2002).

Unveiling was encouraged through public representations of the ideal republican woman who did not wear a veil and through dress codes that restricted the wearing of religious attire in institutional spaces of the state, such as schools, universities, courtrooms, and the parliament (Özdalga 1998). These dress codes were enforced in particular spaces at various points of Turkish history (Secor 2002, 9). In the period following the 1980 military coup in an environment shaped by what Yavuz (2003, 69) calls a redefined "Turkish-Islamic synthesis," new opportunity spaces were created for Islamic cultures and politics.[24]

These new spaces were utilized by female university students who came to classes wearing headscarves. The military, state representatives, and a secular public perceived the presence of veiled students at universities as a sign of divergence from the military-determined secular and nationalistic "Turkish-Islamic synthesis." In response, new dress codes that prohibited the wearing of headscarves were instituted and implemented more vigorously beginning in the 1980s (Özdalga 1998).[25] The wording of this prohibition illustrates the connection made between dress and modernity. The dress code of universities is "modern clothing" (*çağdaş kiyafet*), banning "un- or anti-modern" outfits (ibid., 42). As this regulation stands today, for the most part the veil is excluded from the category of the modern. Veiling or unveiling has since then become a divisive political issue central to "the disciplinary administration of bodies," to "the regulation of populations" and thus to governmentality in Turkey (Secor 2005).

Piety and Modernity

Since the transition to a multiparty democracy in the mid-twentieth century, difficulties became apparent in implementing the project of modernity in its entirety and ensuring state control over Islamic knowledge and practice, as populism, partly based on religion, entered the realm of official politics. In the aftermath of the 1980 military coup, the particular geopolitical context of the Cold War combined with restructurings of neoliberalism created new spaces and opportunities for religious knowledge, expression, production, and mobilization (Ahmad 1993; Yavuz 2003; Zührer 1993). These openings and opportunities have been utilized by a diversity of religious or Islamic-oriented cultural groups, businesses, and political parties (Buğra 2003; White 2002). Islamist politics and capitalism have notably been on the rise (Yavuz 2003). Since 1994, Islamist political parties (surviving bans through multiple reincarnations) have been successful in local and national elections. As Islamist politics have become more prominent so have disagreements and arguments about the specific terms and principles of Islamism.

The fragmentation of political Islam was signaled by the replacement of the traditional Islamist party beginning in the 1960s (in its various reincarnations) by two very different political parties in 2001 (Insel 2003; Yavuz 2003). Although the more conservative branch of political Islam represented by the Felicity Party (Saadet Partisi) did not succeed in the national elections of November 2003, the more moderate Justice and Development Party (JDP) emerged victorious in national elections (Gülalp 2003). The JDP is led by Recep Tayyip Erdoğan, the former mayor of Istanbul from the banned Welfare Party, who was charged with inciting political hatred and imprisoned for eight months. This party does not claim an Islamic identity but only a democratic one (thus "Muslim democrats") and has carried out a series of extensive reforms of democratization and liberalization required by the European Union.[26]

Islamist communities' cultural battle with the terms of state modernity has been fought by contesting the equation of the modern and the secular and of the state's reach into private spaces. Pious middle-class individuals and intellectuals have been instrumental in producing a popular culture that presents Islamist alternatives to secular modernity through television stations, radios, films, magazines, newspapers, and novels (Göle 1997b, 1999, 2002; Öncü 1995; Saktanber 1997). They have upheld Muslim lifestyles in new, emerging spaces of residential enclaves and gated communities in Istanbul (for Ankara, see Saktanber 1997, 2002) in addition to the existing, more informally defined conservative neighborhoods. The secularist stereotypes about religiosity as backwardness, provinciality, and low-class status are contested by this increasing visibility of a new Muslim middle-class lifestyle in Istanbul. Shopping malls as the site for performing modernity have become important within this context of creating "Muslim moderns." Holiday villages along the Mediterranean organized according to professed principles of Islam and based on gender segregation at gyms, pools, and beaches have opened to cater to the Muslim middle class (Bilici 1999; Yavuz 2003, 98).[27] Novelists, journalists, politicians, and entrepreneurs have circulated images of pious women who are able to combine their Islamic beliefs and values with modern technologies, knowledge, and sense of self (Göle 1997b). This "new Muslim woman" is also presented as modern, competing with the ideal of the secularist republican woman.

Veiled Women in Mall Space

In my research the construction of shopping malls as modern spaces in Istanbul has generally been confirmed and reproduced by a diverse group of participants who differed according to age, gender, migrant status, religious identity, and socioeconomic standing. Many of my research participants deliberately used the word "modern" to describe mall space. Yet, probing questions that involve comparing different shopping malls have exposed a much more complex picture of the hierarchical construction of mall space and women's bodies that "belong." The distinctions broadly made by the secularist segments of the public and many of my research participants are expressed very starkly and succinctly by Ahmet, a middle-aged lawyer from Istanbul, as he compares Akmerkez mall to Capitol mall (which opened the same year as Akmerkez):

> There is Capitol on the Anatolian side [of Istanbul]. Capitol is completely . . . full of] people from the varoş [see below]. We see this [because] we go there. For instance we go to the movie theater [in Capitol]. [Capitol] is extremely crowded on the weekends. But 90 percent of this crowd is from the varoş. Veiled women . . . wearing *türban*. Probably because they don't have anywhere else to go. They think going to [Capitol] is an entertainment. But the quality is very different in Akmerkez. . . . In terms of geography, [there is a difference between the] Anatolian side [and the European side]. [Capitol] is on the Anato-

lian side . . . [Capitol] is Anatolia. (Ahmet, Gökarıksel interview, 21 February 2000).

In ranking different malls in terms of quality, Ahmet mainly bases his judgments on how he perceives the crowds that frequent different malls. He uses *varoş*, a term coined after violent incidents in the mid-1990s (Demirtaş and Gözaydın 1997) to describe the kind of crowds he sees at Capitol. This term emphasizes the perceived threat posed by the poverty-ridden areas of Istanbul where mostly rural migrants live and is directly connected to the elitist antimigrant discourse that has been influential in the past decades (Öncü 1999, 2002). Ahmet establishes a direct relationship between veiling and the perceived poverty and danger of the *varoş*. For him, the veil is a symbol of vulgarity and provinciality. The veil is "out of place" in malls—a view shared by my other research participants of similar sociopolitical standing. Moreover, the existence of headscarf-wearing women is enough to taint the supposed modernity of Capitol mall.

Ahmet's views resonate with wider public discourses of secularism and secular identity and starkly expose the class dimension that often remains hidden in these discourses. His interview openly illustrates the elitist appropriation of secularist state modernity to create the terms of social distinction and to construct an urban, secular, and modern middle-class identity in relation to a "veiled Other" (Ayata 2002, 30). Ahmet's point of view also interestingly demonstrates how Turkey's European-oriented modernity finds an immediate and material spatial reflection in Istanbul. The Bosphorus, the border between Asian and European continents, divides the city of Istanbul into two parts. Traveling daily between these two parts or continents via the two bridges or ferries is not unusual for an average Istanbulite. Ahmet rhetorically uses this geographical division to highlight a perceived cultural or "civilizational" difference between West and East, Europe and Asia. He formulates a geographical correspondence of Istanbul's European side (overlooking squatter settlements and *varoş* in this part of Istanbul) to the high quality, upscale, and explicitly secularist Akmerkez mall. In contrast, for him Capitol mall's perceived low quality, religiosity, and provinciality—all embodied by headscarf-wearing women—represents Istanbul's Asian side and more broadly, all of Asia Minor (in other words, Anatolia). Through these assertions, Ahmet, like many others in Turkey, guards the terms of secularist middle-class hegemony in mall space and in Istanbul.

The hegemonic construction of mall space as secular and veiled women as out of place is confirmed by the accounts of my veiled research participants who feel marginalized, neglected, or outright discriminated against in shopping malls. Veiled women's presence in malls engenders them subject to scrutiny, to disapproving gazes, and sometimes to verbal abuse. Gül is a young seamstress who has come to Istanbul from rural northern Turkey and dresses in fashionable and colorful *tesettür*. She describes her experience as follows:

> I feel it in this [mall] type of places. When you are in such a place, people look at you oddly. They don't have to say anything. They look at you [in a way that puts you down]. I went to . . . a restaurant of a hotel. They treated our [unveiled] friends who were with us [so well]. They treated them with respect. As if because we're veiled we don't know anything. You're treated like a *görgüsüz* [see below]. But what does [veiling] have to do with it. It doesn't mean that if your head is covered or if you're wearing a coat that you're a hick who doesn't know anything. I have been treated similarly many times. [That's why] I don't usually like to join the society. I involve myself only with those who are close to me (Gül, Gökarıksel interview, 18 March 2000).

Gül portrays shopping malls (and similar upscale places associated with the secularist state modernity) as places where class distinctions are reproduced and social boundaries are enforced in urban daily life. It is the service personnel at restaurants and shops and in department stores, as well as other customers present in the same spaces, whose secularist values are felt by Gül. The hegemony of secularism is established and reproduced in public spaces through these daily practices that impose secularist values. Gül argues she is perceived and treated as inferior in public spaces such as malls mainly because of her headscarf. The word she uses is *görgü*, which is similar to Pierre Bourdieu's concept of "cultural capital." Cultural capital, along with economic capital, constitute "habitus" and shapes one's taste, mannerism, dispositions, views, and practices (Bourdieu 1984). Gül's objection here is to the hegemony of the secularist definition of social status. It is this definition that posits veiling as a practice that signifies the lack of cultural capital and pushes veiled women to the bottom of the social hierarchy.

Michel Foucault highlights the significance of seeing and being seen as part of the modern apparatus of power and discipline (Foucault 1979). Gül's discussion reveals the power of the gaze of the secularist middle class to tell her what is not her "proper" place and that she does not belong to the mall. Interestingly, it is also workers at the mall who may have similar migrant and working-class backgrounds that become the agents of this boundary-delineation. Gül's interview not only demonstrates the definition of cultural capital in contemporary Istanbul but also her resistance to treatment as a *görgüsüz*. Her objection is both to the Turkish state project of modernity and the secularist middle-class appropriation of this vision of modernity to define the terms of cultural capital that constitutes middle-class identity and to construct its cultural hegemony.

Constructing Veiled Women as Muslim Middle-Class Subjects

Gül's sense that her veil marked her as görgüsüz in secular modern spaces is confirmed by Zeynep and Esra who feel similar discrimination. But Zeynep and Esra tap into the economic and cultural resources at their disposal to construct a Muslim middle-class identity. Zeynep and Esra are two young women who are homemakers born in Istanbul to migrant parents from northern Turkey. They are in their own words, *kapalı*(covered), dressed in *tesettür*. I interviewed them at the Capitol mall described negatively as "Anatolian" by Ahmet and many others. They lived near Capitol mall and frequently visited it and other malls. It was also to the Galleria shopping mall that Zeynep went on her first date with the man who became her husband. Both women pointed out that their favorite was the more "elite" Akmerkez mall where their husbands shopped regularly. Their husbands run an import-export business together and travel widely in Europe for business. Their connections in the United States have resulted in their latest project of marketing the Applebee's restaurant chain in Istanbul. Zeynep describes her attachment to malls:

> The issue of moving business centers like Capitol out of the city was brought up in the parliament. This really bothered me. Because I don't just shop here. I also

hang out/stroll around. It's a source of great pleasure especially for housewives. . . . We feel more comfortable [at malls] with the children (Zeynep, Gökarıksel interview, 8 June 2001).

Zeynep did not wear a headscarf growing up or in her early years of marriage. Her husband encouraged her to veil by presenting her with a beautiful silk scarf from Vakko, a very expensive department store in Turkey.[28] This scarf had important significance to him for the first time she veiled. She was very touched by this and she did wear that scarf when she first veiled a few years later. By repeating that her husband did not force her, that it was her own decision to cover, she claimed her agency in this practice and tried to refute the notion that women veil because they are forced to do so by men. Zeynep's story of veiling did not clearly state her reasons for veiling. What she highlighted in her story was the brand name, beauty, and material of her first scarf. She described her veiling experiences in consumerist terms and stated that the attractiveness of the headscarf was important for her decision to veil. This very same consumer item allowed her to have a religious experience, making a transition from consumerism to spirituality, by attaining "peace of mind" after taking up the veil. The new *tesettür* industry targets women such as Zeynep whose veiling choices include attractiveness and fashion (Gökarıksel interviews, June–July 2004).

As was the case with this first Vakko scarf, throughout the interview both Esra and Zeynep mentioned the middle-upper class brand names for which they shop. Esra and Zeynep presented themselves as well-informed and tasteful consumers, expressing their ownership of economic and cultural capital required for a middle-class identity. From Esra and Zeynep's perspective, mall space is significant to the construction of a middle-class identity that is simultaneously modern and religious. Esra and Zeynep's narrative as sophisticated consumers was accompanied by the complaint that they were not being treated as such in public spaces. Like Gül, they attributed this mistreatment to their veil. The discrimination they faced testifies to the hegemonic production of shopping malls and similar spaces as secular. Their marginalization as veiled women in these spaces shows the limits of democracy and liberalism in Turkey.

In line with the prime minister's definition of public space based on difference and tolerance (Yalçınkaya 2004; Zaman 2004), Esra and Zeynep underlined the significance of accepting and respecting difference for "real" democracy. In doing so, they draw from the liberal human rights discourse to claim their rights to dress according to their beliefs and reject the state's intervention into the private space of the body. Just as they experienced inequality and discrimination as consumers, they also sought their rights as citizens based on their power as consumers. Their resistance to discriminatory acts is also as consumers, in the form of taking their money where they are treated well, regardless of the religiosity or secularism of business owners. They are both powerful and discriminated against as consumers. Their practices of consumption bring them face to face with the hegemonic ideology of secularist modernism embodied by salespeople, storeowners, and fellow shoppers.

Contrasted with Gül, Esra and Zeynep's narratives reveal a neoliberal conception of citizenship, that of the "consumer-citizen," where subjects relate to the state and to society mainly as consumers of products and services and feel that they are entitled to operate in markets as able and informed consumers. In an analysis of the idea of "consumer-citizen" as it emerged in the 1980s–1990s United Kingdom, Yuval-Davis (1997) notes the notion implies a free market model but in fact is constrained by moral and legal measures that prevent marginal groups from exercising their rights. My research participants' narratives speak of their forced positioning at the margins of spaces of consumption and social life that are constructed as secular. In response, they voice their entitlements to rights endowed by citizenship, that is, full membership in the community (Marshall 1950) and seek equal status. The status of consumer-citizen enables them to claim equality and seek rights as citizens and consumers while also making it possible for them to articulate their difference in terms of religion and class. These narratives point to the construction of middle-class identity and distinction within Islamist communities in contrast both to the secularist identification of veiling with low-class status and to the proclaimed "classless" society of Islamist politics (White 1999, 2002).

Conclusion

This chapter underlines the spatial workings of secularism and modernity and shows that the definitions of the secular and the modern have been intertwined with the production of gender and class identities. The focus on the space of shopping malls exposes the everyday constitution of bodies that are seen as "in" and "out of place" according to a hegemonic definition of modernity as secular in Istanbul. This hegemony does not go uncontested as the narratives of women who wear *tesettür* fashions reveal. The discourse of political and economic liberalism provide the repertoire of values for these women to object to their marginalization and to assert themselves as equal citizens whose religious beliefs and choices should be respected. These values are the same ones claimed by the general public and political leaders. However, the issue of veiling exposes the exceptional status of secularism within this widespread support for equality and democracy. Like many nongovernmental organizations that focus on "the headscarf issue," veiled women use the limitations on headscarf-wearing as the basis of their critique of the secular state and democracy in Turkey.[29] My research participants do not only target the legal limitations on headscarves such as the ban in public institutions; they also draw attention to and criticize the cultural and social limitations on veiling and the day-to-day discrimination headscarf-wearers face in modern urban public spaces. This, in turn, points to the gendered construction of secular public spaces as women, whose secularity or religiosity is assumed to be visibly marked by their dress, easily become the targets of discrimination while men do not.

In addition to the political basis of claiming rights as citizens, there is the notable salience of the economic logic of neoliberalism in the quest for equal rights. Neoliberalism has influenced the way the leaders of nongovernmental organizations and Islamist thinkers in Istanbul formulate their argument against the headscarf ban in public institutions. For example, more recent discussions on this topic underline that veiled women pay taxes just like their unveiled counterparts and as "tax-paying citizens" they are entitled to have equal access to public institutions, services, and spaces (Balta 2004; Bulaç 2004). As veiled women are constituted thus as "consumer-citizens," my research also shows that they seek to claim a legitimate presence in public through acts of consumption.[30] Shopping at malls becomes instrumental in constructing a middle-class identity that is modern and religious simultaneously. These acts combine seemingly contradictory values of Islamism and neoliberalism and raise questions about the implications of the making of "pious" selves in increasingly consumerist forms. How are the professed ideals of spirituality, communitarianism, and egalitarianism in Islam to be reconciled with the increasingly commodified construction and expression of class difference within the Muslim community? This analysis shows the current prevalence and power of political liberalism's human rights and discrimination discourses and of neoliberalism's consumer-citizen discourse in contemporary Turkey. Such discourses point to the need to analyze Islamisms and Muslim identities in Turkey and elsewhere as articulated within transnational processes that transform the very means of cultural struggle over secular and religious spaces and bodies.

5

In the Lady's Seat

Cosmopolitan Women Travelers in Pakistan

Kathryn Besio

Female travelers to foreign countries visit religious sites such as cathedrals and mosques, gazing upon religious landscapes.[1] Yet they do far more than just "gaze" upon religious places (see Urry 2002), they also eat, sleep, and do all those day-to-day activities that visitors do, with a range of people in a diverse array of spaces. An embodied analysis of travel and tourism (Veijola and Jokinen 1994) leads to thinking about the ways that female travelers experience places such as Pakistan where Islamic practices inform everyday activities such as how and where women sit on a bus. Day-to-day travel presents women travelers to Pakistan with numerous opportunities to experience the country from an embodied position of knowing by wearing "modest" clothing and adopting to bodily norms and spatial practices that conform to those practiced by Pakistani men and women.

Women travelers to Pakistan commonly come from metropolitan areas of Europe, North America, Japan and Australia, and have a wide range of backgrounds, knowledge, and travel experiences (for introductions to females traveling in developing nations, see Apostopoulos, Sonmez and Timothy 2001; Kinnaird and Hall 1994; and Swain and Momsen 2002). I adopt the term "cosmopolitan women travelers" (after Breckenridge et al. 2004) to describe these highly mobile subjects. In doing so, I hope to overcome, if only partially, the difficulties inherent in labeling this diverse group "western" women travelers. However, I also recognize that the term "cosmopolitan" comes with its own set of baggage.[2]

How cosmopolitan women travelers might comport themselves in Pakistan is the subject of much confusion for many of them. There is great diversity of Islamic practices between Muslims in Islamic countries and within Pakistan, and two practices recommended to Pakistan-bound travelers are the wearing of loose-fitting, Pakistani clothing and using spaces that spatially segregate women from men in public. By conforming to Pakistani norms of travel in public spaces, cosmopolitan women travelers to Pakistan have a chance to perform femininity in ways that might be quite different to how they experience it "at home" in societies that present themselves as secular and modern. I suggest that "modern" practices of cosmopolitan femininity are underlain implicitly if not explicitly by secular values that are, perhaps, nonsecular at closer scrutiny.

Timothy Mitchell (2002, 1) states that societies that developed understandings of modernity from the western Enlightenment tradition characterize it as a period that has progressed from nonsecular irrationality to secular rationality, or what he calls "the unfolding of an inner secular force." Following from Mitchell, modern subjects value rational scientific thinking over other epistemologies, Christianity remaining a silent and potent referent that underwrites a secular modernity. For example, within secular societies, representations of religiosity and irrationality are often embodied in Islam, and Muslim people are represented frequently as nonmodern and fundamentalist. I look specifically at cosmopolitan women travelers' representations of their mobility vis-à-vis Muslim women's mobility, as a marker of their modern condition. In short, to be mobile is to be modern and secular, which is in contrast to representations of inert and invisible Muslim women.

Modernity encompasses a wide range of processes, practices, and knowledges that are well beyond the scope of this chapter (T. Mitchell 2002). Here my focus is on how cosmopolitan women express their identities as modern subjects through travel. This is seen especially vividly in how cosmopolitan women travel in a Muslim—read religious, nonmodern—country such as Pakistan. The persistence of Orientalist representations of Muslim women as immobilized by Islam are found in contemporary guidebooks. Muslim women function paradoxically as invisible—they are perceived as absent from public spaces, yet visible in the background as the symbols of women's oppression—Others for cosmopolitan women travelers.

Ironically, guidebooks and other official sources of information such as governmental guidelines for travelers suggest that cosmopolitan women travelers embrace one aspect of Muslim femininity: the wearing of long-sleeved, full-body clothing and head coverings in public spaces. For cosmopolitan women travelers, for whom the hypermobility of travel is a marker of gender equality[3] and who perceive these clothing suggestions to limit their mobility, this particular advice for culturally sensitive clothing choices can cause a kind of gender dissonance. To some women travelers, conservative clothing and head coverings are emblematic of Pakistani women's oppression and non-modernity, evidenced by their immobility and apparent invisibility in public spaces due to the ways that they dress.

In spite of Orientalist representations of Islam as innately oppressive to women, many cosmopolitan women travelers choose to adopt Islamic modes of dress, covering their heads with scarves and using women-only spaces. As Edward Said describes it, Orientalism is "a style of thought based upon an ontological and epistemological distinction made between the 'the Orient' and (most of the time) 'the Occident' (1978, 2), now usually glossed as 'the West' and 'the East.'"[4] Representations of irrational religious fanatics, effeminate eastern men, and oppressed women are a few examples that pervade Orientalist texts, and there are numerous instances from the colonial writings of explorers, travelers, and missionaries that construct Islam as essentially oppressive to Muslim women (Cook 2003; Garcia-Ramon 2003). Yet, regardless of enduring Orientalist discourses of Islamic determinism (Bernal 1994), cosmopolitan women travelers choose clothing that is culturally sensitive but that they may interpret as the clothing of the "oppressed."

By adopting local dress and spatial segregation practices, cosmopolitan women travelers may enable themselves to move more easily through public spaces in Pakistan, ironically reaffirming their identities as mobile and modern subjects. Those women who choose to assert their modern identities by wearing fitted clothing and adhering to their own social-cultural norms of bodily comportment and spatial interaction may find travel in Pakistan challenging.[5]

Cosmopolitan women travelers can only metaphorically put themselves in the place of Pakistani women through such practices as covering their heads and separating themselves from males in public spaces.[6] Some cosmopolitan women travelers nevertheless seem to take from their travel experiences in Pakistan a renewed sense of cultural superiority that values their gender identities over what they perceive to be religiously based and "nonmodern" Muslim identities (see also Cook 2003; Cook 2006).

This chapter draws upon a range of data to understand better cosmopolitan women travelers' construction of their modern identity vis-à-vis Pakistani women. It includes ethnographic data, Lonely Planet guidebook advice, survey data, and my own reflections on being a cosmopolitan woman traveler in Pakistan. Conducting research, especially ethnographic research on tourists and travelers, is difficult. The inclusion of my observations as a researcher-tourist and participant-observer—more participant than observer in this instance—are especially relevant to this analysis. My hope is that by bringing together these various data, I address the materiality of women travelers' experience, along with the discursive production and consumption of a cosmopolitan woman traveler's identity.

The ethnographic research that informs this research took place in various parts of Pakistan between 1996 and 1998, using primarily participant observation of male and female travelers, survey questionnaires (N = 71), and informal discussions with travelers in Baltistan, a region in the Northern Areas.[7] My research with travelers occurred while I was conducting ethnographic research with women in Askole, a village located along the main trekking trail to the Baltoro Glacier and K2. The project with which I was involved looked at the links and effects of the adventure travel economy on women and girls in the village and was part of a larger research project that examined the political economy of portering relations in the Northern Areas (see MacDonald and Butz 1998; Butz and Besio 2004; Besio and Butz 2004).[8]

My research with Northern Areas travelers involved surveying them about their choice of guidebooks. Lonely Planet guidebooks were commonplace and the most popular choice among travelers. In my questionnaire of travelers, nearly 46 percent of those surveyed carried a Lonely Planet guidebook, either the country guide or guide to trekking in the Karakoram, and 12 percent carried another guidebook to Pakistan. The remaining 42 percent of the respondents carried no guidebook at all, probably because they were on guided tours. However, of those travelers who carried a guidebook, Lonely Planet guides were their overwhelming favorite.

I therefore look at Lonely Planet guides to understand the travel advice given to cosmopolitan women travelers—how the books inform how women dress, behave, and perceive themselves in Pakistan. Lonely Planet travel guides balance providing gender-specific advice to travelers, while simultaneously scripting women travelers' practices. These guidebooks attempt a difficult feat. They provide advice specifically for women travelers and, as such, provide a valuable service. Yet they also must meet the demands of their readership for lively writing, accompanied by in-depth information on where to stay, etc. Moreover, guidebook authors are bound to stringent word restrictions, for the practical reason that these are pocket guidebooks: a tome to travel in Pakistan is hardly useful to travelers on the move. I recognize guidebook writers' restrictions and intend the comments in this chapter in the spirit of encouragement for the continuing improvement of Lonely Planet guidebooks.

I read from two Lonely Planet publications that were in print during the time I conducted my ethnographic research: *Pakistan* (King and Mayhew 1998) and *Trekking in the Karakoram and Hindukush* (Mock and O'Neil 1996). I examine the "dos & don'ts" offered to cosmopolitan women travelers bound for Pakistan.[9]

Finally, I address briefly cosmopolitan women travelers' reception of the information in the guidebooks. First, I draw from participant-observation and survey data with cosmopolitan women travelers, albeit not entirely complete survey data. Second, I work from my own personal reflections as a cosmopolitan woman traveling in Pakistan using a Lonely Planet guidebook. I include my experiences as a woman traveler in Pakistan, to both reflect my own positioning as a cosmopolitan traveler and reflexively to call attention to my embodied and situated position in the research process (see also Besio 2005; England 1994; Al-Hindi and Kawabata 2002; Rose 1997).

My chapter revolves around the themes of clothing and spatial interactions, although the latter to a lesser degree. For cosmopolitan women travelers to access public women-only spaces in Pakistan such as ladies' only seating areas and family dining rooms, they must be dressed in ways that will not offend Pakistanis. Manner of dress and gendered spatial interactions are linked closely. I focus more on the former than the latter, because my survey gave more attention to cosmopolitan women's dress than their spatial practices.

In the concluding section, I return to my main theme that Lonely Planet travel prescriptions and women's reception of the guidebooks *both* reinscribe *and* contest Orientalist assumptions about Others. Second and perhaps more to the point of this volume is that while modernity seems to be a secular force, it reveals its nonsecular dimensions, especially in representations of Islamic religiosity, which is represented as impractical and oppressive. This is particularly apparent in my reading of gender and mobility among cosmopolitan women travelers in Pakistan. Before turning to the "dos and don'ts" of travel, I now turn to some background information on travel and colonialism and my choice of data.

Travelers, Memsahibs, and Guidebooks

Feminist geographers and contributors to this volume pay close attention to what Sara Mills has called "discourses of difference" (Mills 1991) voiced by western women writing during the colonial era (see Blunt 1994; Blunt and Rose 1994; Morin, Longhurst, and Johnston 2001). Mills interrogates how colonial women writers negotiated their gender identities vis-à-vis patriarchy, colonialism, and class, teasing apart the spatial and material differences of women's representations of self and Other (Mills 1991, 1994). Like Mills, I am interested in how women represent themselves as selves vis-à-vis their Others. Women travelers' perceived gender identities are as varied as the women themselves, and here I address only a small piece of the gender construction puzzle for cosmopolitan women travelers in Pakistan, that of mobility.

Unlike Mills (1991), I do not focus on women's travel writing as expressions of gender identity. Instead, I focus upon how contemporary travel guidebooks prescribe practices *to* women travelers, and how some women respond to this prescription. Being a body with freedom of movement is particularly important to the gender constructions of cosmopolitanism, in part because the trope of cosmopolitanism (Breckenridge et al. 2004) relies upon a hypermobile subject. As Dean MacCannell (1999) notes, the tourist is perhaps the most modern of subjects, expressing mobility through tourism or travel. Somewhat ironically, the subjects whom I interviewed preferred to call themselves travelers over tourists, choosing traveler in part because it connotes slower, more immersed travel over the shallow, hypermobile tourist. I use the term "traveler" over "tourist" for specific reasons in this chapter, one of which is based on findings from empirical research with travelers in Baltistan. For many visitors to

Pakistan, the term "traveler" implies "explorer," which seems to be a preferable construction to the contemporary, debased "tourist," and I address this more below. Lonely Planet guidebooks also market themselves to "travelers," not "tourists."

I regard today's travelers and tourists as very similar constructions. While in the nineteenth century, travelers and explorers differed from, for example, Thomas Cook's legions of tourists (Turner and Ash 1975), Lonely Planet's distinction is primarily a marketing move. Their assumption seems to be that "travelers" stay longer in destinations and immerse themselves in destinations, whereas "tourists" stay only a short time and have only a superficial understanding of the places they visit. Lonely Planet's preference for the term traveler is a means of distinguishing "good" from "bad" forms of tourism, although the adventure travel or backpacker travel that Lonely Planet promotes merely raises different ethical issues (Scheyvens 2002; Sorensen 2003).[10] Lonely Planet suggests that travelers, including backpackers and other long-term visitors, experience places more fully than do tourists because their experiences are supposedly less commercial and they, like explorers before them, immerse themselves in local settings and have closer encounters with local populations (Allon 2004; Desforges 1998; Jenkins 2003). In Pakistan, such assumptions overlook the material and exploitative relations of colonial travel and exploration that precede contemporary adventure travel (see Besio 2001; Butz 1995; MacDonald and Butz 1998).

Thus, while I use the term traveler with my respondents' and Lonely Planet's nomenclature in mind, I do so with the relations of colonialism in mind as well. I do not intend to imply that colonial explorers and contemporary travelers access identical discourses, although, at times, the discourses found in contemporary guidebooks are belated expressions of colonial era, Orientalist discourses whereby difference is hierarchically organized around "race" (Behdad 1994; Holland and Huggan 1998). To call the contemporary historical period "postcolonial" in the sense of historically "after colonialism" is problematic, especially in the Northern Areas, because it remains an internal colony of the state. Residents of the Northern Areas do not have voting rights, because they are in "disputed territory" between Pakistan and India. Thus, travel in northern Pakistan is postcolonial in the sense that the term foregrounds colonial relations as part of contemporary relations, although with differences. Although numerous linkages between colonial and postcolonial travel could be drawn out in more depth, my particular focus in this chapter is on how contemporary discourses that could be described as Orientalist are complicated by gender relations.

For example, more women tour now than in the colonial period and are from a wider range of class and race positions, although "white" women and relatively more affluent women are still in the majority of those who travel. Women travelers in Pakistan are often paying members of group excursions, even if they do so "on their own." And contemporary adventure travel in Pakistan, like colonial exploration, is a commercial endeavor. Thus, while colonial and postcolonial travel are both different from and similar to one another in the Pakistan context, one point of similarity I draw out here deals with Orientalist representations of Others in travelogues and guidebooks.

In contemporary guidebooks, the image of a mobile and intrepid western female traveler lurks alongside that of the fearful colonial memsahib. A memsahib can be an honorific term used for women, although when applied to white women, it has a particularly colonial connotation of domination and oppression (Besio 2003; see also Ortner 1999). Yet although the colonial memsahib was part of the colonial establishment, she was represented as fearful of Other men, a fear that focused upon representations of overly sexualized nonwestern males. Blunt suggests (1994, 38), citing Margaret Strobel, that western women such as colonial memsahibs were ambivalently positioned as both racially superior *and* sexually vulnerable. This expression of sexual vulnerability surfaces in the cracks in the section on women travelers in Lonely Planet's *Pakistan*:

> Because many [Pakistani] men are isolated from what westerners consider normal interactions with women outside the family, their views of "other" women come mostly from popular culture and the media. Moreover the average male imagination is inflamed by films full of guns, violence and full-hipped women. (King and Mayhew 1998, 87)

The supposedly aggressive Pakistani male's (sexual) imagination, the guidebook suggests, is similar to the dangerous and supposedly lascivious "eastern male" of colonial fiction and postcolonial film who cannot control his libido when confronted by western women and under circumstances westerners consider "normal." Upon reading passages like this in the guidebook, a contemporary women traveler might recall the "rapes" of Adela Quested from a *Passage to India* (Forster 1952; Lean 1984), or Daphne Manners from Paul Scott's *Jewel in the Crown* (Scott 1966),[11] or even more recently, Dervla Murphy's wary representations of Balti men (1995). Read in this way, guidebooks perpetuate racist fears of nonwestern males and their apparently uncontrollable and abnormal libido.

In contrast to colonial fiction, contemporary guidebooks also provide numerous references to Pakistani males that are positive, for example of males' hospitality and helpfulness toward western women and their interest in meeting foreign visitors. For instance, "plenty of local men will speak to or help a foreign woman, with no other motive than to be hospitable" (King and Mayhew 1998, 86). Statements such as these provide a more "balanced" portrait of Pakistani males and express guidebook authors' desire to depict Pakistan as a sought-after destination. Moreover, guidebook authors may desire to overcome some of the negative perceptions that North Americans have of Muslim countries.[12] Guidebook authors assert that "the risks [of sexual harassment] are clearly less than in most western countries" (King and Mayhew 1998, 87), placing some of the burden for responsibility upon cosmopolitan women travelers. That is, if women travelers dress appropriately and sit in prescribed places, Pakistani males will treat them favorably and with respect.

Unfortunately, the specter of the fearful colonial memsahib lingers on in guidebook advice, because its subtext is that safety is achieved through cosmopolitan women's vigilance in dressing unprovocatively and staying away from Pakistani males.[13] In this reading, Pakistani men are still unable to control themselves around cosmopolitan women, rendering them irrational and uncontrollable, much like Orientalist representations of their colonial predecessors. In spite of guidebook authors' aims in presenting Pakistan and Pakistanis positively, the specter of colonial relations remains present. Although guidebook authors make attempts toward promoting better relations between Pakistani men and cosmopolitan women travelers, they cannot overcome deeply ingrained anti-Islamic and Orientalist sentiments in some segments of the tourism market, specifically, the North American market.[14]

In order to look more closely at how postcolonial guidebooks *both* trouble and reinscribe Orientalism, I draw from participant-observation data from northern Pakistan and also use my own reflections as a female tourist and researcher and as someone who used a Lonely Planet guidebook. My reasons for drawing upon autobiographical material as data are threefold, although I am aware that I run the risk of "methodological individualism" (Moss 2001, 2).

First, my subject positioning as someone who traveled in Pakistan is significant to my analysis. Like many of the cosmopolitan women travelers I encountered during the course of my research I, too, came to know ways of performing my gendered identity in Pakistan that were quite different than what I had experienced previously. When I began my research, I had never been to Pakistan and had numerous preconceptions about how I should act in an Islamic country. Although I knew that modest dressing would be appreciated in Pakistan and that *shalwar kameez* are worn in India by non-Muslim women, my knowledge of clothing and how to behave in Pakistani society were next to nil. Second, like the travelers with whom I spoke, I relied upon my Lonely Planet guidebooks for information. Thus, I shared with them similar epistemological terrain: Lonely Planet guidebooks helped us to learn to practice our femininity in this particular place.

Third, I draw upon my reflections to add to my analysis of the surveys I conducted. I did not survey travelers about their opinions on the information that they found in Lonely Planet guidebooks. In my questionnaire, I asked them whether they carried Lonely Planet guidebooks, what kind of clothing they wore while traveling and trekking in the Karakoram, and whether they covered their heads, and if so, where. Thus, my questions were specific to my particular interests about trekkers' interactions with village women. In this chapter, I do not include extended quotes from conversations with women travelers, and I work primarily from survey data. Hopefully, my reflections fill in some of the gaps in understanding how the guidebook's suggestions are received by cosmopolitan women travelers, although I recognize and call attention to the ways that my reflections are my own and are not intended as representative of the women with whom I surveyed and spoke. I now turn to some of my own first reflections and my own positionality in the research (England 1994; Rose 1997; Valentine 2002).

Cover Gal: Clothing

From how and where to eat in Islamabad to which bus station would take me to Rawalpindi, my Lonely Planet guide was indispensable, and not just for the maps. To me, carrying a Lonely Planet guide just for the maps is analogous to subscribing to *Playboy* for the articles. Most travelers really *do* want to read what is inside, but like *Playboy* readers, cannot admit it for fear of being marked as voyeurs, in this case, ironically, tourists. I hoped that my guidebook would tell me how to behave as a female in Pakistan, something about which I had only the sketchiest idea, although I was certain it differed from how I had been performing my femininity in Honolulu where I had been doing graduate study. Like nearly all the other travelers I met, I relied upon my Lonely Planet guidebook for its apparently no-nonsense, culturally sensitive advice.

On my first research trip in 1996 I was based in Islamabad, although subsequently I was based in the Northern Areas. Even in urban Islamabad, I was aware that I had to "cover-up" and that I would need to present myself as having respect for Muslim values of dressing modestly. In Pakistan, men and women wear clothing that covers their arms and legs, which informants told me was advised by the Koran. Islam is very much geared toward daily practices of religiosity such as food choices, daily prayer, ablutions, and dressing modestly. All of these are expressions of faith for many Pakistani men and women. I was told by my male advisor and co-researcher to bring baggy western clothing to wear for the first days and then buy *shalwar kameez*. Literally "pant-shirt," *shalwar kameez* are worn by men and women alike, and although the styling is different for men and women, they look like a long shirt worn over baggy pants. I was on my own when I first arrived and, like other women travelers, I combed the pages of my guidebook for where to buy *shalwar kameez*. I carried with me the *Trekking in the Karakoram and Hindukush* guidebook (Mock and O'Neil 1996, 62) and found the following information for women trekkers:

> Conservative dress is very important. It would be difficult to overstate the sensitivity of this matter. Dressing in a culturally appropriate fashion shows respect and increases your own comfort level. Wear loose, long-sleeved, non-revealing shirts and full-length pants. Most Western style pants still show

the outline of the body, hence are not the best choice. Even loose skirts or dresses are not a good choice, unless they are ankle length.

This advice seemed very helpful, although it did not give me the information I wanted, since I had already decided that I would wear *shalwar kameez*. It did, though, explain why western style clothing is inappropriate to Muslims, because western style clothing is often shape revealing and hence not conservative by Pakistani standards informed by Islam. For non-Pakistani women who may not have been in my position and for whom wearing *shalwar kameez* was not a foregone conclusion, the authors' suggestions provide helpful context and explanation. In a more recent edition of Lonely Planet's *Pakistan* (King and Mayhew 1998, 53), the authors give this advice to male and female travelers:

> Nowhere is it easier to offend or insult Pakistanis (and Muslims in general)— and nowhere have more foreigners done so without thinking—than in matters of dress. It's simple: to a devout Muslim, clothes that reveal the flesh or the shape of the body are roughly equivalent to walking around in your underwear in the West—ridiculous on men and scandalous on women.

Like the trekking guidebook authors, King and Mayhew (1998) state that revealing one's body shape is offensive to Muslims because it reveals the human form. In the most recent edition of *Pakistan and the Karakoram Highway* (Singh et al. 2004, 43), the authors explicitly advise men *and* women to dress conservatively, noting that male travelers who wear dirty clothing, shorts, and "singlets" are as likely to offend Pakistanis with their clothing choices as are women travelers. Lonely Planet's visual travelogue reiterates this advice, although the video is more explicit about having clothing made. In a scene in their 1998 video, *Pakistan*, the host of the program demonstrates to potential visitors how to buy and wear a *shalwar kameez*. He shops for fabric and finds a tailor to make him a suit in less than an hour (Lonely Planet 1998).

My own experience of buying *shalwar kameez* was far more involved and, I add, far more enjoyable than that depicted in the video. Once I had located a fabric shop, I was faced with stacks and stacks of fabrics of every hue and weight. The shopkeeper kept pulling down bolt upon bolt of "three piece suits"—*shalwar, kameez*, and *dupatta*—for my perusal.[15] I decided on two suits to start with. The shopkeeper called in a male tailor who took my measurements (I did not learn for another year that many women advise going to a "women's shop" and having a female tailor make the suits) and told me to return in three days for my clothing. I was thrilled: I had bought my "appropriate" clothing on my own.

By the end of my first summer of research, I left Pakistan with my suitcase full of *shalwar kameez*. I had also become the butt of many jokes from the librarian at the archives where I had spent my summer. He thought it amusing that I had bought so many *shalwar kameez* to take home to Hawaii, a place where I clearly had no need for "modest clothing." Yet, as the guidebook authors suggest, I had found that the men with whom I interacted in the library were receptive to me and commented favorably on my choice of clothing. The guidebook states:

> Wearing local-style *shalwar-qamiz*—with light scarf to cover the hair and chest in conservative company or in a mosque or shrine—wins a warm response, and can make things easier. It's also comfortable, cool, and easy and cheap to have made in the bazaar. (King and Mayhew 1998, 88)

It all seemed so simple and so easy: if western visitors dress in local clothing, Pakistanis will appreciate them for the respect that they show their religion.

The guidebooks are clear on the importance and effect of dressing in Pakistan. Yet, the problem is that for many western travelers, a show of respect for Islam may be difficult. To be modern is to be secular, and for cosmopolitan women travelers, deferring to Islamic practice may run contrary to their modern identity as both mobile and nonreligious. My circumstances differed from other travelers in that as a researcher, I had strategic reasons for garnering respect. My research depended upon it.

The following summer I began doing research among cosmopolitan women travelers in the Northern Areas. It was then that I came to realize how problematic travelers' dress was for both travelers and local communities.[16] For travelers, the guidebook presents Islam as "conservative" and Muslims as "devout." Such representations of Pakistanis as dogmatically religious stand in contrast to travelers, who by their very presence in Pakistan and their curiosity about Islam display a kind of enlightened curiosity for the cultural beliefs of

Others. Unfortunately, curiosity about other people's lives does not necessarily lead to tolerance for the ways that they dress. This is especially the case, as I came to find out, when Other's values impinge upon cosmopolitan women's mobility and their notions of equality. It also preys upon their fears of Pakistani males' sexuality. Leaving that fear aside, I take up issues of equality and mobility as they relate specifically to the single article of clothing that seems to be most contrary to mobility for cosmopolitan women, that of the veil or *chador* or *dupatta*.

There is a large and growing body of literature on veiling and its diversity, and I do not address it at length here (see chapter 4 for one example but also see el Guindi 2000, Mernissi 1975; Secor 2002; Yeğnoğlu 1998). I understand the term *purdah* as generally referring to spaces of seclusion, or the home spaces that are predominantly family- and female-oriented (Pakistani women who practice *purdah* may interact with family members). Many Pakistanis told me that for women, covering their heads shows respect to women and God and protect them from unwanted stares and advances by unknown men. The terms *hijab* and "the veil" refer more specifically to the ways that Muslim women practice modest dress in deference to Islam. The terms *purdah, hijab,* and the veil often are used interchangeably, although Fadwa el Guindi (2000) suggests that the words connote different types of practices of spatial and bodily seclusion. In Baltistan, the word *hijab* is used more commonly than *purdah,* perhaps because of the word's Arabic roots.

Yeğnoğlu (2003, 542) states that "it is no surprise that there are countless accounts and representations of the veil and veiled women in Western discourses, all made in an effort to reveal the hidden secrets of the Orient." By whatever name the scarf that covers one's head and shoulders is called, this article of clothing is perhaps one of the most Orientalized articles of clothing in history, representing in turn, the "mystic and unknowable" nonwestern woman and all that is "oppressive and conservative" about Muslim males. Cosmopolitan women travelers' views of the "veil as a symbol of oppression" become apparent in their reluctance to cover their own heads. Many women trekkers with whom I spoke and observed stated that they knew that should cover their heads in public spaces, although they did not embrace it. In response to the question, "Do you cover your head in public places?" 23 percent (N = 21 female trekkers surveyed) covered their heads "all the time," with an equal number stating that they never covered their heads. The response of "infrequently" was the most common in my survey: 52 percent. The infrequent response suggests that travelers chose when and where to cover their heads. Regional and sectarian differences in how and where Pakistani women cover themselves complicate the ability of cosmopolitan women to make this decision (Besio 2001).

For example, cosmopolitan women travelers in Baltistan told me they were aware of regional (urban versus rural) and sectarian (Sunni versus Shia) differences in attitudes toward veiling. Yet contrary to travelers' notions of urban women veiling less than rural women, in Baltistan, a predominantly Shia region of Pakistan, women practice veiling most carefully in the regional capital of Skardu where there has been more Islamization of the population. Relative to rural Balti women living in the surrounding villages, Skardu women practice seclusion and do agricultural, reproductive, and productive work in the confines of their households.[17] These urban Shia women are considered more modern *because* they veil, and are in contrast to urban down-country Pakistan women in places like Islamabad and Karachi and rural Balti women who do not veil in the same way.

In contrast to urban Balti women, rural Balti women, such as those women in the village where I undertook research, do not remain in seclusion in quite the same manner as those in Skardu, although they do cover their head, wear modest clothing, and use a scarf or *dakhon*, the Balti word for *dupatta*. They do not practice a strict *purdah* and this is not for lack of modesty, but because the demands of their agricultural workload make seclusion difficult (see also Azhar-Hewitt 1999). In the written space of the guidebook, it would be a challenging task for guidebook authors to make known to travelers the urban-rural and class distinctions of Balti *purdah* practices. Unless travelers have the opportunity to meet and spend time with Balti women, they would not come to know the nuances of what are modern practices of *purdah* in Baltistan (Besio 2007). Thus, cosmopolitan women travelers make a complex decision about where and when to cover their heads, especially with limited knowledge and information about regional variation of *purdah* practices. For example, one respondent said that she never covered her head in Skardu, but did so in "the villages" of Baltistan.

Narratives of "traditional dress" and "conservative places" that travelers' glean from their guidebooks and other sources are central to informing the ways travelers dress and, in turn, construct their "modern" identities. For western travelers, *purdah* is a marker of immobility and is in contrast to their own dress and spatial practices. In the sample of trekkers I surveyed, 57 percent told me they wore "loose fitting western style clothing and athletic clothing," and 20 percent combined athletic and loose western clothing with *shalwar kameez*. Very few Pakistanis would expect an *Angreezi*[18] woman to wear a head covering or dress in *shalwar kameez* while trekking on glaciers or on the trails, nor does the Lonely Planet trekking guide advise it.[19] Baring their heads while trekking is certainly understandable and wearing a *chador* makes walking difficult in icy conditions. My survey findings suggest that minority of trekkers wear locally made clothing, opting instead for their own versions of modest dress.

In Nancy Cook's research (2003) on western women expatriates working in the Northern Areas of Pakistan, her subjects echo the comments I heard from cosmopolitan women travelers about why they did not like *shalwar kameez* and head coverings. Cook spoke with them extensively about their clothing choices. Her research participants went to great lengths to discursively disassociate themselves from "tourists" and "travelers," yet they share with them a disdain for covering their heads and an appreciation for wearing western clothing, even though they acknowledge that wearing *shalwar kameez* and covering their heads are appreciated by Pakistanis. In fascinating detail, some but not all of Cook's research participants tell her about their need for western clothing, particularly jeans, and the ways that wearing their own clothes help them reaffirm their identities as "free" and "modern" subjects (ibid., 209). These same women—who were all based in and around the town of Gilgit—did not want to cover their heads or wear a *dupatta*.

Unlike Baltistan where I surveyed travelers, in the public spaces of Gilgit head covering is not required for a number of reasons, one of which is that the region has a large population of Ismaili Muslim women who have another definition of modest dress and behavior from Balti Shia or urban Sunni women of Pakistan's big cities. Cosmopolitan women working in Gilgit appreciate that they can forego head coverings. However, to be properly dressed, they must still wear a *dupatta* draped over their shoulders and breasts. This still causes annoyance. One expatriate woman told Cook, "the *dupatta* is just a useless piece of material that does nothing except get in the way. So I just hate it, chiefly for practical reasons. Symbolically I hate it too" (ibid., 211). Whether the *dupatta* is over their heads or around their shoulders, it symbolizes the oppression of Others, although it not just the *dupatta* itself, the article of clothing. It is apparently women's movement that the *dupatta* constrains ("it gets in the way"), and in this instance, spatiality itself is Orientalized. Implicit in this reading is that because Pakistani women are essentialized as less mobile than western women, they accept the inconveniences of *dupattas, chadors,* and *shalwar kameez.* In this construction, Pakistani women are represented as immobile and nonmodern, in contrast to the supposedly mobile cosmopolitan women traveler.

In the Lady's Seat: Spatiality

One way that both cosmopolitan women travelers in Baltistan and Cook's (2003) participants express their understanding of oppression is through the notion that clothing, especially the *dupatta,* impedes their mobility. Their discourse of "practical western clothing" suggests that cosmopolitan women wear clothing that allows them freedom of movement, whereas Pakistani women wear clothing that impedes their mobility. The trekkers I surveyed echoed clothing choices that Cook's participants made. However this begs the question: are cosmopolitan women's fashion choices "at home" simply practical, or is this again an Orientalist framing of Muslim women? Any woman who has worn tight-fitting jeans, high-heeled shoes, and short skirts acknowledges the inconveniences to movement that these fashion statements make. Moreover, on a hot summer day in Gilgit or Baltistan, a *shalwar kameez* is comfortable and perspiration dries quickly. Nevertheless, Pakistani women's immobility and nonmodern identity are essentialized by what is perceived to be an "impractical" clothing choice understood through the lens of *purdah.* This reading of Pakistani women's clothing is magnified by their apparent invisibility to cosmopolitan travelers in public spaces.

In this section, I complicate my reading and examine the ways that cosmopolitan women travelers are advised to remain segregated from Pakistani males by using "family rooms" and sitting in the "lady's seat," thus occupying the public spaces of seclusion. Women travelers who adopt the supposedly nonmodern and Islamic-based norms of gendered spatial segregation may find that wearing local dress and donning head coverings, along with using women-only spaces, *enables* their mobility, which, ironically, has the effect of reaffirming their identities as modern subjects. However, cosmopolitan travelers' mobility must be tempered with the caveat that as guests *(mehman)* in Pakistan, they are being treated hospitably, which is not the same as being treated with respect.

In keeping with the theme of invisible and immobile Pakistani women, Lonely Planet *Pakistan* states:

> Travel in Pakistan can be hard work for women. In conservative Muslim families, wives and daughters stay out of the sight of other men—in the house, behind the veil, in special sections of buses, and in the "family" areas of restaurants. That's one reason why women travelers are regarded with such amazement, bafflement or sometimes hostility and are constantly asked, "Where's your husband?" (King and Mayhew 1998, 87)

Like many women who travel on their own, I had reservations about being on the road by myself and initially was wary about going it alone in Pakistan. Lonely Planet (King and Mayhew 1998, 87) states, "Women travelers should also note that the risks are clearly less than in most countries and that isolating yourself is hardly the way to learn about the place you're visiting!" As the guidebook states, I reasoned that if I were traveling anywhere as a woman alone, I would face what I considered to be risks, although this did not stop me from voicing my specific concerns to one of my co-researchers who promptly chastened me for my latent Orientalist fears. I wore *shalwar kameez* and covered my head nearly all of the time while in Pakistan, exclusively so when I worked in the village.[20] Once I got used to it, travel by myself became more comfortable, but I would never say that it got easy. Whenever possible, I sat in the "lady's seat" and ate in family rooms.

One of the reasons that Pakistani women may seem less visible to cosmopolitan women travelers is that Pakistani women who do travel utilize public spaces for women only. Thus, in the spaces of public transportation, there may be fewer women present. Most bus terminals, airports, and restaurants provide separate spaces for Pakistani women. These take the form of seats that are at the front of the bus and also rooms that are designated for families where they can eat and stop for prayer.

Lonely Planet authors describe the "lady's seat" as follows:

Unaccompanied women are expected to sit at the front of the bus or in the front two seats of a minibus. The good news is that men will normally vacate these seats for women and cram themselves into the rear with the other men, and you can make a fuss if they don't. The bad news is that if these seats are already full of women, the bus might not even stop for you. (King and Mayhew 1998, 87)

Once I learned to demand the lady's seat, solo travel became more accommodating. I found that traveling alone literally opened the door to some women-only spaces and places that I would otherwise have not learned about, given that much of my research was in a village where there are more fuzzy spaces of gendered segregation.[21] It was in the public spaces of bus stations, airports, restaurants, and hotels that I experienced the overwhelming generosity and hospitality of male bus drivers, families with children, and fellow passengers, up and down the Karakoram Highway. Whenever I traveled alone, I was ushered into the family rooms, where I had my meals or tea paid for under protest. Whether I was treated well because I was wearing *shalwar kameez* and kept my head covered, or just because I was a woman alone, I do not know. I only know that as a guest, I was taken in and cared for if needed.

Many cosmopolitan women travelers feel quite safe while traveling in Pakistan, regardless of how they are dressed and where they sit on a bus, although it does help to understand regional differences in women's occupation of public spaces. For example, in my survey I did not ask trekkers if they were well received in public spaces, only if they ever felt concerned for their safety while in Pakistan. Of the women I surveyed, only 19 percent had any concerns for their personal safety in Pakistan, with the majority stating that they had no concerns, 79 percent (2 percent had no opinion).

One of those who said she had experienced concerns for her public safety noted it was because she was walking alone on a public roadway in Skardu and children threw rocks at her. While such an occurrence is rare, this cosmopolitan woman traveler's spatial behavior was "out of place" (Cresswell 1996) in Skardu, because of aforementioned gendered conventions of spatiality in the urban, regional capital of Skardu. Like those cosmopolitan women who veil more assiduously in villages instead of Skardu, this traveler's understanding of the spaces of seclusion was incomplete. In Skardu, local women who travel in public spaces do so along the back lanes of residential areas or shop in the "old" bazaar, which has a *purdah* bazaar, a woman's shopping space,[22] and would not, as a rule, walk the streets alone or with a male. As a rule, only tourist women—and this includes down-country Pakistani women—would travel along the main bazaar and public spaces of Skardu. Although the rock throwing is not justified, given the norms of gendered spatiality in Skardu, it is nevertheless not surprising.

Conclusion

Cosmopolitan women who adopt practices such as covering their heads and sitting in gender-segregated spaces may find that travel brings them into contact with women with whom they would otherwise, in all likelihood, have limited opportunity to meet in day-to-day tourist spaces. These interactions may often be superficial and communication strained by language differences. Nevertheless, by sharing spaces such as family rooms, Pakistani women become more visible to travelers, thereby challenging their understandings of public spaces as devoid of women, and that Pakistani women are immobile or invisible. They are not. Instead, they move through their daily spaces and places differently than do cosmopolitan women travelers. The examples of trekkers' veiling practices and walking along public roadways alone illustrate an understandable ignorance on the part of visitors. However, by following guidebook descriptions in adopting the "dreaded" *dupatta,* becoming more aware of the use of women's only spaces, and by using space more like local women do, cosmopolitan women travelers may find themselves more mobile than they might be if left to their own understandings of space.

In this chapter I have looked at how guidebook prescriptions suggest particular forms of dress and spatiality to cosmopolitan women travelers in Pakistan. Suggestions to wear loose fitting, locally made clothing and using women-only spaces may, indeed, ironically, enable travel for cosmopolitan women travelers to Pakistan, making them more mobile and more modern. Yet travel prescriptions for dress and spatial segregation remain underlain by more pervasive Orientalist discourses that depict gender and sexual relations between Pakistani men and women as riven by an uncontrollable male libido, reinforcing Orientalist representations that continue an alarming pattern of using Muslim bodies as referents for nonmodern Others. The most ironic and perhaps expected outcome from this chapter's analysis is that whatever way cosmopolitan women travelers enact travel prescriptions, that is, if they veil or not, if they use the lady's seat or not, walk alone or not all on public roadways, their religious nonmodern Others remain the enabling Other to modern gendered subjects. That is, if cosmopolitan women travelers chose to cover their heads all the time and use women's only spaces, they become the modern, mobile subjects that they aspire to be. If they reject local dress codes and spatiality in the name of their perceptions of modernity, they reaffirm their supposed superiority because of a negative travel experiences. Either way, a western, Enlightenment modernity continues its colonizing force, recapitulating itself in new ways through different embodied experiences (see T. Mitchell 2002, 2000, 1988).

Part Three . . .   New Spaces for Religious Women

6

Missionary Women in Early America

Prospects for a Feminist Geography

Jeanne Kay Guelke and Karen M. Morin

Mar. 10. [1846] Recreation-day. We had our usual missionary meeting it was conducted by Miss Curtis. She took up the subject of Home Missions. Also read a letter received last week from Mrs. Lydia Grant, who left four months since for South Africa. They had a quick passage, & a favorable voyage. . . . After this letter was read, Miss Thurston made her appearance dressed in the Sandwich Island's [native Hawaiian] costume. This as usual excited much interest.[1]

The above summary of a typical weekly meeting of students at Mount Holyoke Female Seminary (now College) in western Massachusetts illustrates some intriguing aspects of women, religion, and space in nineteenth century America: the use of evangelical Christianity to broaden women's geographical horizons, religious women functioning collectively in a society committed to the ideology that "woman's place is in the home," and missionary activity as a focal point for higher education for women (Porterfield 1997).

Historical geographies of American missionary and communitarian religious women of the nineteenth century offer opportunities to examine how religious women "produced space" and negotiated geographical scale in order to pursue their religious and personal goals. Female missionaries and communitarian women particularly interest us because their spatial practices departed significantly from traditional domestic and workplace norms for women and also because these groups skillfully combined spatial and religious concepts to create enlarged spheres for women's activity. We argue in this chapter that religious women's autonomy and increasing spheres of action reflected their ability to marshal community-level resources and to align with their church's global evangelical project, notwithstanding prevalent ideologies that positioned women within the household. Their distinctive geographical expressions manifested at a range of scales, from the body (such as the nun's habit) to the residential community (cloisters and campus) to global outreach (overseas missionary work.) We foreground our themes and examples with a feminist interpretation of American Christian missionary and communitarian women in the nineteenth century, finishing with a brief case study of Mount Holyoke Female Seminary of western Massachusetts, which had a missionary agenda and campus under female and communitarian management.

Mission and Community

American Christian missionary women during the nineteenth century negotiated conventional gender norms that ideologically and materially restricted middle-class women to their homes, and once "in the field" amid unfamiliar societies, missionary women faced the prospect of either reinscribing the conventional standards for femininity and space in their new location or else of negotiating new norms for women's "proper place" (Higham 2001; Lindley 1996; Ramusack 1990; Robert 1993; Rowbotham 1998). In a period when metropolitan authority conflated Christianity with "civilization" and thus Euro-American middle-class fashions in education, housekeeping, hygiene, diet, and clothing styles, female missionaries played a particularly important role as purveyors of middle-class white feminine culture to women and girls in their mission fields. As Americans overseas or in colonial contact zones within the borders of the present-day United States, some missionary women supported the American political and military agenda of conquest, colonization, and territorial dispossession of indigenous peoples. Female missionaries' practices in socializing indigenous people and settlers consequently have been interpreted as interfering in traditional cultures and contributing to cultural genocide (Comaroff and Comaroff 1991; Huber and Lutkehaus 1999; Adeney 2002).

Religious women of the nineteenth century who served as missionary teachers deserve special attention. The denominations of most Euro-American women excluded them from ordination, but they increasingly found a scope for their religious expression in teaching both secular and religious topics to women and children overseas, or in the case of missionary women in American territories, to indigenous pupils and settlers living in places remote from their nation's infrastructure of churches, schools, and government. Male Protestant missionaries voluntarily relinquished the instruction of females in mission fields where gender norms thwarted their efforts to work with local women, and under the social reform movements of nineteenth-century America, "women's work for women" added to missionary women's sense of moral capital (Wills 1997).[2]

A few female missionaries nevertheless occupied an ambivalent position with respect to imperialism, resisting European or American political or economic expansion by siding with Natives on land claims issues, for example, and in opposing their own governments' expansionist agendas (Morin 2000; Morin and Berg 2001). Presbyterian missionary teacher and wife Mary Ann Riggs (Leonard 1996, 244–45), for example, decried the plight of Native Americans in Minnesota where she and her husband labored in 1862, when Dakota (Sioux) living near her mission faced territorial dispossession and execution as the federal government's punishment for their recent uprising (original orthography retained):

I clip a snip out of yesterday's Pioneer [newspaper] about removing the Indians. I don't wonder people feel thus, but I think the Indians who have not participated in this rebellion should not suffer with the guilty. . . . Mr. L. W Pond thinks this late war would never have taken place if the *Mdwakantons* had been kept on their old grounds & not put so near other bands & the Winnebagoes. . . .

I feel very much afraid that the Indians sense of justice is too blind & dull to see the righteousness of their own people being executed. . . . I do not think it would benefit white people to see them shot or hung. . . .

Whether or not they explicitly endorsed U.S. expansionism and colonialism, missionary women interpreted their activities in terms of a Western Christian geopolitics whose objective was global conversion of the world's population to Christianity (Robert 1996). In locations remote from the Euro-American ecumene, missionary women often represented little-known nations and cultures to congregations, teachers, and mission administrators back home via letters, memoirs, tracts, and souvenirs. As such, they developed a kind of "religious women's geography" (Porterfield 1997; Robert 2002) parallel to the Victorian women's tradition of writing travel narratives or natural history in an era when women were excluded from professional science (Guelke and Morin 2001). Missionary work was the lens through which many religious American women learned about other places. Lucy Larcom (1986, 256–57), who worked in the textile mills of the Merrimack Valley, Massachusetts, reported around 1840:

> The needs of the West were constantly kept before us in the churches. We were asked for contributions for Home [U.S.] Missions, which were willingly given; and some of us were appointed collectors of funds for the education of indigent young men to become Western Home Missionary preachers. There was something almost pathetic in the readiness with which this was done by young girls who were longing to fit themselves for teachers, but had not the means. . . . An agent who came from the West for school-teachers was told by our own pastor that five hundred could easily be furnished from among Lowell mill-girls. . . . The missionary spirit was strong among my companions.

In rejecting the essentialist notion that religious women naturally expressed themselves in uniquely feminine genres, we nonetheless propose that women who were excluded from the government-sponsored expeditions or university posts that led to scholarly monographs could nevertheless write about foreign areas in ways that supported the socially sanctioned goal of promoting Christian missionary work, while writers simultaneously demonstrated the type of femininity that was acceptable to their society.

Women's missionary activity became a panoramic organizing principle that entailed three distinctive female populations, each with their respective but overlapping fields of work: the missionaries themselves, the "objects" of their conversion efforts, and the support groups of co-religionists back home (and sometimes in the mission field itself). Because missionaries required formal support groups of administrators, charitable associations, fund-raisers, donors, and educators as well as informal networks of supportive friends and neighbors, both overseas and Western American missionaries activated a great deal of collective or community-based effort on their behalf, often by groups of women in the eastern states (Ginzberg 1990; Robert 1996; Lindley 1996). Female support networks subverted the notion that women's highest calling was to be married with children and more or less focused upon the household. "Stay-at-home" mothers and single women who did not become missionaries but who actively supported their work via local fund-raising chapters that met in members' homes further challenged the notion of a private domestic space separate from the mission field. Missionary letters such as those penned by Mary Ann Riggs to her mother in 1837 (Riggs 1996, 22) reveal how stay-at-home family members and neighbors as well as missionary organizations participated vicariously in missionary work by providing basic necessities:

> I wish you would secure for me two yards of gingham like my dress and send it the same way (in a small box or packet to the American Board of Foreign Missions, Boston.) . . . Do you suppose the good people of Hawley [Massachusetts] would feel like filling out a small box for the Dakota mission sometime? If not you can send me anything for, as I mentioned before, I have not procured any bed quilts yet. . . .

A church membership by definition entails some community-level aspects: the Roman Catholic parish and Protestant congregation are local ecclesiastical units with geographical borders that typically contain mutually supportive social networks of families, neighbors, friends, and perhaps auxiliary associations. Religiously motivated nineteenth-century American women were notable for their collective and charitable venues of action, and it was activity at this community scale, whether a cloister or a club, that is critical to our analysis (Ginzberg 1990; Moore Milroy and Wismer 1994; Coburn and Smith 1995; Lindley 1996; Cott 1997; Fast 1999; Fessenden 2000; Spain 2001; Eason 2003). Ginzberg (1990) and Spain (2001) revealed the urban "redemptive landscape" of hospitals and accommodations for the poor, built by Protestant charitable organizations such as the YWCA, to which one could add schools and hospitals staffed by Catholic nuns (cf. Heaney 1993). The contributions of women's organizations to the urban fabric of the United States are notable during the nineteenth century, when individual women faced serious legal restrictions to owning land, restrictions they could avoid through the collective identity of charitable organizations (Ginzberg 1990).

The communal lifestyle of Catholic nuns and the Protestant female seminary with its common dining and dormitory facilities are examples of more significant breaks with conventional household models for women in centuries past, because the convent with its grounds (Heaney 1993) and the seminary campus (Horowitz 1984; Mihesuah 1993) housed same-sex or homosocial subcultures that also constructed buildings, landscape architecture, and real estate. Communities of religious women produced spaces under their control, and these spaces in turn helped to constitute particular kinds of social roles for women beyond traditional marriage and motherhood, and in distinct contrast to the available secular alternatives to family life such as female domestic or industrial labor. Restated, one can infer from denominationally based women's auxiliaries, the cloister, or the campus, that religious women were actively involved in the *production of scale* at a community level in defining new spaces for women, which in turn often transformed women's religious activity in the household or at the larger scale of the mission field.

Sister Blandina Segale (1990, 241) of the Cincinnati Sisters of Charity, posted to Trinidad, Colorado Territory, described in 1872 such a religious women's landscape in her description of her mission grounds and co-residents:

> The Purgatoire River . . . is the boundary line to land and house given by Don Felipe Baca, one of the leading citizens here, to the Sisters for a school. The land on which the Academy is built (now in the course of erection) was donated by a Mr. Heone, who lives a few miles outside of Trinidad.
>
> This gentleman and Dr. Beshoar, our physician, have pews in the church—if you can call eight planks nailed together, pews. The Sisters use the choir loft. The church is an adobe structure—with a pretense of a gable roof and a double pretense of having been shingled; mud floor, mud walls, wooden candlesticks. . . .
>
> The graveyard is in the rear of the church with a street between graveyard and convent. There is a long stretch of an adobe wall from convent (academy) to public school, the only one here and taught by the Sisters.
>
> . . . The Sisters are: Sister Marcella, in charge and music teacher; Sister Martha, Housekeeper; Sister Eulalia, Factotum; Sister Fidelis, Select School; Sister Blandina, Public School Teacher; Sister Eulalia, Assistant.

Colonial and postcolonial theorists have widely addressed the colonial and imperial relations of missionaries and their subjects, including in the U.S. contact zone with Native Americans. In directing attention to missionary women's attempt to advance personal, professional, and religious goals through "the production and politics of geographical scale" (Smith 1992), we now build upon Marston's (2000, 2004) recommendations for more research at scales where women's influences were more obvious and meaningful. As Marston argues, there is a pressing need to move beyond economic and political approaches that privilege global capitalist production over studies at the scale of the household or local. Purcell (2003b, 328) adds: "[What] is required is a more synthetic critical human geography . . . [and] a specific methodological agenda on the part of all human geographers that broadens the scope of their analysis beyond its traditional bounds."

Religion, Women, and the Production of Scale

In encapsulating recent scale research in human geography Sheppard and Mc-Master (2004, 15) assert that

> if scale is socially constructed, then we cannot simply take for granted the exis-
> tence and importance of the geographic scales usually involved in human geo-
> graphic writing: Neighborhood, city, regional, national and global. Rather, we
> need to understand not only why their relative importance may vary over space
> and time, but also whether these are even the right scales to be thinking about.

Religions, like political and economic systems, produce scales, but in ways that differ from geographers' conventional hierarchies based upon economics and political divisions. Many of them predate the capitalist and national systems upon which much current human geography studies of scale are based.

Probably the most noteworthy aspect of religiously constructed scales is in their framers' efforts to stress their simultaneous effects. Christianity, for example, is dedicated to regulating people at the level of the body or individual through proscriptions about sexuality, but does so with a cosmological project in mind, articulated through intermediary ecclesiastical structures. Prayer is an individual or congregational act that is meant to influence the cosmos. The whole concept of the "Christian home" (McDannell 1994) shows the influence of an ideology that is global (or supernatural) in scope upon the scale of the household. As we discuss in more depth later, the Protestant Evangelical prose-lytizing mission was based upon integration at a number of scales, including at a cosmological scale.

If women's traditional contributions to society have been through the body, home, and community, religion gave women (and men) a rationale for them through a much larger sphere of influence, via, for example, the Vatican or through the Boston-based Protestant agency, the American Board of Commissioners of Foreign Missions (Robert 1996). During the nineteenth century U.S. religious authorities primarily expected women to be "consumers" of information about the wider scales, not producers of it. Female missionaries radically transformed this agenda.

The activities of missionary women (and the community-based women with whom they interacted) do not fit well within contemporary geography's customary focus on geopolitical and economic scales that follow one of an assortment of nested hierarchical models (Herod 2003; Sheppard and McMaster 2004). Not only do ecclesiastical scales tend to differ from secular models (individual < parish < diocese or mission field < global Catholic Church < cosmos) but also because some religious women actively "jumped scale" from the conventional household or home to larger fields of endeavor (Wills 1997). They often redefined the meaning of those scales in the process; such as the convent's hybrid space of the residence and community or Spain's (2001) "redemptive landscape" of urban hospitals and poor houses sponsored by Protestant women's organizations.

Sister Blandina (Segale 1990, 241) in Colorado Territory, for example, immediately following her above quotation on her mission buildings and grounds, described the dramatic extension of her scale of activity:

> Here, if you have a largeness of vision, you find the opportunity to exercise it; if a cramped one, the immense expanse of the plains, the solid Rockies, the purity of the atmosphere, the faultlessness of the canopy above, will stretch the mind toward the Good. . . . I wish I had many hands and feet, and a world full of hearts to place at the service of the Eternal.

The prospects for locating studies of religious women within geographical theory and paradigms are enhanced by attention to scale, rather than viewing religion simply as a unique source of difference (Kong 2001; Hervieu-Léger 2002; Park 1994). In noting that scales are inextricably nested and interconnected—providing the platforms or "scaffolding" upon or out of which social roles and relations are produced—we next consider five interconnected scales that missionary women actively produced or contested for their religious and personal ends: the body, the residence or dwelling, the site of worship, the community or town, and the geopolitical scale. Recent scale research can especially help retool a predominant model in human geography today, that of public and private space as separate spheres, because public and private space tends to overlap more than to exist in separation. In our conclusion we offer some suggestions for how such retooling can proceed when examined through the lens of missionary women's lives and work.

American Christian Women and the Politics of Scale

Recent geographical feminist research (reviewed by Nagar et al. 2002) applies Smith's (1992) concept of the *politics* of scale to global processes affecting women. For example, women with little political power at the local level may subvert their authorities' indifference and gain global support through transnationally disseminated publicity about their situation, or what is termed the "rescaling" (changing scale) or "upscaling" (moving an issue up the hierarchy of scale) during a dispute. Scholars thus note the processes by which those without power can move across scales, "tak[ing] advantage of the resources at one scale to overcome the constraints encountered at different scales in the way more powerful actors do" (Staeheli 1994, 388; quoted in Marston 2000, 222).

Marston (2000, 236) argues that for U.S. women in the late nineteenth and early twentieth centuries, home "was the site from which other scales were addressed and occupied," developing a link between national trends in production of household goods and household trends in consumption of nationally advertised products. We ask why and how religious women attempted to shift scales (rescale or upscale) in terms of women's domains of intellectual purviews and agency. Without denying the agency of individual religious women, histories of American women and religion (Ginzberg 1990; Lindley 1996; Fast 1999; Coburn and Smith 1999) indicate that the scale of the community, more than the individual home, was the platform from which they sought a wider sphere of action on the regional, global, and even cosmological stage. Although Protestant women often met in one another's households, what they were doing on a temporary and flexible basis was "creating their own politics of scale" (sensu Smith 1992) by creating a group of believers intent on a particular purpose, such as self-improvement or fund-raising for missionary efforts. Lucy Larcom (1986, 174–75, 220), for example, reported how "mill girls" in Lowell, Massachusetts, set up their own "Improvement Circle" that met in members' rooms and developed their own literary magazine in support of their larger goals:

> Many of them were supporting themselves at schools like Bradford Academy or Ipswich Seminary [Protestant female seminaries] half the year, by working in the mills the other half. Mount Holyoke Seminary broke upon the thoughts of many of them as a vision of hope. (Larcom 1986, 223)

We consequently argue that many missionary and communitarian women created their own "politics of scale" to negotiate patriarchal-centered scale constructions. Although we do not view missionary women as oppositional or even resistant to their patriarchal religions with which they associated themselves—they were, after all, "bargaining with patriarchy" (Kandiyoti 1988; Ebaugh 1993) in order to help that very patriarchal system succeed—through the production of scale they nonetheless opened new space for women that gave them opportunities to live with other women, exercise their talents and skills, increase mobility for women, increase female literacy through their schools, and improve women's health through their hospitals.

From Body to Cosmos and Back Again

In this section we elaborate a bit further on the mutual constitution and integration of scales relevant to the study of religious women. Our intent is to emphasize both the "simultaneous effects" of religious women's activities as well as the politics of scale they deployed to accomplish their religious and personal goals. Most significantly, religious women used the community scale to support local benevolent work, but their distinctive types of communities (benevolent society, convent, or seminary) also transformed women's religious activity at larger scales, such as the mission field. All of our examples show women's potential to elide and maneuver scales in creative ways.

Religious women in early America marked and enacted religious beliefs while enhancing their religious stature at the scale of the *body* through numerous bodily or corporeal restrictions and embodied acts and practices. Their clothing (see chapters 3, 4, 5, and 8) had an important spatial logic. In addition to the nun's habit and rosary providing a portable "sacred space" for women as they conducted their work within the public or "profane" spheres, some Protestant women's dress identified them as members of particular denominations, notably the Salvation Army and the Amish (cf. Dwyer 1999b; Secor 2002; Alvi, Hoodfar, and McDonough 2003 on the Muslim veil or bourka). During the Victorian era, the modest dress of Euro-American Christian women became the standard through which missionary women pressured indigenous women to cover their bodies and adopt their practices of celibacy or monogamy (Grimshaw 1989; Zwiep 1991), thus connecting the scale of the body to their global conversion effort.

The centrality of the family *household* to normative American women's religious practice appears in many nineteenth-century advice manuals (Margolis 2000; Tonkovich 1997; McDannell 1994). Victorian associations of monogamous mothers within the reverent "Christian home" (ideally complete with parlor organ and sheet music for hymn playing) and the home shrines of some Catholic women nevertheless pose interesting contradictions to the sharp separation of sacred and profane space (sensu Eliade 1959), where the former is to be distinguished by specially designated, male-oriented religious buildings and precincts. In a Catholic advice manual to women of the late nineteenth century, Monsignor Bernard O'Reilly (1894, 7) reinforced the belief that devout women convert the home into sacred space:

> All the institutions and ordinances which God has created in civil society or bestowed upon his Church, have for their main purpose to secure the existence, the honor, and the happiness of every home in the community. . . . There is nothing on earth which the Creator and Lord of all things holds more dear than this home . . . in which a mother's unfailing and all-embracing tenderness will be, like the light and warmth of the sun in the heavens.

As already noted, the concept of the Christian home demonstrates the simultaneity, if not erasure, of discrete spatial scales; as home-based religious acts such as Bible-reading or bedtime prayers simultaneously link the body, the home, and God or his divine intermediaries in the mind of the believer.

Communitarian religions by definition all but erase boundaries between the household and the community and sometimes the house of worship. For example, as a religious women's space the Catholic convent takes on numerous sacred and metaphorical meanings, as a space of refuge for women seeking a retreat from parents, marriage, or motherhood or a space constructed to promote a life of contemplation and prayer. Roman Catholic sisters adopted a variety of communitarian living arrangements, ranging from the strictly cloistered to teaching orders who allowed the "outside" world to enter their convents, where their work extended beyond religious devotion to the education of young girls in convent schools. The Roman Catholic Ursulines provide a good example. The Ursulines were the first officially sanctioned religious group of missionary women established in North America. They came to Quebec in 1639 and a century later, in 1727, another group from France founded the convent in New Orleans, which in turn founded the oldest school for girls in the United States (Choquette 1994; Clark 1998, 2002; Heaney 1993). Resident Ursuline nuns practiced a communitarian type of living arrangement with other sisters and had as their central purpose the school education and Christianizing of settlers' daughters, slave girls from neighboring plantations, and Native girls.

Temporally and spatially, much of what constitutes "official" Christian religious practice takes place within specifically consecrated *church buildings*. During the nineteenth century when few American denominations ordained women or encouraged them to speak in church, itinerant female preachers gave sermons in people's homes or outdoor meeting grounds (Brekus 1998), both examples of innovative sites of organized worship for women. Harriet Beecher Stowe met African American preacher Sojourner Truth in 1863 and reported how Truth simultaneously changed the scale of preaching while locating her ministry outside of conventional churches (Sterling 1984, 151):

> I went to the Lord an' asked him to give me a new name. And the Lord gave me sojourner, because I was to travel up an' down the land, showin' the people their sins, and being' a sign unto them.

. . . I journeys round to camp-meetin's, an' wherever folks is, an' I sets up
my banner, an' then I sings, an' then folks always comes up round me, an' then I
preaches to 'em.

Roman Catholic nuns cannot conduct mass, and nuns in settler communities typically relied on the sometimes sporadic visits of priests to do so. And yet,
women such as the Ursulines of New Orleans were responsible for the funding,
construction, and maintenance of the chapels and other church buildings
within their missions (Choquette 1994; Clark 1998, 2002; Heaney 1993) as well
as classroom-based religious instruction. Protestant women's prayer circles
that took place in homes or seminary campuses are other examples of sites for
women's worship that occurred without the need for a church and ordained
(male) minister.

Religious women enlarged their sphere of religious work through their
local *communities,* including those in established religious orders, via voluntary social services at the scale of parish or congregation as well as through the
establishment of female-sponsored schools, hospitals, and orphanages. Religious women in settler communities, including those in established religious
orders, often enacted their notions of communal identity via such voluntary
social services. In addition to their teaching mission, the Ursulines also ran
hospitals and orphanages and were among the largest real estate developers in
francophone North America (with land charters from the King of France),
meanwhile providing for their own subsistence. The Ursulines were not only
effective educators—they raised the literary rate of women in the New Orleans
to one of the highest in colonial America (Clark 2002, 4)—but independent
businesswomen, architects, and builders (Clark 1998, 2002).

The work of the gospel, as Christian missionary women and their support
groups understood it, was evangelical, and consequently, in today's terms it was
geopolitical. Missionary women's activities and influences extended well beyond the local level, and missionary work gave ordinary women a chance to
participate as agents at the national or global scale. To some female missionary
teachers a "home" mission within the U.S. colonial interior, entailing work with
Native or settler children, was not as demanding as (and was consequently less
prestigious than) working in Asia, although it equally centered upon incorpo-
rating non-Christians into white Christian mores (Higham 2001; Mihesuah

1993; Craig 1997; DeRogatis 2003). Others eagerly sought to "rescue" benighted women in the nineteenth-century American West (Pascoe 1990; Yohn 1995) and Hawaii (Zwiep 1991). The Social Gospel movement in the late nineteenth century (Spain 2001; Eason 2003) convinced other Protestant women and Catholic nuns that "charity begins at home," and they sought to help the disadvantaged in their own cities through settlement houses, social work, and orphanages. Once in a foreign or home mission, missionary wives typically saw their duty as reproducing "the Christian home" as they knew it and to encourage indigenous women to follow their example (Grimshaw 1989; Hill 1985; Hunter 1984; Robert 1993). Thus each type of Christian outreach entailed some aspect of self-justification based upon the perceived nobility attached to the scale and location of the ministry.

Missionary women conceptualized the earth in distinctly Christian ways. Many believed that their collective efforts would redeem the earth from its "fallen" state and prepare it for the Second Coming (Hitchcock 1858). Many viewed the world through scriptural lenses, frequently deploying phrases derived from the Bible in their letters and memoirs. Others considered themselves part of God's plan for their home communities or mission fields. Consequently no consideration of scale in the geography of religion can ignore that religious people are motivated at levels of scale on a *spiritual plane,* well beyond the global. Their denominations' concepts of God, heaven, the hereafter, or the millennial kingdom inform and guide their practices at all levels. Women's acting upon explicit Christian precepts to donate the "widow's mite" from their household allowances in order to spread the gospel via missionary work simultaneously brought larger-scale concerns into their homes and communities while women constructed the household and local scales as domains within which women could contribute to municipal, global, and indeed universal visions. In that sense they rewrote the "content" of the home itself. Similarly, use of a home-derived metaphor—"sisterhood"—inspired women at the community and broader scales as well.

We suggest that women's organizations on the margins of male authority and concern, with the reduction of surveillance over women's activities, promoted some degree of women's independence. The Roman Catholic convent may regulate religious women and place them under male ecclesiastical authority, but as a female space of administration, economic subsistence, intellectual advancement, and sometimes retreat, the convent may provide a space for female resistance, however politely that resistance may be expressed. Coburn and Smith (1999), for example, describe a Missouri community of sisters of St. Joseph de Carondelet and show how the nuns resisted their local parish priest's control by "upscaling" in claiming that they reported to a higher authority in the church—located conveniently well removed from the sister's daily operations (see also Ebaugh 1993).

Cloistered nuns seem particularly adept at playing off various scales against one another in order to retain their autonomy. Rachel Daack (2004) discusses Blessed Virgin Mary sisters as moving their seat of operations from Philadelphia to schools in the West in order to minimize male ecclesiastical control. When ordered by the local bishop in Missouri to adopt particular rules, the nuns "jumped scale" by arguing that their order fell under papal authority; they thus foiled the local priest's attempts to control their operations.

Scales of religious organization and ideology indeed interact with political and economic scales, but often in a way that subverts today's conventional secular models. Nineteenth-century theorist Catharine Beecher, for example, simply attempted to invert the conventional top-down hierarchy: the Christian home to her thought became the foundation of the state and religion (Sklar 1973). Although feminists convincingly argue that political, economic, and religious systems simultaneously exert significant social control over women, and although the cultural genocide intended by Christian missionaries further negate any valorizing of the religious women we studied, it seems fair to argue that they achieved greater autonomy through, and not despite, their reworking of scale via their religious beliefs.

We agree with theorists of scale such as Smith (1992) and Marston (2000, 2004) that creating a politics of scale is much more than a geographical abstraction, because scales have material consequences. In the examples cited above, Ginzberg (1990) and Spain (2001) noted that nineteenth-century Protestant women's ability to upscale from the individual and the home scale to the community-based (or sometimes even nationally based) organization gave them the legal possibility of owning land for their charitable work; a right denied to them as individual women. Similarly, globally based Roman Catholic female religious orders permitted their convents to amass considerable landholdings and encouraged individual nuns (such as the Mother Superior) to exert considerable administrative influence. Mount Holyoke Female Seminary, which we turn to next, addressed a New England problem of a demographic surplus of unmarried women—who would otherwise live as economically vulnerable dependents of fathers or brothers—by giving young women teaching skills that were marketable locally, in the western territories, or overseas in missionary schools (Sweet 1985; Conforti 1993).

Case Study: Mount Holyoke College

Mount Holyoke Female Seminary (now College) in western Massachusetts had a communitarian dimension and strong commitment to missionary work that highlight the production and politics of scale by a group of religious women. Mary Lyon (1797–1849) of western Massachusetts is often cited as the founder of higher education for women for the United States as well as internationally (Green 1979). Whether her founding of Mount Holyoke Female Seminary in 1837 qualifies for this honor is a matter of some debate among scholars (and alumnae), but Lyon clearly advanced the cause of academic as well as missionary women. As a devout member of the Congregational church, the outgrowth of Massachusetts Puritanism, Lyon was able to co-opt tenets of Puritan theology, such as the Protestant work ethic, for her own purposes during the 1830s (Conforti 1993). The industrial revolution, New England's newly emerging middle class, and the demographic circumstance of "surplus" young women created a situation where middle-class women gained increasing leisure time. Lyon deplored the trend of leisured women's education as ornamental rather than useful and developed the project of higher education for women as a means of fitting them to become better Christians, school teachers, or mothers of future Christian citizens (Sweet 1985; Green 1979).

A confirmed evangelical, Lyon enlisted locally prominent men such as ministers to champion her cause and serve as trustees, thus somewhat mitigating the sharp criticism that she had stepped out of her proper sphere. Her strategy of recruiting male advocates for her seminary also enabled Lyon to extend her reach into venues where women were excluded. As she conspired with a female associate in 1833 (Hitchcock 1858, 172): "It is desirable that the plans relating to the subject should not seem to originate with *us,* but with benevolent *gentle-*

men. If the object should excite attention, there is danger that many good men will fear the effect on society of so much female influence."

Lyon deployed the biblically based evangelical principle that the great work required of all Christians was global conversion, overseas as well as within the United States and its territories, where both Natives and secular white settlers appeared in serious need of salvation. Educating future teachers and mothers in a Protestant seminary was critical to her essentially geopolitical goal (Lyon 1839). Mount Holyoke student and teacher Susan Tolman in 1846 reported on Mary Lyon's intentions:

> Our prayer meeting was appointed in Room B. at $8^1/_2$. . . . She wanted we should pray for the conversion of all this family, that so Christ's kingdom might be built up & the world be converted, also for the missionary societies & the American Board [of Foreign Missionaries] . . . pray for the different stations, & for all the Missionaries, especially ours, those that have gone out from us, pray for them by name, pray that more laborers may be raised up, & the missionary spirit increased all over our land.[3]

In the above quotation, the unconverted among the "family" refers to students who did not have a personal spiritual experience of the Christian faith. Cole (1940, 102) aptly called Mount Holyoke at its founding in 1837 a "Puritan convent." Here a small community of female students and teachers lived and studied together in a single campus building designed by Mary Lyon expressly to promote the work of the gospel, as she defined it. (See also Green 1979; Sweet 1985; Horowitz 1984; Robert 1993, 1996; Conforti 1993; Porterfield 1997; Thomas 1937; Sklar 1979.) Preparing young women to become mission teachers if single, as well as missionary wives, soon joined the original plan of educating local teachers and the seminary subsequently became a magnet for missionary daughters as well. Like the Catholic convent, the female seminary afforded its residents scope for considerable religious autonomy apart from male surveillance (Fisk 1866, 148):

> It was during this year [1841] that little daily prayer meetings were commenced. . . . the meetings being conducted by the pupils themselves. . . . Mon-

day was given to Foreign Missions, and she who had the care of the meeting said a few words suggesting particular subjects under this head. . . . Tuesday was given in the same way to Home Missions. Wednesday, to prayer for the Bible and Tract Societies. Thursday, to home churches and friends. Friday, to our own and other seminaries, while on Saturday we pleaded for Abraham's seed.

Mary Lyon believed that good health was essential if women were to become effective teachers and missionaries; they required "piety, a sound constitution, and a merry heart" (Gilchrist 1910, 322). Calisthenics therefore had a central role in her Mount Holyoke curriculum (Green 1979, 220). In this way reform at the scale of the body was intimately connected to that of the mission field. Developing a tight-knit female Protestant community at Mount Holyoke as an aid to redemption was Mary Lyon's principal objective, and she designed the campus accordingly (Horowitz 1984). Lyon's writings reveal that she intended an erasure of the boundaries (scales) between the household, community, and house of worship. For example, she viewed the original Mount Holyoke Female Seminary building both as a home and as temple (Horowitz 1984; Hitchcock 1858). She designed the shared rooms in the residence hall with the belief that the more pious students would support the faith of their less spiritually inclined roommates. Closets were designed in the residence areas as monastic cells for prayer, rather than for wardrobes. Mary Lyon's use of the classroom lectern to deliver sermons in an era when Congregational women were forbidden to preach (Hitchcock 1858) is an example of innovative spaces for women's worship outside the official church building.

"Town-gown" relations were also important to Lyon. She strove to develop a sense of pride of ownership in her seminary among congregations in western Massachusetts, when she solicited them to donate furnishings to campus rooms (Hitchcock 1858; Green 1979). This represents a shift of interest from the local to the regional, particularly in that her students simultaneously thus saw themselves and their dormitory rooms as more than personal space, connected rather to a larger, regional community.

Geography instruction was an aid to Bible study and to prayer for missionary workers overseas (Gilchrist 1910, 437–41). Former teachers and students in missions overseas shipped natural history specimens of pressed plants and stuffed birds (Levin 2005, 73) as well as letters about life in Persia, China, and

India to Mount Holyoke, whereby missionary women contributed a kind of Christian geography back to the college (Porterfield 1997; Stowe 1887; Levin 2005). Their "imperial geography" is particularly clear for those who worked among native Hawaiians and the Cherokee nation (Grimshaw 1989; Mihesuah 1993) during the Five Civilized Tribes's period of removal to Arkansas and subsequently to Oklahoma. The Cherokee National Female Seminary and seminaries overseas, for example, were established by Mount Holyoke women on a plan that replicated their alma mater (cf. Porterfield 1997; Mihesuah 1993). The goal of Mount Holyoke College's alumnae "home missionary" wives and teachers was assimilation of Native girls to white women's models of religion as well as decorum, dress, family, and housekeeping; essentially cultural erasure. Yet these women also associated with ministers who protested government treatment of Native people (cf. Chaudhuri and Strobel 1992; Riggs 1996).

Our capsule description underlines the findings of "women and religion" scholars that many religious women experienced considerable autonomy in their lives and work. Mary Lyon was a master at rethinking traditional concepts of scale and related affiliations and social roles. Girls from Massachusetts farms were to be educated about global salvation and then would move into the wider world as teachers or missionaries. Lyon asked each town in western Massachusetts to contribute furnishings to her new college so that each would think of the college as "their" college, shifting their scales from the local to the regional (Stowe 1887). Lyon also played the meaning of home as a site of pious domesticity against one where middle-class women had too much leisure and too little sphere for constructive contributions. Through missionary activity, communal arrangements, or charitable work as well as religious zeal, they exemplified striking alternatives to conventional norms for American femininity and domesticity.

Conclusions: Beyond Separate Spheres

Some Christian women in the United States, even within the more restrictive norms of the nineteenth century, deployed their faith's own proof texts and concepts of morality to negotiate with churchmen in support of enlarged spheres for women. These women used New Testament verses beyond Paul's mandates for obedient wives in Ephesians to underscore their faith's goal for the entire world as a land converted to their vision of Christianity (Robert 1996; Wiesner-Hanks 2000). It was difficult for patriarchal Christian men to refute determined and devout women's arguments that Jesus's mandate of global conversion required women to become more proficient in Bible-reading, and better educated as teachers, so that they could more effectively bring the gospel to their own children or young pupils (Lindley 1996; cf. Hitch-cock 1858). Thus some Christian women piously demonstrated a need for women in education, benevolent societies, and evangelical projects as well as in the local fund-raising activities necessary to support them.

Although religious women's methods of enhancing their status are inter-connected and hence difficult to delineate independently, it may be fair to say that Christian women's involvement in missionary work—and the attendant production and politics of scale that it entailed—historically has been their principal means of modifying the more patriarchal aspects of religion for themselves, if not for the objects of their proselytizing efforts. Missionary work was an acceptable and perhaps even empowering way for nineteenth-century European and North American religious women to escape home boundaries and to travel to other, sometimes exotic, locations while working and fulfilling their religious commitments. Women who did not become missionaries them-selves frequently formed Christian societies that raised funds for missionary men and women and eagerly attended returning missionaries' lectures, thus participating vicariously in missionary work (Robert 2002).

If their church's doctrines concerning global Christianity required or-dained male missionaries to preach the gospel and baptize the convert, then de-voutly religious women also argued effectively that these clergymen required Christian women's support services (Robert 1993, 1996). Depending upon the denomination, time, and place, women's support services might range from wives at home who managed household affairs in their missionary husbands' absences, to missionary wives "in the field" who kept house for their husbands in mission stations, to more autonomous women who managed mission schools, hospitals, and the economic means to operate them. Because some in-digenous non-Christian societies denied male missionaries' requests to prose-lytize local women out of concern for propriety, some denominations concluded that missionary women were essential to their global conversion project. Although missionary women often replicated their familiar domestic patterns in the mission field, they did so in locations that their contemporaries often regarded as exotic and with a spirit praised simultaneously as enviably adventuresome and piously self-sacrificing.

Nineteenth-century American Christians at home indeed found mission-ary work to be prestigious and exotic: male- and female-authored missionary books on remote locations, unfamiliar cultures, and the physical dangers en-countered in hostile environments were popular fare, as were sermons in church by returned missionaries (Robert 2002; Porterfield 1997). An ancillary result of missionaries' faith-promoting books and lectures was that these com-munications provided significant geographical information to co-religionists back home, albeit with a distinctively sectarian tone (DeRogatis 2003). Simi-larly, geographical education was a key part of some denominations' mission-ary project, in order to foster knowledge of mission fields among prospective missionaries as well as among their financial supporters (Stowe 1887). Mis-sionary life was understood to be fraught with physical hardships and spiritual disappointments, yet these could serve to accentuate women missionaries' ap-propriate feminine virtues of self-sacrifice and patience (Robert 1996; Higham 2001; Hill 1985).

As institutions engaged in educating future missionary women or provid-ing workplaces for them overseas, Christian women's seminaries, cloisters, and hospitals might be construed as simply "ghettoizing" women in locations where their taken-for-granted attributes of nurturing and self-sacrifice still marginalized them from the real sites of (masculine) political power. However, women's "places on the margins" of centers of ecclesiastical or government au-thority can become sites of female empowerment where the classroom or mis-sion, especially in remote settlements, affords sufficient isolation from centralized patriarchal supervision and surveillance. It is worth noting that the classroom took women out of the domestic household and into a more public, community-level domain, at the same time that women taught subjects such as geography and religion that were dedicated, at least abstractly, to transporting global awareness into their pupils' homes and communities.

Religious women's worldviews, their facility with religious ideology and language, the very powerful feelings of spirituality and even mysticism that some women experienced, and a sense of sisterhood (a metaphor both Catholic nuns and Mount Holyoke seminarians used), tended to give ambitious women more scope and authority to pursue their goals and to give disadvantaged women the ideological means of valorizing their plights (Griffith 1997). We have argued that it is important to understand the scales that both influenced and expressed these women's endeavors. The admonition "Go where no one else will go. Do what no one else will do" is not a recent feminist manifesto (or *Star Trek* slogan), but is attributed to Mary Lyon, an exemplar of Christian piety and founder of higher education for American women. The belief that women could become successful hospital administrators and land managers, without a conventional home life and family, does not date from 1970s liberal feminism but has influenced Roman Catholic convents since the Middle Ages. In these examples, religious women emerge as producers of religious hermeneutics, spaces, and ultimately of secular social innovations and not merely as docile consumers of male-oriented religious belief and practice.

7

Korean Immigrant Women to Los Angeles

Religious Space, Transformative Space?

HaeRan Shin

This chapter draws upon in-depth interviews with Christian Korean immigrant women in Los Angeles to explain how they accommodate constraints in spatial practices, careers, and family decisions. My subjects initially turned to their Christian theology as a positive "adaptive mechanism" for their limited situations in an unfamiliar country. At the same time, their Christian faith buffered these women from the abundant personal frustrations that arose from their situations as recent immigrants. This strategy for adjustment, however, eventually became a constraint to their participation in wider social and economic life.

The importance of the ethnic church or other house of worship to immigrants' group identity and adaptation to a new environment is well known through studies of diasporic communities (Hume 2003; Hagan and Ebaugh 2003; Cottrell 1999; Lehr and Katz 1995), including through studies of Korean immigrants in Los Angeles (Min 1992). New immigrants in the United States typically participate in religious activities more than in their home countries because religious affiliation offers "meaning to their new lives, a sense of self-awareness, and belonging in the host society" (Kwon 2000, 1–2). Korean immigrant women's mobility, in both public and private, is strongly influenced by their Christianity (Kim 1996; Kim 1997). In Los Angeles, the majority of Korean immigrants are religious or at least participate in religious rituals (Min 1990, 18; 1992).

Gender, however, is seldom a consideration in studies of religious immigrants (but see Kim 1997). At the same time, a number of studies consider changing gender identities due to immigration, yet leave out the significance of religion. Hondagneu-Sotelo (1994) and Dyck and McLaren (2004), for example, focus on the process of reconstructing gender through immigration and settlement, but do not look at religion as an essential part of their female subjects' culture.

Gender and religious practice are nevertheless mutually constituted in religious immigrants' identities and adjustments to a new place, notably because religious immigrants often transfer traditional beliefs about gender to their new destination, and traditionalists may be particularly concerned to monitor the behavior of women within their immigrant community (Kostovicova and Prestreshi 2003; Kim 1997). Claire Dwyer (2000, 1999b) has taken this intersection of gender, religious affiliation, and immigrant status a step further, in interviewing young Muslim women in Britain about their hybrid identities both as diasporic Muslim women and as British subjects. Anna Secor (2004, 2002) interviewed secular and religious immigrant women in Istanbul, Turkey, about the spatial strategies (Secor 2004, 353) they used in everyday life to express their sense of belonging or alienation. Only a few scholars of religious immigrant women, such as Kim's (1996) study of Korean women in New Jersey, however, interviewed their subjects in depth about how prayer, their scriptures, and their "operative view of God" (ibid., 89) permeate their daily lives or contribute significantly to their assimilation or social exclusion (as defined by Hiebert and Ley 2003).

With the aim of investigating the role of religion in the spatial practices of Korean immigrant women, I conducted in-depth interviews with forty-two Korean immigrant women who are "active" Christians, between the ages of forty-one and fifty-three, who live in the Los Angeles metropolitan area. I discovered how these women established their daily lives to accommodate the constraints incurred by immigration, and, in the process, how they emphasized, interpreted, and used certain Christian tenets as guiding principles for their accommodation process.

In interpreting each interview I focused upon the cultural identities expressed through Korean women's everyday lives (cf. Dwyer 2000). I also considered how religious affiliation, belief, and practice influenced women's job choices, their family life, and ultimately, their *capability*. Sen (1992, 1997, 1999) argued that poverty is not a question of how many resources people are able to command ("functioning") but of what they are actually able to do or to become ("capability"). Capability reflects personal choice; a person's freedom to lead one type of life or another (Alkire 2002). Although some of my subjects were poor in the financial and functional sense, others in households with secure incomes expressed religious beliefs that nevertheless limited their personal capabilities, that is, their mobility and potential for entering the Los Angeles economic and cultural mainstream, even in a highly multicultural city where 45 percent of the residents are also foreign-born (Agnew 2004).

Protestant beliefs and participation in Korean Protestant churches have long stood at the center of Korean immigrant communities in the United States in general (Hurh and Kim 1984; Kim 1981) and Los Angeles in particular (Min 1992; Kim 1997). The Korean churches have served as places of survival, where the majority of the Korean immigrant families who live in Los Angeles are able to keep their senses of themselves as Korean intact.[1] They have provided many benefits to their congregations, including opportunities to meet with other Korean immigrants, education for the second generation, material assistance, and Christian faith life counseling (Min 1992). Especially for Korean immigrant women in the Los Angeles metropolitan area, church involvement has helped to mitigate the difficulties caused by immigration to the United States at the same time that, as I discuss below, it constrains women's mobility, career choices, and their entry into social and economic life in Los Angeles.

Culture, Adaptive Career Preferences, and Place

How might religious beliefs assist immigrants in their adaptations to new places? Swidler's (1986, 273) definition of culture as a " 'tool kit' of habits, skills, and lifestyles from which people construct 'strategies of action' " is widely used by sociologists (Small and Newman 2001, 35). Culture, from this point of view, provides people with a ready-made set of solutions for human problems so that individuals are not required to begin all over again with each new generation (Lewis 1966). The essence of religion as an aspect of culture, in this sense, lies in its positive adaptive function.

Jon Elster (1983), Amartya Sen (1997), and Timur Kuran (1995) have dissected the preference formation process. Elster sees "adaptive preference formation" as the adjustment of wants to possibilities. Behind adaptation, for low-income individuals, is the drive to reduce the tension or frustration that one feels in possessing desires that one cannot possibly satisfy. Low aspiration helps to reduce frustration, and the legitimization of short-range self-satisfaction. The interviewees in the study by Lewis (1966) of urban poverty nevertheless experienced spontaneity and enjoyment. Lewis's biggest contribution stems from his discovery of poor people's flexibility and resourcefulness (Harvey and Reed, 1996). Regardless of their level of income, Korean Christian women in my study displayed several of the characteristics of the poor that Lewis identified. These included adoption of low expectations in order to minimize frustration with difficult personal circumstances.

Religion is a big part of the lifestyle and daily culture of the faithful; it influences deep-rooted notions of masculinity and femininity (Mills and Ryan 2001, 62), attitudes toward abortion (Boggess and Bradner 2000), sexual activity (Brewster 1994), and the socialization and defining of women's role as caregivers (Taylor, Mattis, Chatters 1999; Levin, Taylor, Chatters 1994). The community activity of religious women—usually housewives—is locally based on religious institutions. For Korean immigrant women especially, Protestantism is one of the critical factors that influence their ideology, behaviors, and attitudes toward themselves and the society in which they live (Kim 1997), in short, their adaptations and expectations regarding their new situations.

The conservative Christian subculture has long been challenged by alternative voices that argue for women's equality (Ingersoll 2003, 2). Feminist scholars have pointed out that the Christian valorization of making sacrifices has helped legitimize women's inferior socioeconomic positions and their roles as wives and mothers (Rigby 2000). Christian women seem to undergo a gender socialization process that emphasizes patience, forbearance, and restraint (Taylor, Mattis, Chatters 1999, 537), thereby limiting their freedom or options when making lifestyle choices. Patriarchy is hardly limited to Christianity: Kim (1997) noted that gender beliefs transferred readily from Confucianism to Korean converts to Christianity. At the same time, Ingersoll (2003) and Griffith (1997) discussed how evangelical women reshaped the concept of submission to create a space of empowerment. It is important to view devout Christian women, therefore, as more than mere victims of patriarchal oppression.

The Interviewees

This chapter is based on in-depth interviews (Glaser and Strauss 1967; Weiss 1994; Lewis 1966) and participant observation of forty-two Korean immigrant Christian women who live in the Los Angeles metropolitan area. The subjects have either resident alien (green-card) status or U.S. citizenship, having stayed in the United States since the 1970s or 1980s. The fieldwork occurred over an eight-month period, beginning in October 2003. The interviews were tape-recorded with the interviewees' consent and were fully transcribed for all forty-two participating individuals. All interviews and interactions occurred in the Korean language; the quotes appearing in this chapter were selected from the transcripts and were then translated. In this study, I use pseudonyms of the subjects in order to protect their privacy.

The interviewees were between forty-one and fifty-three years of age, and all were involved in Protestant religious practice, especially Presbyterianism. Presbyterianism is the biggest denomination among Los Angeles Korean immigrants, although the Korean Methodist Church predominates in some other parts of the country (Kim 1996). I selected women within this age range because they are more likely to be in stable career situations than are women who are between twenty and forty (Felmlee 1984), a consideration that becomes particularly important given their immigrant status. They are presently married except for two divorced and two widowed women.

Interviewees were purposively selected to obtain instances of all the important dissimilar categories of the subjects (Weiss 1994, 23) according to job, class, education, and length of residence in the United States. To identify women, I relied upon personal networks as well as Presbyterian churches for a nonrandom snowball sample. For selecting subjects I focused on large ethnic churches such as Young Nak Church, West Hills Presbyterian Church, and Love Church. The interviewees came from a range of financial circumstances.

The conducted interviews were semi-structured to allow for rich first-person accounts from women in diverse environments. I did not interrupt their stories nor did I limit their accounts to my research interests in the hope that unexpected aspects of women's religion and space might be revealed. At the same time, the interviews possessed some semblance of structure, with prepared questions given to guide interviewees. Each interview was approximately three hours in duration, and some interviews were spaced over two meetings. In such instances, information from the first meeting was used to redesign questions for the second meeting.

Interviewees were asked about their labor market participation preferences, their domestic positions, their ambitions, their religious and cultural aspects toward femininity and family ideology, their religion and work values, their role models, their daily schedules, their parents' married life and education, their child-rearing habits, their household division of labor, their labor support from parents or relatives, and their amount of "bargaining capability" at home. The focus was placed on how religious practice and faith influence their family ideologies and activities, and ultimately, how all of this may lead to freedom or constraint, in terms of career decisions and how the interviewees interpret or legitimize their actions.

To promote trust between the interviewer (myself) and the subjects, I made efforts to become personally acquainted with the study's subjects by participating in several church worship services before beginning the interview process. To avoid oversteering the interviews, I asked very general questions first and then let interviewees spend as much time as they wished on interpreting each question in their own manner (Mueller 1992, 98). The women I interviewed were generous enough to give me their life histories and experiences with respect to their occupations, their marriages, and their religious activities.

My own experience and positions seem to inevitably have influenced the interviews. As a Korean-American doctoral student, former Christian, married woman without children, I could bring my own experience to bear on my research. On one hand, when they told me about their faith, their Korean culture, and their Korean-American culture and its influence on their daily lives, I, as a former Korean Christian woman who grew up in Korea and recently lived in Los Angeles, knew firsthand what they meant. This insider kind of advantage is also seen in Ingersoll's (2003, 10–11) research on conservative Christian women. On the other hand, in talking to me, the respondents sometimes tried to persuade me to become one of them, meaning they attempted to convince me to become a Christian, to have a baby, and to remain in the United States after graduation. The fact that I was a doctoral student seems to have influenced my subjects in various ways. Some women seemed to assume that I did not understand why they were staying at home,[2] so they tried hard to explain why, seeking not to "lose face" in front of me and to look "positive" regarding their career decisions (Ingersoll 2003). Aware of this limitation, I reassured them that judging their lifestyle was not my intention at all. I also actively responded to their talk but in a neutral manner. In qualitative interview studies, the demonstration of influence depends on the description of a sequence of events that can be visualized, where each event flows into the next (Weiss 1994, 179). My research shows a relationship between an earlier event and a subsequent event by attempting to uncover the process through which women's religious factors express themselves in career decisions.

Women's Security and God's Plan

The subjects' involvement in Korean churches symbolizes their efforts to seek identity security; the churches are the central institution of "Korea in the United States" in that they provide mental relief and a social network and define family norms, including such tenets as no drinking and no gambling. In this sense, the church seems to be an informal education center for immigrants. Korean immigrants are likely to become afraid if they "lose heart" about their potential for success, if their children are too involved in the Western culture's liberal and materialistic lifestyles, and if their family becomes fragmented. With these fears, their religiosity is likely to become increased. Some who used to be non-Christians become involved in Christianity when it was introduced to them by their families, relatives, and Korean neighbors.

Praying proved helpful for controlling both the subjects' anxiety, which arose from their unpredictable and unstable immigrant lifestyles, and their anger, which was caused by marriage problems, including disappointment with their husbands and conflicts with their families-in-law. Jang Un Lee (aged fifty) said that she prayed when she felt like falling down after her husband was shot by a gang. She could manage the tragic situation by believing that the taking of her husband was God's will. The interviewees are present-tense-oriented, as seen in Lewis's (1966) studies of the urban poor. The women do not worry about the future, they said, because God has a plan for them. The financial insecurity and assimilation difficulties experienced by immigrants made it hard for them to survive "today." As a result, they have learned to pray for their security in the belief that God will take care of them in the future. Many of them have met a "real God" during their difficult times in the United States, even though they were already Christians in Korea, they said. They went on to say that after they met this real God, they not only received peace of mind but also realized what the goal of their life should be—being His people. Being His people objectified their life and made them more relaxed about their situation than they had been before.

It was strikingly common that since childhood, these women have had neither personal goals nor role models for their careers. Even with respect to marriage, many of them said they did not have an opinion but thought simply that they were "supposed to get married" in their early twenties. Only a very few of the women ever dreamed of becoming a nurse, a hair-stylist, or other professional. Most dreamed of becoming a *Hyn-Mo-Yang-Cheo* (a wise mother and docile wife).[3] Their education was often sacrificed in favor of male family members, whose success, their parents told them, was the whole family's dream. Kun-Hyun Park, a former hair-stylist, said:

> My father wanted me to become a hair-stylist because he thought that it would be a good job for a woman in case she should ever have to take care of herself. There was a widowed woman who has a hair salon. It looked good to my father, I guess. So, I finished high school and got trained to be a hair-stylist. . . . My brothers? Of course, they went to college. Their education was placed above anything else by my parents. You know, they are sons. (Kun-Hyun Park, Shin interview, 28 February 2004)

Some of the subjects went to college, thinking that doing so would be helpful in meeting a good husband on the marriage market. One woman was encouraged to go to college by her mother, who believed that her daughter's attendance would increase the likelihood that her son (the college-attending young woman's brother) would find a bride with a higher education degree.

The subjects expressed "no thoughts about the future." Regarding marriage and jobs, they took it for granted that a woman would work outside the home until marriage. If their fathers or grandfathers thought that women should not develop lives outside the household, however, they stayed at home. All of these women's families were strongly involved in the plan for their future.

As these women continued their stories, one of the common expressions they frequently brought up was "His plan." It is almost like they, as observers, see what plan God has in mind for them as His people. Young-Shin Jun (forty-six), who is a housewife, said that she was very curious about God's plan for her because it seems that He has one other than working outside the home:

> I thought of holding down a job many times; however, every time I tried to get one, something happened. I felt so uncomfortable, and if I quit, I felt good. As I was about to start the new job, my children would get sick. . . . So now, I almost gave up. I think He has another plan for me. . . . He lets me know what He wants, either by making something happen or by making me feel uncomfortable. (Young-Shin Jun, Shin interview, 25 March 2004)

When she did not like what she was doing, she interpreted her explanation by stating that her having the job was simply not in God's plan for her.[4] In reality, the reason why she and her three children can survive without a job was that she received $3,000 a month from her ex-family-in-law and $2,000 a month from the government. She does not want to have a job that pays more than $800 a month because then she will have to give up the welfare money the government provides, but she still interprets the situation as a part of God's plan. She is now worried that she will not receive money from the government after her children reach eighteen years of age. Having voiced this concern, she said she was afraid of God's plan for her and was apprehensively waiting for it to reveal itself.

Such a religious interpretation for these subjects' unclear decisions is also presented in Nam-Hee Choi's case. She did not see her husband many times before their marriage so she did not know going into the partnership that her husband was an alcoholic. She said her marriage was planned by God because neither of them had wanted to get married nor come to the United States. She believes that God gives a good opportunity to grow and learn by allowing His people to experience troubles. Her family is not well-off, as her husband is a construction worker and she is an unpaid housewife, with three children to support on one meager income. She said:

> I don't think I could live like this if I were in Korea. All my friends are very well-off. I think, oh God loves me so much that he makes me live in the U.S. where I

have no friends. I don't have contact with my friends. They envy me because I live in the U.S. I never bring them here. (Nam-Hee Choi, Shin interview, 16 April 2004)

She has suffered tremendously since she got married as a result of her husband's drinking. Once she decided to divorce her husband, she prayed overnight. In praying, she heard God calling her name and saw a bloody cross. It was like God was saying, "My son bled for you, but you cannot even tolerate your husband's drinking?" The next day, her husband drank again; however, unlike before, this time she felt comfortable.

Low Aspiration: Adaptive Preferences

I repeatedly found in the course of these interviews that, despite the differences in legitimating their employment status, the subjects had low employment aspirations. The interviewees thought their jobs and income were "extra" to the family's income. Some of them even said, "I am not working," although they were. In so doing, they were, in effect, presenting their work as "just helping my husband" or "just helping others." Many of them said they work so as not to be bored. One woman, who once went to an emergency room because she repeatedly worked too hard, said, "I work because I would be bored otherwise."

Sweeney (2002) argued that women with good prospects in the labor market are less likely to marry than are women with relatively poorer prospects. However, the characteristics considered important in a marriage market have today become more symmetrical for husbands and wives. If having an income adds to women's attractiveness on the marriage market, marriage can increase women's likelihood of being employed at least until marriage. For lower-class couples, a double income is not optional but rather required to survive financially. Hence, being paid adds to a woman's attractiveness as a marriage partner. These characteristics are often seen among immigrants who struggle to survive in a host society. The Korean immigrant women's low career aspiration reflects their adaptation to typical immigrants' employment constraints as well as to Christian values regarding women's appropriate roles as wives and mothers.

Most women in my sample made a job decision based not on their career ambition but on the convenience of location, their husband's suggestion, and offers from someone they knew. They preferred a part-time job that did not distract from their role as the home caretaker. Sook-Hee Park, who is working in a factory, said:

> I enjoy working. It is not that I have to work. No one cares if I work. If I say I don't like my job, even though my husband may want extra money, he wouldn't say anything against it. So I can quit, even tomorrow. But my job doesn't bother my ability to take care of my family. I would be so bored if I stay at home. And [by] working, I can have a social life, some extra money, and excitement. I feel sorry for men. They have to work because of responsibility. (Sook-Hee Park, Shin interview, 16 December 2003)

The low aspiration, ironically, enables these women to get jobs earlier than their husbands. When they arrived in the United States, they did not intentionally try to get a job, they said. When someone offered them a very low-income job, their low aspiration enabled them to take it, without hurting their pride. Because they think that a job is not very important to women, they are not very bothered by the low-income jobs they are offered. Their husbands, with their high aspirations and ambition to be successful in a foreign country, however, were depressed by the low-income jobs available to new immigrants.

Elster (1983, 43) explores "by-product" as something that can only come about as the derivative of actions undertaken for other ends. The women's immediate employment was often the by-product of their willingness, with no impact on their self-image, to take any job as a nonbreadwinner. Their income was essential for their survival in the early stage of migration, but as their husbands got "real jobs," these women's jobs remained "extra." This situation seems to have formed their adaptive preference (Elster 1983; Kuran 1995) of viewing their jobs as merely an additional source of family income and in light of Christian ideology of the husband as household head.

Constrained Mobilities and Spatial Practices

My interviewees' spatial practices and mobility were constrained by four interrelated phenomena: (1) their tendency to live close to or even in the same home as their immigration sponsors, who are typically relatives; (2) their economic status; (3) the characteristics of transportation in Los Angeles; and (4) ideological constraints on their mobility arising from their Christian beliefs. The relocation of the subjects as a result of their international migration from Korea to the United States has profoundly influenced them. It impacts the boundaries of their day-to-day mobility, such as their daily schedules and their accessibility to transportation. Mobility and religious participation are also mutually constituted: the women's travel to church and activities in churches play dual roles. First, church activities reinforce the conservative gender-based culture, but second, they enable Korean housewives to move beyond the domestic sphere on a regular basis.

Many of the interviewees were invited by their families or their relatives to migrate to the United States, in a characteristic chain-migration pattern. Typically, one invited immigrant family settles down near the inviter's family or relatives. As a result, in their initial stages of migration, the majority of these subjects' families have lived in the same neighborhood, the same apartment complex, or even the same house as their inviter's family. In so doing, these immigrants can get help from their guardian families and relatives in locating a place to live, finding jobs, raising children, and receiving emotional support. In the process, their lifestyles, including their spatial mobility, has been substantially influenced by their guardian's lifestyle.

Geographical proximity to guardians, combined with the Korean family ideology, has also caused trouble in these women's lives. The interviewees described a dichotomy in their living situation. Although they stated it was great living near their relatives, they also hinted that the proximity made their relationships with each other complicated. In particular, those who migrated to the United States to follow their families-in-law said that they have been bothered by expectations of a traditional extended family relationship. In the circumstances where these immigrants almost entirely depended on their guardian families and had few other acquaintances, their troubles with their in-laws often led to loneliness and marital problems.

Although men's careers were prior factors in the migration decision-making process, the expectation of women's careers was flexible, according to the family's economic situation. Yon-Woo Choi (forty-three), who is now a floral arranger, was told by her father-in-law "not to go around." In obedience, she stayed at home for six years, until her family's financial situation declined. She has lived with her parents-in-law for thirteen years. As she was interviewed in her home with her mother-in-law present, she almost whispered her responses, even after we moved to her bedroom. By way of explanation, she stated that it had become her habit to do things quietly.

The immigrant women's level of dependence and closeness in the guardian relationship is also reflected in their mobility and the churches they attend. In the initial stage of immigration, when the interviewees lived with their guardian families and relatives in the same neighborhood, all members of the familial clan attended the same church. As the interviewees became more independent and frustrated by their obligations, however, they often moved to another community and started attending different churches. Sometimes the resulting different opinions about religion and church caused even more distance between members of the expanded family.

Driving, too, is a critical factor in women's spatial practices. In the 1970s and 1980s, when they first left Korea bound for the United States, driving automobiles was not a popular Korean custom and Korean women drivers were very rare. In addition, in the initial stages of their migration to Los Angeles, where driving is an everyday part of life, one immigrant family could afford only one car and the driver was always the husband. Many of these women worked side-by-side with their husbands, either cleaning houses or working in the same factory, so their weekday mobility was almost always the same. Also, on the weekend, these wives and their husbands went to a Korean market and church together. As a result, these women's independent mobility has been limited to the home, work, and church, which are often located near each other. More specifically, these women's career decisions are frequently based on nearness to home, so that they are still able to pick up their children from school and cook their family's dinner. Finding a job based on family location was possible because many of these women took low-skilled jobs that did not require major commuting, a result also noted by Hanson and Pratt (1991).

As a means of coping with such spatial constraints, many of these women proudly went on to say that their husbands did not allow them to drive on the freeway. Some of them, saying they are scared, never drive, even though they have a driver's license. In so doing, they showed culturally appropriate feminine appreciation of their protective husbands. Soon-Im Park (forty-eight) worked in a nearby Koreatown store during her first year in the United States

(1981). Each day, her husband took her to her workplace and back home. This process was exhausting to both of them since her husband had a job that was far away from her place of employment. Moreover, one time when her babies were sick, she quit her job altogether and never had one again. She had learned from her church that God teaches that a woman's first role is to take care of her family, so, in rationalizing her decision, she said she appreciated quitting the job a long time ago.

These women's activities in their churches and group meetings charge them with the courage to go beyond their private sphere and to socialize with others. Many of them said that except for their family lives and their jobs, which are just a means of earning money, their churches have become almost the entire world to them. They appreciate the fact that they can have friends and perform meaningful activities within their churches. The church activities in which they engage have become these women's main access to the public sphere. While on one hand these women's conservative family ideologies and gender roles are reinforced in the church, on the other hand, their participation in church activities has empowered them.

Husband as Head of the Family

The subjects said that the husband is the head of the family, that wives should submit to their husbands, and that husbands should love their wives; beliefs with major impacts for immigrant women's mobility and adaptations to a new nation. It is unclear how much Korean women actually act according to these beliefs in their daily lives, but the assertions seem to have become a consensus in these women's communities. Their expressed perception of their husbands' position in the family seemed influenced by three things: their Christianity, their Korean traditional ideas, and their migration process. Their Korean traditional ideas, as influenced by both Confucianism and Christianity, reinforce women's conservative family ideologies.

In addition, having gone through the migration process, the interviewees seem to have adjusted their perceptions of their husbands and developed a survival strategy. They believe that it is important for them to allow, or at least pretend to allow, their husbands to think of themselves as the center of the family. Although some researchers of religious immigrant women report that they have at least the potential to experience greater autonomy in their more liberal, secular host society (Dwyer 2000; Kim 1996; Kostovicova and Prestreshi 2003), my Korean subjects insisted on traditional gender relations that extended intact via Christianity and Confucianism for many generations in Korea. This characteristic seems to be associated with "Koreanized" Christianity (Min 1992, 1391), which focuses on marital counseling services.

First, conservative Christians argue that in the Bible, husbands are "the heads" over their wives. While biblical feminist works interpret the notion of "head" as "source" (the head of a river, for example), conservative people respect the literal passage in Ephesians (5:21–33) that commands wives to submit to their husbands. While the implicit connection between orthodox theology and the patriarchal family structure has been maintained by conservative believers and scholars, many Evangelical feminists embrace the practice of modifying all biblical language for gender inclusiveness (Ingersoll 2003, 19). Few subjects looked uncomfortable with the concept that husbands can be like friends. Moreover, they stated that they want to keep an equal relationship between a man and a wife. They said the interpretation of the Greek origin of the Bible is wrong, as biblical feminists argue. One woman even made a joke of the situation, saying "my husband is the head and I am the neck, so the movement of the head is controlled by the neck." The interviewees said submission should be mutual, and the husband is the head of the family if his behaviors are appropriate.

Second, even those Korean women who became Christians after they grew up accepted such notions of family hierarchy because they are supported by traditional Korean ideologies (Kim 1996; Kim 1997). Such interviewees said that the assertions in the Bible are identical to what they heard from their parents and others as they grew up. When many of them left Korea in their twenties during the 1970s and 1980s, a father was considered the head of the family. Under Confucianism, a father is supposed to be as respected as a king or teacher. The interviewees vividly recalled, as children, how submissive and respectful their mothers were to their fathers. They were educated to obey their fathers, whose authority stemmed simply from their position as fathers.

Third, some of the interviewees' attitudes toward their husbands nevertheless indicated a sympathetic and more egalitarian perspective that was created in the migration process.[5] These women said that Korean immigrant men in the United States are "poor things" rather than real men who have established social positions. When they compared Asian men's image with that of Asian women in the United States, they concurred that Korean men experience downward mobility even in their societal image. They think Korean immigrant men, who work hard but rarely succeed in mainstream society, are not as attractive as they would be in Korea had they not migrated. These women have been disappointed even by their husbands' transformations into more sensitive and more religious men than before because those changes did not reflect the expected images of a strong, head-of-the-family man. As a result, this group of women has tried to encourage their discouraged husbands to have more self-confidence. In making that effort, consideration of their husbands as the heads of family is the essential strategy. It was also important for these women to educate their children to think of their father as the center of the family.

Ultimately, the most desperate need of the husband as head-of-family belief seems to lie in these women's strategic effort for family security. Time and again, they expressed fear that their husbands would become discouraged by immigrant life. Women who earn higher incomes than their husbands were afraid that their roles had been "switched" and that, as a result, their husbands would lose their motivation to be ambitious and responsible men. That fear derived from observations that in some cases, discouraged husbands could not "make a peaceful family" because of their complaining and fighting.

My interviewees expressed three different reactions regarding that fear. The most common reaction was for the women to work but to remind themselves and their children to respect their husbands as head of the family. As a result of this belief, they make their children ask their father's opinion and do not involve themselves in major decision-making processes. Hee-Young Kang, a forty-six-year-old woman, said:

> I try to make my husband look as strong as possible at home. If my children ask me for buying something big, I say, "Go ask your dad." I don't have a strong voice in such big things as buying a house, buying a car, and moving. And I don't let him do dirty things like cleaning the bathroom. . . . The Bible says that women should be submissive to their husbands. (Hee-Young Kang, Shin interview, 1 November 2003)

The second reaction to such fear is for women to be respectful because they believe it is strategically helpful for their family life. Such subjects often said that they decided not to work because the harder they worked, the less their husbands worked. Three women said (respectively):

And, you know, it is very nice to be submissive to your husband. It means no responsibility to you. (Hae-Kyung Park, Shin interview, 12 November 2003)

The husband is the head of the family, because a man, everyman, wants to be the head. I learned this through my life. (Mi-Ja Lee, Shin interview, 28 October 2003)

Once you respect my husband, he is willing to work to feed me and my children. Then you don't have to work, so this is the better way. (Yong-Shin Moon, Shin interview, 15 January 2004)

As seen in Brasher's (1998) study of religious fundamentalists, Korean Christian women in my sample are not bothered by their inferior position within the family. Some say they are even happy with the fact because it gives them more freedom from the demands of employment and more power in the domestic sphere. Young-Soon Kim (forty-eight) said that because her husband's religiosity leads hers as well as her marriage life, though they are relatively poor, she is happy and is envied by her brother-in-law and his spouse, who are much more affluent. Another reason for her peaceful married life, she thinks, is that her husband is much older than she is. As a result, "He thinks he wins even if he loses."

Third, women prayed to God to help their husbands and believed that any suffering they experienced in their marriages was part of God's plan for them. They complained about their husbands and said they have consciously decided to divorce many times. What stopped them from going through with that decision was their religious commitment to the belief that a Christian should not get divorced. Even though they are frequently upset with their husbands, they believe that God cares for them and even appreciates that they are spiritually growing as a result of their troubles. Kuk-Sun Yang, who has an alcoholic husband, said:

> I know that my husband really tried. So many times I thought a divorce is the only way I can survive. But when I pray, I feel taken care of by God. He is so warm that I don't worry about my family too much. I am even grateful. I guess this trouble was planned by God so that I can become more dependent on him. (Kuk-Sun Yang, Shin interview, 25 January 2004)

As seen in Ingersoll's (2003) study of conservative American Protestantism, gender roles in the family are not fixed, static, and monolithic. Rather, they are constantly changing as proponents of the faith interpret the Bible or their reality in different ways. The differences seem to stem from different educations, family backgrounds, and churches, but the common thread was that each woman used her own interpretation to legitimize her situation or her responses to the situation. It should be pointed out that I was left to wonder if those women either intentionally or unintentionally tried to look optimistic about their situation because I was an outside researcher, whom they might think of as opposed to an unequal relationship between a husband and wife (Ingersoll 2003, 6). However, they also may have been trying to convince themselves of their happiness by legitimizing their situations and the choices they have been forced to make. Although these Korean women's deference to their husbands surely would not be considered a feminist response to immigration pressures, it tends to support concepts of the immigrant church as a space where traditional attitudes flourish and fulfill emotional needs and cultural continuity among minorities. Moreover, the male head-of-household trope can be construed as a feminine coping mechanism for the stresses of immigration, in that it removes responsibility from the wife for the outcome of the move and the family's changing fortunes.

Religious Unification of the Family

Most interviewees stated that religious unification of the family is very important. They stated that "a couple should be one both spiritually and physically" and that different religions encourage different directions, especially with regard to children's education. Their highest expectation for their children is that they become sincere Christians and find sincere Christian spouses. This notion owes its origin to these women's belief that "being a sincere Christian" naturally means being an honest and diligent person. Young-Shin Jun, whose non-Christian husband died eleven years ago, understood her husband's sudden death as God's plan to help her send her children to Christian preschool. She said, "That's why He (God) hurried up. My husband became a rotten seed to grow four of us (her and her three children)."

Some of the subjects regret that they married non-Christian men, saying that the religious war they experienced within the household was unbelievably difficult. They said that a family in which all members share the same religion has a "something special" that ties all the members together with a love for God and for each other. Because they believe that an unbeliever eventually goes to hell, the interviewees said they feel so sorry about their husbands' non-Christianity. Moreover, they were disappointed by their husbands' religious standards, ultimately holding the belief that a non-Christian is simply not a good person. In an attempt to alleviate their guilt, they have tried to bring their husbands to church on Sunday and have prayed to God in the hopes that their husbands' minds would be opened to finding the meaning of life in God.

Sun Im Cha (forty-eight), another former hair-stylist, said that when her husband was deeply involved with gambling every weekend, she met a nice guy. She thought, however, that infidelity was not beautiful in God's eyes and so stopped herself from having a love affair with him. Turning to her religious life for solace, she became more sociable with other church members. As she became more involved in her faith, she began to regret that early on in her religious life, she loved only singing and praying and had failed to read the Bible. She said that, according to the Bible, a believer should marry a believer and her ignorance of this tenet was to blame for her unhappiness.

Another reason these women desperately wanted their husbands to be religious was that they believe that the husband should be the religious leader of the family as well as the principal provider. Otherwise, the balance of the family hierarchy is ruined. Some men who are not active in church activities do not want their wives to be too deeply involved in such activities, these women sometimes pointed out. Many of the women I met were worried they could not respect their husbands because these men tended to focus only on meeting their wives' basic financial needs rather than leading a religious life. Hye-Jin Oh (forty-nine), after complaining about her husband's pickiness and abuse of her, said that she nonetheless respected him because she and her husband are religiously very similar and enthusiastic in helping others. Whatever the underlying reason, the group of religiously intermarried women have been constrained from enjoying religious and social lives in church, not only because their husbands have not liked their church activities but also because they avoided becoming the religious leader in the family. This idea of male spiritual authority is equivalent with some interviewees' comfortable feeling toward their husbands' superior occupations and social standing.

Conclusion

This study of forty-two Korean immigrant Christian women focused on religion as a rationale for their responses to the issues they faced with their new immigrant status. With due respect for their religious faith, I observed their various ways of legitimizing their situation by explaining it as an expression of God's will. Their religious faith influences their important life decisions, but more than that, their interpretation of Christianity and the assertions set forth in the Bible provide them with the necessary courage to face their situations and legitimate their lifestyles. As some of them said, their difficult way of life as immigrants is one of the reasons why Christianity has become such an important institution in the Korean immigrant society.

The impacts of the Korean Presbyterian community on the city of Los Angeles are substantial. Women's low aspirations and family ideologies are formed from their constrained conditions, and these lead to women's unemployment or underemployment. Even if these women manage to get jobs, their consideration of domestic responsibilities can limit the area in which they are willing to work or the amount of time that they can allocate to their careers. Hence, they are underemployed. When they try to participate in the labor market—usually when their families break up or when their children grow up—a lack of job experience may at first appear to be a barrier to employment, whereas the actual barrier may be the religious subculture itself. The subculture acts as a positive adaptive mechanism for women who are dealing with situations beyond their control (Lewis 1966). Their career preferences and attitudes toward participating in the job market are an adjustment of wants to possibilities. Behind this adaptation lies the drive to reduce the tension and frustration that one feels in having desires that cannot possibly be satisfied.

Afterword

Anna Secor

> So there are two quite different Islams, an Islam that is in some sense a woman's Islam and an official, textual Islam, a "men's" Islam. And indeed it is obvious that a far greater gulf must separate men's and women's ways of knowing, and the different ways in which men and women understand religion, in the segregated societies of the Middle East than in other societies—and we know that there are differences between women's and men's ways of knowing even in nonsegregated societies such as America. . . .
>
> No doubt particular backgrounds and subcultures give their own specific flavors and inflections and ways of seeing to their understanding of religion, and I expect that the Islam I received from the women among whom I lived was therefore part of their particular subculture. In a sense, then, there are not just two or three different kinds of Islam but many, many different ways of understanding and being a Muslim. . . . Now, after a lifetime of meeting and talking with Muslims from all over the world, I find that this Islam is one of the common varieties—perhaps even *the* common or garden variety—of the religion. It is the Islam not only of women but of ordinary folk generally, as opposed to the Islam of sheikhs, ayatollahs, mullahs, and clerics. (Ahmed 1999, 123, 125)

What is the relationship between religion, gender, and space? In her memoir of growing up in Egypt and her journeys beyond, Leila Ahmed writes of how her own religious education among women in her family consisted of Islam as a spoken, rather than textual, heritage. This Islam, which itself consists of many local and familial varieties, shows little regard for the pronouncements of the religious scholars. Instead, Ahmed recognizes the Islam of her childhood as a broad ethos, a way of living and being in the world. Ahmed describes how this spoken Islam is produced through the gendered spaces of everyday life. At the same time, she also acknowledges that it is not only women but "ordinary folk generally" who understand and live their lives through the particular oral and aural Islamic knowledges of their families and communities. The spatiality of what she calls "women's Islam" is linked to the everyday practices that produce the segregated spaces of women's and men's worship, learning, and association. Space, gender, and religion are here intertwined—not just in the common sense that religion is seen as prescribing a particular gendered spatiality but in the sense that religious knowledge and practice is itself produced within and through gendered spaces.

By starting with Ahmed's insight into the spatial and gendered production of Islamic knowledge, I hope to open a discussion of gender, religion, and space that will situate the preceding chapters in relation to some central problems. To begin, the idea of "women's Islam" spurs us to ask some critical questions about the multiplicity of religious understandings (whether Islamic, Christian, Jewish, or any other) and the category of religion itself. If religious practices are also gendered spatial practices, what does this mean for an epistemology of religion? And if we accept the idea of multiple "Islams" or "Judaisms" or "Christianities," what stitches together these various understandings so that, at another level, these faiths maintain their distinction and identity? After a discussion of religion as a category, I turn to the question of how religion operates in relation to states and subjects. Can religious identity be understood as a process of *subjection,* that is, a process whereby we both become subject to (in this case) religious law as well as subjects of such law? And if so, how does this help us to understand how religious and state identities intersect, and sometimes compete, with one another?

The theme of religion vis-à-vis state practices and identities can be traced through many of the chapters in this volume, and especially those by Leonard Guelke, Jennifer Kopf, and Jeanne Kay Guelke and Karen Morin (chapters 1, 2, and 6). Another thematic strand that ties together this volume concerns questions of gender, mobility, and (religious) dress. In the chapters by Kathryn Besio, Tovi Fenster, and Banu Gökarıksel (chapters 3, 4, and 5), dress is a cipher for gendered religious identities. Dress also becomes implicated in women's mobility, their spatial passage across literal and figurative social boundaries. I argue that an understanding of religion that foregrounds embodied spatial practice also enables us to understand the critical significance of dress for questions of religion, gender, and space. In the final section of this chapter, I draw into question the ideas of choice, freedom, and self-expression that frequently come into play in discussions of dress and the demarcation of both religion and modernity. In this way, I hope to show how studies of religion, gender, and space stand to contribute to our understanding of the diversity of ways in which subjects may conceptualize their own insertion into the world. What I hope to draw forward is an understanding of religion as no more and no less than what Ahmed describes as the Islam of her upbringing: "A way of holding oneself in the world—in relation to God, to existence, to other human beings" (1999, 121).

Religion, the State, and the Subject

How is it that "religion" comes to constitute a category of social life, practice, belief, and identity? In the context of this volume, such a question draws attention to the production of "religion" as an object of knowledge in relation to gender and space. In his genealogy of religion as an anthropological category, Talal Asad has argued that "there cannot be a universal definition of religion, not only because its constituent elements and relationships are historically specific, but because that definition is itself the historical product of discursive processes" (1993, 29). There are two parts to this statement. First, the statement suggests that when "religion" is deployed as a category and applied across time and space, it brings with it a very particular set of assumptions. When a certain ensemble of utterances and practices becomes labeled "religion," and thus considered to be one instance of a universal phenomenon, the historical specificity of the elements of this ensemble and their interrelations with other elements of life are elided. The second (and related) component of Asad's statement is the recognition that the very definition of religion itself is a historical product. As such, it works to produce and naturalize particular social formations, relations of power, and ideas of the self.

When we begin with certain assumptions about what religion is and how we may know it, we also begin by imposing the assumptions of a particular political and social order. For example, if we define religion as consisting of private belief or faith, we immediately bring to our analysis some assumed distinctions between belief and practice and between public and private realms. Likewise, if we enter our work with an understanding of religious ritual as being composed of symbols that can be read, we have already imposed a particular mode of representation and interpretation onto our subject. In order to break away from what Akhil Gupta (1995) calls the "imperialism of categories," we might begin not with "religion" as a universal category, but instead with the practice and creation of particular ways of being in the world. As Gökarıksel (chapter 4) shows, it is not necessary that we read veiling practices simply or primarily in terms of a religious symbol. Instead, through her study, we come to understand the possibility and intelligibility of the practice of veiling as embedded within a web of historically situated disciplines and forces, some but not all of which have Islam as an organizing principle. Likewise, women's spatial practices, including those of mobility, travel, or enclosure, are best understood as produced through particular historical conjunctures that transect the blurry and porous category of religion (see chapter 6 by Guelke and Morin). To paraphrase Asad (1993, 54), if we unpack the comprehensive concept of what we call religion, we are thus more able to situate everyday practices with regard to broader, historically contingent fields of practice and discourse.

All of this is not to say that we ought not to talk about "religion" at all; rather, it is to suggest an epistemology of religion that recognizes religious ways of being as part of how we come to understand or imagine our relation to the world. As Ahmed suggests, religion can be seen as a way of being inserted into the world, a way of "holding oneself" in relation. In other words, "religion" appears to be one more term (like citizenship) that refers to a way of becoming a subject, both to power and of power. Further, this "submission" is practiced and understood in many ways; women's religious knowledges may be different from men's, rural knowledges may differ from urban, etc. In this way, religions not only enjoin particular gendered ways of being in the world but are themselves defined and practiced in gendered ways. Indeed, as contributors to this book show in their case studies, gendered spatial practice is critical to the creation and enactment of religious subjectivities.

If we understand religion as a way of being inserted into the world and a way of becoming a subject as I have suggested, I believe this gives us a vantage point from which to view the various, historically contingent ways in which state and religion collide or collude. Indeed, the historical studies of colonial practices, gender, and space in this volume (see chapter 1 by Kopf, chapter 2 by

Guelke, and chapter 6 by Guelke and Morin) focus our attention at the intersection of state actors and religious belief and practice. In these studies and others, women are shown to be central to the symbolic and material construction of national and religious identities (see also Moghadam 1994; Yuval-Davis and Anthias 1989). I have argued that religion can be seen as a mode of *subjection,* that is, as a way in which we become both subjects and objects of power (Butler 1997). Just as secular law hails the modern state subject, the religious subject recognizes itself in relation to the call of divine law (Althusser 2001). In all cases, the authoritative Subject (whether State, Islam, Christianity, or other) and its subjects (citizens, Muslims, Christians, etc.) are mutually constituted; they call one another into being. In fact, Althusser's most fleshed out example of the process of "interpellation" (what I am calling simply subjection) focuses on Christianity (2001, 120–24). In short, whether we are talking about the state or religion, we find ourselves tracing out relations of power that define the subjectivity of individuals in relation to law, secular or divine. What the chapters in this volume help to draw out is how this takes place in particular contexts and how gendered spatial practices become critical to both state and religious actors in their performances of power and identity.

Religion, Dress, and Mobility

Mobility and the regulation of dress emerge as recurrent themes in the discussion of gender, religion, and space throughout the chapters of this volume. In chapter 5, Besio examines how Western women travelers in Pakistan negotiate sociospatial gender regimes, especially as they concern women's dress and mobility in public spaces. As an entry point into questions of right and mobility in the city, Fenster (chapter 3) focuses her analysis on a particular spatial regulatory regime, the "modesty walls" that regulate women's dress and thereby assert the propriety boundaries of an orthodox Jewish neighborhood in Jerusalem. While Fenster thus addresses the techniques and effects of gendered spatial regulations, Gökarıksel turns our attention to women's contestation of dominant spatial codings. In her ethnographic study of mall space in Istanbul (chapter 4), Gökarıksel shows how veiled women challenge the dominant meanings of "modernity" in Turkey. Although HaeRan Shin's study (chapter 7) does not deal with women's dress per se, her study resonates with these discussions of dress as part of how religion works to code space. For Shin, religion works as an interpretive lens through which Christian women conceptualize their own spatial practices, especially in terms of their work inside or outside the home. Guelke and Morin (chapter 6) show how the "spatial logic" of the nun's habit and the modest dress of Euro-American Christian women work to imbricate bodily and national scales. By placing questions of dress, conduct, and religion within a broader historical context, Guelke and Morin's chapter helps us to see how questions of dress and conduct are both inserted within and productive of geographical scale. Taken together, these chapters illuminate the knotted question of dress within the field of religio-spatial practice.

Dress is important for understanding gender, religion, and space because it is an embodied practice through which religious ways of being are represented and enacted. As Joanne Entwistle (2000, 2001) has argued, dress "works on the body," thereby mediating experiences of the self as positioned and moving through space. The dressed body, she argues, is actively produced through social practices that link performances of individual identity to social practices of inclusion and exclusion. Drawing on Mary Douglas's (1984) ideas about purity and pollution and the leaky margins of the body, Entwistle suggests that because the boundaries of the body are seen as dangerous, it is no surprise that dress is subject to social regulation and moral discourse (Entwistle 2001, 37). Dress can thus be understood as one of what Asad calls the "systemic practices" through which "particular moral dispositions and capacities are created and controlled" (Asad 1993, 65).

To say that moral subjects (and, I would add, spaces) are not only controlled but also *created* through (religious) dress is to move away from an idea of religious dress as either merely a symbol or an instantiation of "social control." Linda Arthur (1999, 1), for example, puts both social control and symbolic meaning at the center of her introduction to *Religion, Dress, and the Body*: "Dress becomes a symbol of social control as it controls the external body. While a person's level of religiosity cannot be objectively perceived, symbols such as clothing are used as evidence that s/he is on the 'right and true path.' " Such an approach meets with at least two difficulties. First, dress is indeed inserted into regulatory regimes that attempt to control the dangerous, leaky margins of the body, but if "control" is the primary filter through which we view dress, it becomes difficult to recognize its lived complexity. In other words, if we simply understand a woman being forced to uncover her head in a particular space (for example, at a university in France or Turkey) as an instance of social control, we lose not only the historical and political contexts that nuance this regulatory regime, but we also miss out on how this dress code is enacted, experienced, and given meaning by those who negotiate these rules in their everyday lives. Indeed, the chapters by Fenster and Gökarıksel illustrate how dress is constituted in the relationship between subjects and the regimes of "social control" through which they pass in their daily lives.

Second, Arthur's understanding of religious dress emphasizes the *symbolic* aspect of this dress; it is, she suggests, a marker that the wearer is on the right path. Such an approach to dress is in keeping with much work that has focused on the semiotics of dress, understood as an abstract symbolic system that can be "read" (in fashion magazines, for example) (Barthes 1983; Lurie 1992). If we return to Asad's critique of the anthropological category of religion, this reading of dress as a symbol falls into the same difficulties that he identifies as besetting the study of religious rituals as coded texts. In both cases, there is an assumption of "meaning" as separable from practice and of religious meaning in particular as separable from the full range of social relations, discourses, and practices. In other words, the symbolic approach abstracts and decontextualizes (religious) dress, decoding it as though it has a fixed and transcendent meaning. The semiotic approach to dress thus turns out to be inadequate to attend to the messy, contingent, and diverse ways in which dress is practiced in everyday life (Entwistle and Wilson 2001).

Finally, what I am advocating is an approach to religious dress that begins from a particular epistemological position. If religion is understood to be a mode of subjection, a way of being and therefore of being in relation to others and to (secular or religious) law, then religious dress can likewise be understood as a "technology of the self" (Foucault 1988). Dress is a discipline and a way of becoming a moral subject through practice. This is not to shift from an excessively structural approach (the semiotic and social control varieties) to a purely subjective and voluntaristic approach. On the contrary, if we understand dress as a discipline of religious subjection, our analysis may focus both on technologies of regulation (such as the modesty walls of Fenster's piece or the legal headscarf bans in France and Turkey) and on the ways in which dress becomes part of a definition of "the self." Such an approach is in keeping with

Gökarıksel's call (see chapter 4) for analyses of Islam and Muslim identities as articulated within transformative transnational processes. In this way, we may be able to open up the diversity and historical contingency of the ideas of self and body that dress enacts. As Paul Sweetman (2001, 74) puts it, dress is not simply a symbolic process, but instead contributes to the "individuation, rationalization, and socialization of Western and non-Western bodies and selves." As such, religious dress becomes a critical "technology of the self," creating and contesting the boundaries of identity and belonging.

Whose Freedom, Whose Rights?

Why is freedom measured in terms of mobility instead of enclosure? Where do we locate "rights"—in city streets, in the courts, at home? And what implications does this location have for our understanding of the nexus of gender, religion, and space? Where do our ideas about "choice" come from, and what do they imply about who we are—*and what we expect others to want*? Such questions are unavoidable when we strive to do research that does not function as a vehicle for the "imperialism of categories" by replicating and naturalizing particular ideas of self and society, of public and private, of desire and shame. As Nikolas Rose (1999) has argued, freedom is not simply an abstraction, but a material, technical, and historical ethic that proposes particular ways of relating to ourselves and to rule. In other words, being "free" means being regulated in a particular way. Rose argues that the dominant ideal of freedom today is shaped through liberal arts of government. Like religion, freedom is a discipline; it entails the internalization of particular modes of moral conduct, a particular idea of the self, and a relationship to (secular or religious) law. If this is so, then it follows that when we aim to understand the broadest implications of religious ways of being for gendered, spatial practices, we need at once to examine the assumptions about freedom, choice, and self-hood that we may bring to such an analysis. It is not enough to say that religious dress, for example, both enables and constrains mobility; it is also necessary to understand how these practices make possible and enact particular ways of being in the world.

To provide a brief illustration of the contingency of the idea of rights, I draw an example from my work in Istanbul, Turkey. The following conversation took place in 2003 among women who were involved, to one degree or another, in Islamist social, charitable, educational, or political activities. All the women are lower-middle class housewives, and all of them veil in one manner or another. In the following discussion, they consider the question of rights (*hak*).

> *Moderator:* Are there places where you feel your rights to be broader or narrower?
> *Arzu:* Outside you cannot ever be the owner of rights. Of course if you are at home, but outside is very big, very crowded.
> *Havva:* For a year and a half I spent most of my time at hospitals. Because of this my rights were very much under attack.
> *Tahire:* It is most [under attack] in those places and at the door of justice.
> *Moderator:* The door of justice?
> *Tahire:* At the courts.

Like women in many of the focus groups I have conducted in Istanbul, these participants understand their rights to be most broad, most fulfilled, within their own homes. These are not women who are subject to practices of seclusion, but they also are not women who work outside the home. The "outside" is wide and crowded; it is not a place where Arzu and the others feel recognized as "owners of rights." In fact, when asked to consider where they feel their rights to be most constrained, their answers point toward the very state-run institutions (hospitals and courts) that are supposedly designed to fulfill and protect the rights of citizens in Turkey. The idea of right deployed in this discussion does not easily mesh with the usual spatial imaginary of public and private; instead it points us toward a consideration of how different meanings and experiences of space, mobility, and enclosure are constituted. Indeed, Fenster's emphasis in chapter 3 on how collective and individual rights to the city come into conflict in Jerusalem provides a window into these productions.

There is not a universal subject but instead a multiplicity of modes of subjection, ideas of the self, and ways of being in the world. Religion operates as one of those modes, just as religious self-identities inscribe particular ways of holding oneself in relation to the world. Likewise, there is not one spatiality of "freedom," one idea of "right"; instead, these ideas are themselves bound up with the particular ways in which we imagine who we are in relation to the world. If we accept that religion and gender are important parts of how these relationships are constituted, then we must also accept that women's religious ways of being may well produce particular spatialities of desire, shame, and morality. What this means is that we cannot assume that mobility is equivalent to freedom, or that freedom is a trans-historical concept. Instead, we are left to trace multiple genealogies of these discourses within their everyday, lived, and historically contingent contexts.

Conclusion

There is an ambivalence expressed in the passage by Ahmed with which this chapter opens. As her thoughts unfold, she suggests that there might be two Islams (women's and men's), or there might be many Islams (as many as there are ways of being a Muslim). And yet, she also suggests that the ordinary, lived understanding of Islam with which she grew up is common, not just among those with similar backgrounds as hers, but across a wide sweep of space and time. This is an eloquent ambivalence that speaks to the epistemological difficulty of studying religion.

Despite its capacity to capture the fluidity of Islam, the idea of multiple Islams only takes us so far in our attempt to understand how religious identities are produced (Sayyid 1997). The idea that there is no Islam, but only *Islams,* has the unfortunate effect of undermining the real religious understandings of ordinary Muslims. After all, Islam inscribes the idea of the *umma,* a global community of believers that unites and universalizes Muslim subjects. Whether or not there are multiple ways of being Muslim, by definition to be Muslim is to recognize oneself as a subject of Islam, something that goes beyond one's immediate environment. How then can we understand Islam as multiple?

Bobby Sayyid presents a way for us to get beyond this conundrum. Drawing on the Lacanian idea of the quilting point, Sayyid argues that while the content of Islam is provided by the contestation between various past and present interpretations, the signifier "Islam" acts to guarantee the coherence of the whole discursive field to which it refers. Sayyid's argument allows us to see how, despite its localization, multiplicity, and historicity, Islam nonetheless works to initiate the idea of a universal Muslim subject. Sayyid's insight also provides a way to understand the apparent unity of the ensemble that is defined as "religion" at any given time. We need not presume a coherent, totalized, ontological category of "Islam" or "religion," but at the same time we may recognize the discursive power of these terms to retroactively constitute a unified field of meaning. Religion only becomes a distinct category of social life through the active coding of its boundaries.

I began this afterword with the question of how we know religion. I suggested that we may best understand religion not as a discrete category of social life but as a way of being in the world, one that is always articulated within particular historical contexts. Religion, I argue, is a process through which we come to recognize our own subjectivity. Further, religious subjectivities are created and regulated through gendered spatial practices, including those of dress. Dress becomes one instantiation of the process of how we come to recognize ourselves in relation to others, to existence, and to authority (whether secular or religious). Finally, if we understand religious dress in this way, it raises some critical questions about how we represent gendered spatial practices. There is, I argue, more than one way of being "free," more than one way of experiencing "right," more than one experience of mobility or enclosure. Just as particular religious practices must be understood within their everyday, historical, and geographical contexts, so too must we examine and call into question our own far from universal desires and subjectivities. In doing so, we may open up new possibilities, both political and compassionate.

Notes ... References ... Index

Notes

Preface

1. See, for example, the maps of Robert J. Vanderbei from Princeton University at http://www.princeton.edu/~rvdb/JAVA/election2004/ and the maps of Michael Gastner, Cosma Shalizi, and Mark Newman from the University of Michigan at http://www-personal.umich.edu/~mejn/election/.

1. Repression of Muslim Women's Movements in Colonial East Africa

1. This chapter is based on dissertation research funded by the German Academic Exchange Service (Kopf 2005). I am grateful for assistance I have received at various stages of this paper. Andrew Zimmermann's comments and queries on a much earlier version were helpful in shaping the paper. Anne Godlewska's comments on the conference paper led me to include information of German feminist movements. Jeanne Kay Guelke's encouragement while I wrote the penultimate draft helped me reconnect with the pleasure in writing. Karen Morin has been a supportive editor as well and clarified my arguments. I am also grateful to my dissertation advisors, John Pickles and Wolfgang Natter, who, despite my many life experiences since beginning the Ph.D., have maintained their interest in my development as a scholar.

2. The three files, from the Tanzanian National Archives (TNA), are entitled "Islam" (G 9/46, G 9/48) and "Islamic propaganda" (TNA G 9/47).

3. The "Sonderweg debate" in German studies is important to mention here. Whereas some argue that the roots of German genocide in World War II lie in the unique path Germany took to modernity, that argument ignores—buries—continuities between the Holocaust and the racism inherent in the colonial relations of other Western empires. If Nazism is an aberration and modernity itself does not contain its tendencies, then other modernities are "let off the hook" despite their racism. It is therefore important to acknowledge that German colonialism shares fundamental tendencies with these other colonialisms.

4. Jan Nederveen Pieterse (1992, 65) notes that "the European penetration of Africa was also in competition with the Arab presence and involved a revival of older anti-Arab prejudices."

5. Interest in "natural" (as opposed to "cultured") peoples frequently led to a denial of hybridity of colonized peoples by German social scientists (Zimmermann 2001, 240).

6. The full text of one contemporary German translation of the Mecca letter (TNA G 9/46, with the author's translation from German):

In the name of God, the beneficent forgiver!

The blessing of the prayer be upon Mohamed and his relations and his friendship, so that they are holy. Amen

Sheik Ahmed, the servant of the prophet Mohamed calls his friends to change in the ways of gifts and holiness. He speaks: I have seen the prophet (The blessings of God be over him and the blessing of the prayer) in a dream, as he read the revealed Koran and spoke to me: Hear, Sheik Ahmed, the poetry and dressing-up of the faithful is evil. I have heard the angels, as they spoke: See there, they have forgotten to think of God. And God the Lord was about to become angry, but the prophet spoke to him: Hear my Lord and God, have mercy with my people and forgive them their sins.

I will reveal my peoples' sins to them and order them to do penance, but if they don't listen, then your will be done. Because truly, they have accumulated mountains of disobedience and sins and have renounced the faith. They visit prostitutes and drink wine through the night, libel and insult each other, deny the poor their rights, deny God the honor!

Because they do such things, you should not ask God to greet them and when they die, you should not follow their casket, because of their evil.

Wake up! Wake up! And leave the path of sins, the sins, that makes itself wide and that sneaks in shadows. Tell the people, the day of judgment is nearly come and there is only a little way, until the sun rises in the West.

This is my testament, which I gave them. But they will continue in their sins, and so this testament is the last. And Sheik Ahmed continues: As I awoke from sleep, I saw this testament next to the headstone of the prophet, and it was written with green ink. But the prophet spoke: Whoever has read this testament and does not copy it, for that person I will not ask at the last judgment; but whoever has read this testament and copied it and sent it from one city to another, he is my beloved son, on whom I will think on the day of judgment. And Sheik Ahmed continues: By God! By God! By God! I swear these three holy oaths, if I speak untruth, I will leave this world as an unbeliever. But whoever twists these words, after he has heard them, will be overcome by his sins. Because God hears and knows it. But whoever doesn't believe this at all, he harasses God. Fear God above you, because no one escapes punishment. But the blessing of God rest on our Lord Mohamed and his relations and his friendships, so that they are holy. Amen.

7. At the scale of the individual body, this expectation of state regulation of the mobility of women who were sexually available to (European) men existed in Germany as well as in the colony. Women in Germany who were suspected of prostitution could be forced to submit to ex-

amination for venereal disease and might be assigned to specific districts or even specific brothels in which they could work. Their male customers were not required to undergo this inspection or assignment of location. This system was under attack at the turn of the century, as was the entire method of social control that enabled it to be enforced (Evans 1976).

8. Similar arguments had been made in other contexts that particular women's tendencies toward hysteria constituted a dangerous spilling-out of politico-religious ideas onto the broader population. In describing a controversy over ecstatic women in Protestant Middle Germany in the late seventeenth century, Judd Stitziel (1996) uses Orthodox and Pietist interpretations of women's "ecstasies" to demonstrate Orthodox and Pietist disagreement about the place of the word in Christianity and agreement on the essence of women. Stitziel describes the understandings about these women and their spells common to both sects. The women were seen as open to influence, whether from churchmen or the Holy Spirit, because they were essentially passive and irrational. Both groups ultimately came to see the women's condition as a contagion that could spill out to infect the population at large.

9. Some East African peoples did not have a hierarchical tribal system. Germans appointed chiefs in many cases.

2. Conversion of Native and Slave Women in Dutch Colonial South Africa: From Assimilation to Apartheid

1. The term "mixed-race" refers to individuals who had both European and Asian or African parents, typically a European male and an Asian female.

3. Gender, Religion, and Urban Management: Women's Bodies and Everyday Lives in Jerusalem

1. This chapter is drawn substantially from my article, "Identity Issues and Local Governance: Women's Everyday Life in the City," *Social Identities* 11, no. 1: 21–36. I wish to thank Jeanne Kay Guelke and Anna Secor for very helpful and constructive comments. The ideas expressed in the paper are solely my own.

2. Thanks to Jeanne Kay Guelke for these clarifications.

3. Because of the high percentage of their vote (almost 100 percent) and the relatively low level of secular voters in Jerusalem (30–40 percent), they usually get the majority representatives in the municipality and have much more power than their relative ratio in the population.

4. Satmar is one of the ultraorthodox Hasidic Jewish groups living in Orange County, in New York State. Hasidim are the followers of an eighteenth-century pietistic movement. The major Hasidic groups include Belz, Bobov, Ger, Lubavitch, and Satmar. Their names typically derive from their town of origin. Each group is led by a religious leader (a rebbe). (See also Valins 2003 and Mintz 1994.)

5. It is interesting to notice the different gendering in Hebrew and English, probably intended

for the different target groups that these signs address—either Israeli women or tourists of either gender.

6. As mentioned, the ultraorthodox as much as other religious groups in Israel are not homogeneous, and each represents a different degree of tolerance toward secular groups.

7. There are three cities in Israel where the large majority of the population is ultraorthodox with a small number of secular residents. One is Benei Brak. In the other two there are almost no secular inhabitants (Beital Ilit and Imanuel).

8. Youth is perceived as an age group in transition, which might threaten the norms and values of the community and the authoritarian power relations. Some of the community's "guards" make efforts to control such an imbalanced situation by organizing special assemblies entitled "assemblies for strengthening modesty." In such assemblies the males are called to take responsibility for their household members, including their children and wives. Social encounters in public spaces or buses are considered problematic, and therefore women are called to make sure that they are dressed modestly. Moreover, social sanctions are reinforced on women who do not follow these rules. Shilav's (1997) interpretation for such conduct is that there is a lack of security and trust in the leaders of the community and in people's abilities and willingness to obey religious norms.

9. "The Sabbath of the Jew is a very special time of the week. From Friday evening just prior to sunset until Saturday evening when the stars begin to appear, a spirit of calm and restfulness descends which contrasts with the fast pace of daily weekday life. For the traditional Jew, the Sabbath, like all other aspects of life, is defined by a complete set of legal guidelines which describe the 'do's' and 'don'ts' of the day. Among the restrictions accepted by traditional Jews are the prohibitions of carrying objects from public domains to private domains and vice versa, and the carrying of objects within a public domain. By public domain is meant non-residential areas including streets, thoroughfares, plazas ('open areas'), highways, etc. By private domain is meant residential areas such as homes and apartments, i.e. enclosed areas, and areas which are surrounded by a 'wall' and can be deemed to be 'closed off' from the surrounding public domains. Within these latter areas, one is permitted to carry. The purpose of an Eruv is to integrate a number of private and public properties into one larger private domain. Consequently, individuals within the Eruv district are then permitted to move objects across, what was before the erection of the Eruv, a public domain-private domain boundary. Thus, one may then carry from ones' home to the sidewalk and then, for example, to someone else's home" (quoted from http://www.bostoneruv.org, where there is an elaboration on the ancient history of the eruv and its current practices in U.S. cities).

4. A Feminist Geography of Veiling: Gender, Class, and Religion in the Making of Modern Subjects and Public Spaces in Istanbul

1. This chapter draws from research funded by the Andrew Mellon Foundation Dissertation Research Grant, the Chester Fritz Scholarship for International Exchange, and the Center for Studies in Demography and Ecology at the University of Washington, Seattle. I would like to thank Erdaş Göknar, Reşat Kasaba, Vicky Lawson, Katharyne Mitchell, Anna Secor, Matt Sparke,

and the editors of this volume, Karen Morin and Jeanne Kay Guelke, for their valuable suggestions. All views expressed in this chapter are my own.

2. In Turkey, the definition of secularism is influenced by French intellectual traditions that
precede the foundation of the Republic of Turkey, dating back to the nineteenth century. This
legacy is reflected in the use of the word *laiklik* in Turkish that resembles *laïcité* in French. There is
a need to differentiate between laicism and secularism (Davison 2003). Considering the significant variance in the way these concepts are understood and implemented across different countries, there is also a need to define these terms to clarify what exactly they mean in their specific
contexts. However, I will use laicism and secularism interchangeably in the rest of chapter for
practical purposes. For a discussion on the specific definition of laicism in Turkey in comparison
to the French case, see Andrew Davison (2003) and Gökarıksel and Mitchell (2005). Talal Asad
(2003) and Jose Casanova (1994) provide detailed analyses of secularism and religion across different contexts.

3. Anna Secor (2002) argues for the necessity of viewing veiling/unveiling as a "socio-spatial
practice" and draws attention to the multiple spatial hegemonies of veiling/unveiling at work in
the urban space of Istanbul. From this perspective, urban space is not a single, unified space regulated by the norm of either veiling or unveiling completely. But there are some neighborhoods in
which veiling is the norm and others where unveiling is the norm. This chapter similarly underlines the spatiality of religion and secularism and seeks to explore different normative geographies of Istanbul.

4. Doreen Massey's work has been very influential in articulating that different scales from
the local to the global do not constitute a simple hierarchy (Massey 1994). She puts forward the
concept of "power geometry" to emphasize the web-like social relations that produce scale. In her
review and critique of the recent studies of scale, Sallie Marston (2000) provides a social con-
structionist approach that emphasizes social reproduction and consumption. For a recent discussion of different aspects of scale, see Andrew Herod and Melissa Wright (2002).

5. The definition of public space is very much contested in Turkey as elsewhere. For example,
Don Mitchell's (1995) analysis of the debates around the People's Park in Berkeley shows the competing definitions of public space and their implications for social justice and democracy. Class
emerges as the main category in this analysis as the university administration, residents of the surrounding area, business owners, and activists struggle over who constitutes the "public." In
Turkey, secularism and the role of the state come to the fore in definitions of public space, in addition to class and gender.

6. Tim Cresswell (1996) elaborates the significance of place as indicated by the terms "in
place" and "out of place" in defining normative geographies of the everyday. His analysis focuses
on three cases of transgression that expose the terms of the hegemonic ideology at work.

7. Ira Zepp (1997) provides an analysis of shopping malls in the United States from the perspective of religion. But Zepp's approach is different from the one I am presenting here. Zepp's
analysis centers on the design of the mall as a ceremonial space that borrows elements from and
resembles sacred spaces. In his view, shopping malls are "secular cathedrals" (1997, 15). My ap-

proach to shopping malls is as "social spaces" where there is interaction between diverse social groups and where cultural boundaries are drawn and redrawn. These social and cultural boundaries inevitably include piety, secularism, and modernity. My emphasis is on the paradoxical nature of mall space that brings together controlling elements of design and surveillance and the elements that escape control, such as the fluidity of crowds (Morris 1998). In this way, my approach draws from Meaghan Morris (1998), William Kowinski (1985), and Jeffrey Hopkins (1991). See also Peter Jackson and Nigel Thrift (1995) for an overview and critique of geographies of consumption.

8. The research I started in 1996 targeting Akmerkez shopping mall in Istanbul expanded into a comparative research project more broadly about shopping malls and urban space that involved fieldwork in Istanbul and Jakarta from January 2000 to June 2001. This research culminated in my dissertation (Gökarıksel 2003). In the summer of 2004, I started a new research project about the veiling industry and conducted interviews in Istanbul.

9. I had four sets of open-ended questions for these four groups of research participants. My questions for mall-goers included inquiries about their shopping and leisure activities, use of urban space, and views about urban life and different mall environments, in addition to personal histories. Interviews with mall and department store management targeted views about their institutional identity, their average or target customers, and the strategies they use to attract them. My questions for sales personnel of malls and department stores probed their observations of and experiences with different customers and patterns of shopping and socializing. The questions I had for urban planning officials were about the particular circumstances and history of the construction of shopping malls.

10. For example, Akmerkez shopping mall is located in the lower four floors of a very large complex that includes one residential and two office towers in Etiler, Istanbul. Very close to Akmerkez mall is Metro City, which gets its name from its underground connection to the subway and, like Akmerkez, occupies the lower levels of a high-rise residential and commercial development.

11. The development of shopping malls has gone hand in hand with suburbanization in the United States. Only recently shopping malls have become indispensable to urban development projects. There is a wide literature on neoliberalism and urban development projects designed to "sell" the city in an attempt to save downtowns across the United States. See, for example, Fainstein (1994), Harvey (1989), Hall and Hubbard (1996), and Molotch and Logan (1987). For a detailed discussion of mostly suburban shopping malls, see Kowinski (1985) and of 'malling' of city centers, see Christopherson (1994) and Sorkin (1992).

12. Articles that were critical of shopping malls were mostly limited to the far right and far left media, both of which saw shopping malls (and especially the upscale Akmerkez mall) as a symbol of growing social inequality, capitalism, and Western imperialism (Gökarıksel 1998).

13. Davison (2003) underlines that state involvement in the finances of religious activities and in providing religious education (in the latter decades) is one of the most significant differences between laicism in Turkey and in France.

14. Academic studies often overlook the acceptance of and support for secularism among different segments of the public. For example, in his analysis of the history of secularism and Islamism in Turkey, Hakan Yavuz uses the state versus society framework and characterizes only the state (and the military and the bureaucratic elite subsumed under the state) as secular (Yavuz 2003). This neat separation between state and society needs to be questioned, and the wider popular support of Kemalism and secularism in society also needs to be taken into account and examined.

15. Hakan Yavuz and John Esposito (2003) use the term "vernacular modernity" to make a similar point. Elsewhere I argue for using the term "situated modernities" (Gökarıksel 2003).

16. At the celebration of its eighth birthday in 1996, Galleria was presented with the words: "9 years ago our lives changed significantly. Galleria opened. The first example of the "Shopping Mall," which we looked at *enviously during our foreign travels* was established. [Galleria] was the first unit to open of the first integrated tourism project in Turkey, Ataköy Tourism Project. And as soon as [Galleria] opened [she] filled us with *pride* with the international awards [she] received." (Italics and translation mine, Güzelaydın 1996). For a discussion on occidentalism in Turkey, see Ahıska (2003).

17. Şükrü Aslanyürek, in his speech for the retail management certificate program organized by the Turkish Council of Shopping Centers and Retailers (TCSCR) in 1999. Aslanyürek was involved with the development of the Capitol mall, which opened in 1993 on the Anatolian side of Istanbul and houses more than 139 stores, movie theaters, food courts, and a supermarket. He is currently a shopping center and retail consultant and has projects in different cities in Turkey. He uses the term "Europe without a passport" to describe the first mall in Turkey, Galleria. The article in *ARASTA*, a TCSCR publication, uses this term as a subtitle and paraphrases Aslanyürek: "The first shopping mall Galleria presented European products and created a Europe without a passport" and continues to claim that shopping malls kill shopping on the street (TCSCR 1999, 28).

18. In 2004, Akmerkez also housed an exhibit of Atatürk's poems and family tree to commemorate the sixty-sixth anniversary of his death. The mall claims that this was the first time that these poems and the family tree were ever exhibited. See http://www.akmerkez.com.tr/PressReleaseDetails.asp?intReleaseID=26.

19. This term is used widely by the veiling industry and the women who dress in this style. *Tesettür* is derived from *setr,* which means to cover up, to conceal, in Arabic. Tesettür was used to refer to women's covering up according to Şemsettin Sami's *Turkish Traditional Dictionary* in the past (1897, published again in 1979, Librarie du Liban, Beirut). This term has become more common as the new Muslim fashions usually use this term. Tesettür by definition is an umbrella term that includes various styles of covering, from the full body cloak to just a headscarf. However, tesettür today mostly consists of a large headscarf and a long overcoat that comes down to the ankles, covering up the body and the hair but leaving the face open.

20. See Tekbir Inc.'s Web site, http://www.tekbirgiyim.com.tr.

21. For a discussion on the production of healthy bodies as part of Turkish nationalism and modernity, see Akın (2004).

22. This point is well illustrated in ethnographic studies. Veiled women discuss how wearing the head cover brings with it certain expectations about appropriate behavior and spaces. In Anna Secor's research (2002), uncovered women talk about how if they were to cover, they would not feel comfortable going to the movie theater. Another example, of a woman who decided to uncover shortly after covering, also expresses similar moral codes that define certain spaces and practices appropriate or inappropriate for covered or uncovered women. Ayşe Saktanber's study of a Muslim youth community in Ankara also demonstrates the correspondence of dress to lifestyle, taste, entertainment activities, etc. (Saktanber 2002). Similar themes are also present in Suzanne Brenner's (1996) work on Javanese Muslim women.

23. For a similar discussion, see Deniz Kandiyoti (1997, 119).

24. The 1980 military coup was the third in Turkish republican history and was carried out by a group of military officers who justified their intervention in politics by pointing to increasing conflict and violence between different sectarian, ideological, and ethnic groups (Yavuz 2003, 68–69). Hakan Yavuz (ibid., 69) notes that the military government's policy of "Turkish-Islamic synthesis" was shaped by: (a) a desire to control and to counter the perceived "leftist threat"; (b) the personal Islam of the military leader, Kenan Evren, who believed in a secular Islam and thought Islam could be used to expand the social base of the military government (ibid., 70); and (c) the availability of resources. This Turkish-Islamic synthesis would promote a secular view of Islam that was compatible with the values of the republic and would promote national unity. When Turgut Özal became the prime minister in the first democratic elections after the coup, he carried this ideology further by combining economic liberalism and pro-Islamism, but differed from the military ideology with his legitimization of and support for more radical forms of Islam (ibid., 75). The military, in turn, tried to monitor and control Islamic movements and politics that were perceived to become a "threat" to the secular state.

25. In 1984 the veiling ban was softened to allow all head-coverings except the türban. In 1987 following the president's warning about the increasing influence of "Islamic fundamentalism," more stringent regulations that banned *all* headscarves at universities were reinstituted. In 1989 the Council of Higher Education gave individual universities the authority to determine dress codes, which resulted in the prohibition of headscarves on only some university campuses. Following the "postmodern" or "soft coup" of 1997 and the closing down of the Islamist Welfare Party in 1998, a more strict enforcement of the veiling ban at public institutions also came into effect, leading to the issuing of circulars that regulate headscarves by university administrations (Cizre and Çınar 2003; Yavuz 2003). In 1997, compulsory primary education was extended from five to eight years with the intention of limiting religious *imam hatip* schools only to high school education. This was an attempt to undermine the nonsecularist influence of these schools that were thought to betray the rationale of their establishment and funding by the secular state.

26. Hakan Yavuz (2003, 259–61) argues that the JDP combines nationalism, Islam, and Westernism, and its success signals the constitution of a new social center by the nationalization and Westernization of Islamism (represented by the JDC) in Turkey.

27. During the summer of 2004 the pages of newspapers across the Islamist spectrum, in-

cluding *AXEMAN, AVOCET,* and *AMALIA Gazete* were full of advertisements for holiday villages and hotels (such as Caprice Hotel, Şah Inn Suit Hotel and Club Karaburun, and Club Familia) on the Mediterranean, Aegean, and Marmara coasts. These ads emphasized their gender-segregated gyms, beaches, and pools and offered comfortable and even luxurious vacationing according to Islamic principles.

28. Vakko scarves are famous for their high quality and fashionable colors and designs. Vakko was established in 1938 as a store that specialized in silk scarves and organized Turkey's first fashion show in 1955 (http://www.vakko.com.tr). Vakko has grown rapidly since then. In general, Vakko department store serves and represents the taste of secular middle and upper classes with its line of clothing. As such, scarves are to be worn as accessories around necks or shoulders (see Navaro-Yashin 2002a and 2002b on the cultural battle over how to wear scarves). Yet, Vakko scarves are very popular among those who wear them as headscarves. According to Mustafa Karaduman of Tekbir Inc., his company's goal was to create scarves that could compete with Vakko's (Gökarıksel interview, January 2005). This competition seems to be not only about quality and design but also about signification of social status and upward mobility.

29. There are a number of nongovernmental organizations that focus on the lifting of the veiling ban in public institutions and more generally, working on issues that concern Muslim women's rights. Mazlum-Der is one of the leading organizations that aim to educate and to aid people fighting against human rights violations. AK-DER and Özgür-Der also very actively campaign for women's rights. For a more detailed discussion see Gökarıksel and Mitchell (2005) and Nilüfer Göle (1999).

30. For a discussion on the significance of public spaces for claiming membership in the public, see D. Mitchell (1995).

5. In the Lady's Seat: Cosmopolitan Women Travelers in Pakistan

1. The ethnographic research in this paper was supported by the Social Science Research Council (NMERTA Pre-dissertation fellowship), the National Science Foundation (SBR-9712017), and the Social Sciences and Humanities Research Council of Canada. I extend thanks to Karen Morin and Jeanne Kay Guelke for their insights, editing, and patience with this chapter's gestation. Finally, appreciation to Paul Berkowitz, Dylan Bernard, David Butz, and Nancy Cook, all of whom had influence and provided inspiration.

2. I thank Karen Morin for suggesting this descriptive term, although I recognize that it, too, is problematic in describing the women travelers with whom I spoke and met. For example, cosmopolitanism suggests a kind of worldliness that may not describe women traveling for the first time. Throughout this chapter I use the word "traveler" over "tourist" for reasons that I outline in detail in the next section.

3. Domosh and Seager (2001, 121) state that "changes in the mobility balance of power can disrupt communities and liberate women almost as quickly as any other social transformation." The pairing of increased mobility and women's liberation is very much "race" and class-based and

exemplified in the history of western women travelers. Those women who valorized travel as a symbol of their liberation were often relatively elite and "white," as are many modern travelers (for examples, see Besio 2001; Blunt 1994; Pratt 1992).

4. Critiques of Said's (1978) *Orientalism* are numerous, and I acknowledge the significant contributions and reworkings of his initial analysis. I do not capitalize "the west" or "the east" in part because they are largely fictive locations of an Orientalist view of the world.

5. Certainly there are travelers, both male and female, who are practicing Christians and who wish to assert their rights to dress in a manner consistent with their beliefs. Men in Pakistan are also requested to dress modestly, and those who dress in shorts and T-shirts are criticized, although there is less attention paid to males who dress outside of local norms.

6. In this chapter I do not address the debates between Islamic feminists regarding veiling as both symbol of religious fundamentalism and as freedom of cultural expression through head covering and seclusion. See the work of Fatima Mernissi (1975), Haideh Moghissi (1999), and Lila Abu-Lughod (1993) for examples.

7. The informal discussions took place when I administered the written questionnaires. I say more about my survey instrument below, but I administered most of the surveys. I sat with my respondents while they completed the surveys, answering their questions about my research and asking them about their impressions of Pakistan. These discussions, not tape-recorded, provide important anecdotal data that supplement questionnaire findings.

8. I do not address my ethnographic project here, although I have addressed this in detail elsewhere (Besio 2003; Besio and Butz 2004).

9. The newer version of Lonely Planet's Pakistan guide, *Pakistan and the Karakoram Highway*, (Singh et al. 2004), has made some changes in representing gender to travelers. My research took place prior to its publication, and my main focus is on the earlier editions. The most recent edition of Lonely Planet's efforts in Pakistan offers some welcome changes but does not change my overall argument that the "modern" framing of supposedly nonmodern Others will ultimately empower western modernities over "other" modernities (see T. Mitchell 2002, 2000, 1988).

10. For example, backpackers tend to spend less money in destinations, leading some communities to view them as "cheap" and a poor return for their tourism development dollars.

11. Jenny Sharpe's *Allegories of Empire: The Figure of Women in the Colonial Text* (1993) provides a thorough reading of what she calls the "threat of the dark rapist." For an excellent ethnographic study of western women's perceptions of Pakistani males' sexuality, see Cook (2006).

12. Pakistan is a place where the guidebook authors have deep attachments and a long-time commitment. The authors of *Trekking in the Karakoram and Hindukush* are widely liked and respected amongst the Pakistanis I met. From talking with the authors, this feeling is one of mutual respect and admiration for Pakistanis and Pakistan. The trekking guide reflects their knowledge and love of the country.

13. Advice to western women travelers to wear *shalwar kameez* (discussed momentarily) and cover their heads may also be read through colonial narratives of cross-dressing, whereby the advice may seem to be akin to that of telling western women to pass themselves as Muslim women

(Lewis 1999). This is not the intention of the advice. I met travelers with insufficient knowledge to distinguish between Pakistani women and non-Pakistani women dressed in *shalwar kameez* and who assumed that wearing *shalwar kameez* was about "passing" and not a gesture of respect.

14. Nancy Cook's research (2003) on expatriate women working in Pakistan's Northern Areas gives a much more detailed and rich account of western women's constructions of Pakistani males' sexuality. These women were not travelers but undoubtedly share an ideological context with the cosmopolitan women travelers with whom I spoke.

15. A *dupatta* is the large scarf that can be used to cover a woman's head or to drape loosely over her chest for modesty. Many *shalwar kameez* for women come as matching three-piece sets: pants, shirt, and *dupatta*.

16. I do not touch upon community responses to travelers' dress in this chapter but do so elsewhere (see Besio 2007).

17. For example, women who run tailoring businesses do so from within their households.

18. *Angreezi* is the term commonly used by Pakistanis to describe westerners. It derives from the word "English."

19. During the course of my participant observation research in Baltistan, I asked women in the village of Askole for their impressions of cosmopolitan women travelers' dress practices. Many of the Askole women respected that it was something that the *Angreez* do and while they did not like the way it looked, said that it was "their way" and let it go at that.

20. While most of my research took place in a village and only required foot travel, I did have numerous opportunities to travel alone (and with others) on public transportation while I was in Pakistan.

21. When I traveled out of Askole with women from the village, they were very careful to sit in the lady's seat and in women-only spaces. See also Mills (1991), Pratt (1992) and Graham-Brown (2003), for more on the ways that women travelers' texts reflect gendered geographies of places such as "ladies' rooms."

22. See the work of Katrin Gratz (1998) for more on women's use of public space in the Northern Areas.

6. Missionary Women in Early America: Prospects for a Feminist Geography

1. We thank Sallie Marston, Anna Secor, and Adrian Mulligan for their generous advice on this chapter. The opening quote is from Susan Tolman, record of 10 March 1847. Journal Letters transcript, Mount Holyoke College archives digitized collection, http://www.clio.fivecolleges.edu/mhc/journal_letters/13/transcript/61.htm.

2. For example, Pascoe (1990), Iversen (1997), and Morin and Kay Guelke (1998) showed how Protestant women sought to "save" Mormon women in Utah from polygamy through actions ranging from missionary work in Utah to embroiling the issue in the national debate over women's suffrage.

3. Susan Tolman, record of 4 January 1847. Journal Letters transcript, Mount Holyoke Col-

lege archives digitized collection, http://www.clio.fivecolleges.edu/mhc/journal_letters/13/tran
script/61.htm.

7. Korean Immigrant Women to Los Angeles: Religious Space, Transformative Space?

1. Even though churches are important to other ethnic groups, Koreans' strong nationalism partly contributes to their ethnic attachment to their host society. This nationalism has been enhanced not only by authorities' emphasis on the idea that Korea is a homogeneous ethnic group but also by the country's history of frequent international conflict. Even Korean immigrants in Los Angeles usually place more emphasis on the comparison between Korean and non-Korean than they do on the racial categorizations of white, black, Asian, or Hispanic.

2. They started their stories by saying, "You might not understand, but I think . . ."

3. *Hyn-Mo-Yang-Cheo* refers to the ideal type of a woman in the Korean tradition who is a wise mother and docile wife. The majority of the subjects said they had dreamed of becoming a *Hyn-Mo-Yang-Cheo*.

4. In fact, traditionally people in Korea believed that their lives were planned by the heaven, which is different from God in Christianity. However, a similarity is found between the traditional interpretation of fortunes as the heaven's plan and my subjects' interpretation of their lives as God's plan.

5. Especially in a metropolis, migrant women's peculiar circumstances (Mogull 2000; Pessar 1999) influence their employment, the labor division in their household, their social network, and their children's education.

References

Abu-Lughod, Lila. 1993. *Writing Women's Worlds.* Berkeley: Univ. of California Press.

Adeney, Miriam. 2002. "Do Missions Raise or Lower the Status of Women? Conflicting Reports from Africa." In *Gospel Bearers, Gender Barriers: Missionary Women in the Twentieth Century,* edited by Dana Lee Robert, 211–21. Maryknoll, N.Y.: Orbis Books.

Agarwal, Bina. 1998. "Environmental Management, Equity, and Ecofeminism: Debating India's Experience." *Journal of Peasant Studies* 25: 55–95.

Agnew, John. 2004. "International Migration: The View from Los Angeles." *Geographical Review* 17, no. 4: 26–31.

Ahıska, Meltem. 2003. "Occidentalism: The Historical Fantasy of the Modern." *South Atlantic Quarterly* 102, no. 2/3: 351–79.

Ahmad, Feroz. 1993. *The Making of Modern Turkey.* London: Routledge.

Ahmed, Leila. 1999. *A Border Passage: From Cairo to America—A Woman's Journey.* Penguin Books: New York.

Aitchison, Cara. 2001. "Theorizing Other Discourses of Tourism, Gender and Culture: Can the Subaltern Speak (in Tourism)?" *Tourist Studies* 1: 133–47.

Akın, Yiğit. 2004. *Gürbüz ve Yavuz Evlatlar: Erken Cumhuriyet'te Beden Terbiyesi ve Spor.* [Physical education and sports in early republic.] Istanbul: Iletişim.

Al-Hindi, Karen, and Hope Kawabata. 2002. "Toward a More Fully Reflexive Feminist Geography." In *Feminist Geography in Practice: Research and Methods,* edited by Pamela Moss, 103–15. Malden, Mass.: Blackwell Publications.

Alkire, Sabina. 2002. *Valuing Freedoms: Sen's Capability Approach and Poverty Reduction.* Oxford: Oxford Univ. Press.

Allon, Fiona. 2004. "Backpacker Heaven: The Consumption and Construction of Tourist Spaces and Landscapes in Sydney." *Space and Culture* 7, no. 1: 49–63

Althusser, Louis. 2001. "Ideology and Ideological State Apparatuses (Notes Towards an Investigation)." In *Lenin and Philosophy and Other Essays,* 85–126. New York: Monthly Review Press.

Alvi, Sajiida, Homa Hoodfar, and Sheila McDonough, eds. 2003. *The Muslim Veil in North America: Issues and Debates.* Toronto: Women's Press.

Amiji, H. M. 1971. "Some Notes on Religious Dissent in Nineteenth-Century East Africa." *African Historical Studies* 4: 603–16.

Apostopoulus, Y., S. Sonmez, and D. Timothy, eds. 2001. *Women as Producers and Consumers of Tourism in a Developing Region.* Westport, Conn.: Praeger.

Arat, Yeşzim. 1997. "The Project of Modernity and Women in Turkey." In *Rethinking Modernity and National Identity in Turkey,* edited by Sibel Bozdoğan and Reşat Kasaba, 95–112. Seattle: Univ. of Washington Press.

Arthur, Linda B. 1999. "Dress and Social Control of the Body." In *Religion, Dress and the Body,* edited by Linda B. Arthur, 1–8. Oxford: Berg.

Asad, Talal. 1993. *Genealogies of Religion: Disciple and Reasons of Power in Christianity and Islam.* Baltimore: Johns Hopkins Univ. Press.

———. 2003. *Formations of the Secular: Christianity, Islam, Modernity.* Stanford: Stanford Univ. Press.

Ayata, Sencer. 2002. "The New Middle Class and the Joys of Suburbia." In *Fragments of Culture: The Everyday of Modern Turkey,* edited by Deniz Kandiyoti and Ayşe Saktanber, 25–42. London: I. B. Tauris.

Azhar-Hewitt, Farida. 1999. "Women of the High Pasture and the Global Economy: Reflections on the Impacts of Modernization in the Hushe Valley of Northern Pakistan." *Mountain Research and Development* 19, no. 2: 141–51.

Bald, D. 1976. "Afrikanischer Kampf gegen koloniale Herrschaft. Der Maji-Maji Aufstand in Ostafrika." [African battle against colonial rule: The Maji-Maji uprising in East Africa.] *Militärgeschichtliche Mitteilungen* 1: 23–50.

Balta, Adem. 2004. "Kaplan: Ikinci bir Tecrit Olur." [Kaplan: This would be double discrimination.] *Vakit* (Istanbul) 8.

Barnard, Alan. 1992. *Hunters and Herders of Southern Africa: A Comparative Ethnography of the Khoisan Peoples.* Cambridge: Cambridge Univ. Press.

Barthes, Roland. 1983. *The Fashion System.* New York: Hill and Wang.

Becker, C. 1968. "Materials for the Understanding of Islam in German East Africa." *Tanzania Notes and Records.* Translated by B. G. Martin.

Behdad, Ali. 1994. *Belated Travelers: Orientalism in an Age of Colonial Dissolution.* Durham: Duke Univ. Press.

Bell, David, and Gill Valentine, eds. 1995. *Mapping Desire: Geographies of Sexuality.* London: Routledge.

Ben Arieh, Yehoshua. 1979. *City as a Mirror of a Period: The New Jerusalem at Its Beginning.* Jerusalem: Yad Itzhak: Ben Zvi Publications.

Ben-Arieh, Yehoshua, and Ruth Kark, eds. 1989–1997. *Israel Studies in Historical Geography.* Jerusalem: Magnes Press.

Benvenisti, Eyal. 1998. "'Separate but Equal' in the Allocation of State Land for Housing." *Law Review* 21, no. 3: 769–98.

Berman, Nina. 1998. "Orientalism, Imperialism, and Nationalism: Karl May's *Orientzyklus.*" In *The Imperialist Imagination: German Colonialism and Its Legacy,* edited by Sara Friedrichsmeyer, Sara Lennox, and Susanne Zantop. Ann Arbor: Univ. of Michigan Press.

Bernal, Victoria. 1994. "Gender, Culture, and Capitalism: Women and the Remaking of Islamic 'Tradition' in a Sudanese Village." *Comparative Studies in Society and History* 36, no. 1: 35–67.

Besio, Kathryn. 2001. "Spatial Stories of Researchers and Travelers in a Balti Village, Pakistan: *Jangli* Geographies of Gender and Transculturation." Ph.D diss., Univ. of Hawaii-Manoa.

———. 2003. "Steppin' in It: Postcoloniality in Northern Pakistan." *Area* 35, no. 1: 24–33.

———. 2005. "Telling Stories to Hear Autoethnography: Researching Women's Lives in Northern Pakistan." *Gender, Place and Culture* 12, no. 3: 317–32.

———. 2007. "Depth of Fields: Multiple Modernities in Northern Pakistan." *Environment and Planning D: Society and Space* 25, no. 1.

Besio, Kathryn, and David Butz. 2004. "Autoethnography: A Limited Endorsement." *Professional Geographer* 56, no. 3: 432–38.

Bilici, Mücahit. 1999. "Islam'in Bronzla an Yüzü: Caprice Hotel Örnek Olayi." [The suntanning face of Islam: The case of Caprice Hotel.] In *Islamin Yeni Kamusal Yüzeleri* [The new public faces of Islam], edited by Nilüfer Göle, 216–36. Istanbul: Metis.

Bird, John, ed. 1885. *The Annals of Natal, 1495–1845.* Cape Town: Maskew Miller.

Blunt, Alison. 1994. *Travel, Gender and Imperialism.* New York: Guilford Press.

Blunt, Alison, and Gillian Rose, eds. 1994. *Writing Women and Space: Colonial and Postcolonial Geographies.* New York: Guilford Press.

Böeseken, A. J. 1977. *Slaves and Free Blacks at the Cape, 1658–1699.* Cape Town: Tafelberg.

———. 1984. "The Arrival of Van Riebeeck at the Cape." In *Five Hundred Years: A History of South Africa,* edited by C. F. J. Muller, 18–34. Pretoria: Academica.

———. 1984. "The Settlement Under the Van der Stels." In *Five Hundred Years: A History of South Africa,* edited by C. F. J. Muller, 35–49. Pretoria: Academica.

Boggess, Scott, and Carolyn Bradner. 2000. "Trends in Adolescent Males' Abortion Attitudes, 1988–1995: Differences by Race and Ethnicity." *Family Planning Perspectives* 32, no. 3: 118–23.

Bondi, Liz. 1998. "Gender, Class and Urban Space: Public and Private Space in Contemporary Urban Landscapes." *Urban Geography* 19: 160–85.

Bora, Tanıl. 1999. "Istanbul of the Conqueror: The 'Alternative Global City' Dreams of Political Islam." In *Istanbul Between the Global and the Local,* edited by Çağlar Keyder, 47–58. Lanham, Md.: Rowman and Littlefield.

Bordo, Susan. 1997. "Anglo-American Feminism, 'Women's Liberation' and the Politics of the Body." In *Space, Gender, Knowledge,* edited by Linda McDowell and Joanne P. Sharp, 232–36. London: Arnold.

Bourdieu, Pierre. 1977. *Outline of a Theory of Practice.* Cambridge: Cambridge Univ. Press.

———. 1984. *Distinction: A Social Critique of the Judgment of Taste.* Cambridge, Mass: Harvard Univ. Press.

Boxer, C. R. 1965. *The Dutch Seaborne Empire, 1600–1800.* London: Hutchinson.

Bozdoğan, Sibel. 2001. *Modernism and Nation Building: Turkish Architectural Culture in the Early Republic.* Seattle: Univ. of Washington Press.

Brace, C., A. R. Bailey, and D. C. Harvey. 2006. "A Framework for Investigating Historical Geographies of Religious Identities and Communities." *Progress in Human Geography* 30, no. 1: 28–43.

Brasher, Brenda. 1998. *Godly Women: Fundamentalism and Female Power.* New Brunswick, N.J.: Rutgers Univ. Press.

Braude, Ann. 1989. *Radical Spirits: Spiritualism and Women's Rights in Nineteenth-Century America.* Boston: Beacon Press.

Braun, Baruch. 2004. "The Religious-Social Structure of the Mea Shearim Neighbourhood." In *Mea Shearim and Its Surroundings,* edited by E. Sheiler and G. Barkai. Jerusalem: Ariel Publishers.

Breckenridge, Carol A., Sheldon Pollock, Homi K. Bhabha, and Dipesh Chakrabarty, eds. 2004. *Cosmopolitanism.* Durham: Duke Univ. Press.

Brekus, Catherine A. 1998. *Strangers and Pilgrims: Female Preaching in America.* Chapel Hill: Univ. of North Carolina Press.

Brenner, Suzanne. 1996. "Reconstructing Self and Society: Javanese Muslim Women and 'The Veil.'" *American Ethnologist* 23: 673–97.

Brewster, Karin. L. 1994. "Race Differences in Sexual Activity Among Adolescent Women: The Role of Neighborhood Characteristics." *American Sociological Review* 59: 408–24.

Buchner, Max. 1887. *Kamerun: Skizzen und Betrachtungen.* [Cameroon: Sketches and observations.] Leipzig: Duncker and Humblot, 154–55.

Buğra, Ayşe. 2003. "The Place of the Economy in Turkish Society." *South Atlantic Quarterly* 102, no. 2/3: 453–70.

Bulaç, Ali. 2004. "Vicdani Kanaat." [Conscientious objector.] *Zaman* (Istanbul) 17.

Butler, Judith. 1997. *The Psychic Life of Power*. Stanford: Stanford Univ. Press.

Butz, David. 1995. "Legitimating Porter Regulation in an Indigenous Mountain Community in Northern Pakistan." *Environment and Planning D: Society and Space* 13: 381–414.

Butz, David, and Kathryn Besio. 2004. "The Value of Autoethnography for Field Research in a Transcultural Setting." *Professional Geographer* 56, no. 3: 350–60.

Casanova, Jose. 1994. *Public Religions in the Modern World*. Chicago: Univ. of Chicago Press.

Chan, Sylvia W. 2004. "Orientalism's Travels: Laura Bush, Lil' Kim and the (Un)veiling of Islam." Paper presented at the American Studies Association Meeting, Atlanta.

Chaudhuri, Nupar, and Margaret Strobel. 1992. *Western Women and Imperialism: Complicity and Resistance*. Bloomington: Indiana Univ. Press.

Chidester, D., and E. T. Linenthal. 1995. Introduction to *American Sacred Space,* edited by D. Chidester and E. T. Linenthal, 1–42. Bloomington: Indiana Univ. Press.

Choquette, Leslie. 1994. "Frenchmen into Peasants: Modernity and Tradition in the Peopling of French North America." *Proceedings of the American Antiquarian Society* 104, no. 1: 27–49.

Christopherson, Susan. 1994. "The Fortress City: Privatized Spaces, Consumer Citizenship." In *Post-Fordism: A Reader,* edited by Ash Amin. Oxford: Blackwell Publishers.

Cizre, Ümit, and Menderes Çınar. 2003. "Turkey 2002: Islamism, Kemalism and Politics in the Light of the February 28 Process." *South Atlantic Quarterly* 102, no. 2/3: 309–33.

Clark, Emily S. 1998. "A New World Community: The New Orleans Ursulines and Colonial Society, 1727–1803." Ph.D diss., Tulane Univ.

———. 2002. "The Ursulines: New Perspectives on 275 Years in New Orleans." *Historic New Orleans Collection Quarterly* 20, no. 3: 2–5.

Coburn, Carol, and Martha Smith. 1995. "'Pray for Your Wanderers': Women Religious on the Colorado Mining Frontier, 1877–1917." *Frontiers* 15, no. 3: 27–47.

———. 1999. *Spirited Lives: How Nuns Shaped Catholic Culture and American Life, 1836–1920.* Chapel Hill: Univ. of North Carolina Press.

Cole, Arthur Charles. 1940. *A Hundred Years of Mount Holyoke College: The Evolution of an Educational Ideal.* New Haven: Yale Univ. Press.

Comaroff, Jean, and John Comaroff. 1991, 1997. *Of Revelation and Revolution*. 2 vols. Chicago: Univ. of Chicago Press.

Conforti, Joseph A. 1993. "Mary Lyon, the Founding of Mount Holyoke College, and the Cultural Revival of Jonathan Edwards." *Religion and American Culture* 3: 69–89.

Cook, Nancy. 2003. "Stayin' Alive: The Constitution of Subjectivity Among Western Women in Gilgit, Pakistan." Ph.D diss., Sociology, York Univ., Canada.

———. 2006. "Bazaar Stories of Gender, Sexuality and Imperial Spaces in Gilgit, Northern Pakistan." *ACME: An International E-Journal for Critical Geographies* 5, no. 2:230–57. http://www.acme-journal.org/index.html.

Cott, Nancy. 1997. *The Bonds of Womanhood: "Woman's Sphere" in New England, 1780–1835*. 2nd ed. New Haven: Yale Univ. Press.

Cottrell, Michael. 1999. "The Irish in Saskatchewan, 1850–1930: A Study of Intergenerational Ethnicity." *Prairie Forum* 24: 185–209.

Craig, Robert. 1997. "Christianity and Empire: A Case Study of American Protestant Colonialism and Native Americans." *American Indian Culture and Research Journal* 21: 1–41.

Cresswell, Tim. 1996. *In Place/Out of Place: Geography, Ideology and Transgression*. Minneapolis: Univ. of Minnesota Press.

Crosse-Upcott, A. 1960. "The Origin of the Majimaji Revolt." *Man* 97, 98.

Cuthbert, Alexander R. 1995. "The Right to the City: Surveillance, Private Interest and the Public Domain in Hong Kong." *Cities* 12, no. 5: 293–310.

Daack, Rachel. 2004. "Casting Aside the Veil: Geography, Religion, and the BVM Sister-Teachers." Paper presented at the Annual Meeting of the Association of American Geographers, Philadelphia.

Dahles, Heidi, and Karin Bras. 1999. "Entrepreneurs in Romance Tourism in Indonesia." *Annals of Tourism Research* 26: 267–93.

Davison, Andrew. 2003. "Turkey, a 'Secular' State? The Challenge of Description." *South Atlantic Quarterly* 102, no. 2/3: 333–50.

De Villiers, C. C. 1996. *Geslag Registers Van Die Ou Kaapse Families*. 3 vols. Cape Town: A. A. Balkema.

Demirtaş, Sibel, and Iştar Gözaydın. 1997. "Varoşlar Kente Indi." ('Varoş' Has Entered the City.) *Istanbul* 23: 82–87.

DeRogatis, Amy. 2003. *Moral Geography: Maps, Missionaries, and the American Frontier*. New York: Columbia Univ. Press.

Desforges, Luke. 1998. "Checking Out the Planet: Global Representations/Local Identities and Youth Travel." In *Cool Places: Geographies of Youth Cultures*, edited by Tracey Skelton and Gill Valentine, 175–94. London: Routledge.

Dikec, Mustafa. 2001. "Justice and the Spatial Imagination." *Environment and Planning A* 33: 1785–805.

Domosh, Mona, and Joni Seager. 2001. *Putting Women in Place: Feminist Geographers Make Sense of the World.* New York: Guilford Press.

Douglas, Mary. 1984. *Purity and Danger: An Analysis of the Concept of Pollution.* London: Routledge.

Du Toit, André. 1983. "No Chosen People: The Myth of the Calvinist Origins of Afrikaner Nationalism and Racial Ideology." *American Historical Review* 88: 920–52.

Durakbaşa, Ayşe. 1998. "Cumhuriyet Döneminde Modern Kadın ve Erkek Kimliklerinin Oluşumu: Kemalist Kadın Kimliği ve 'Münevver Erkekler.'" [Construction of women's and men's identities in the republic: Identity of the Kemalist woman and 'enlightened men.'] *75 Yılda Kadınlar ve Erkekler.* [Women and men in 75 years.] Istanbul: Tarih Vakfı [Historical Foundation], 29–50.

Dwyer, Claire. 1997. "Contested Identities: Challenging Dominant Representations of Young British Muslim Women." In *Cool Places: Geographies of Youth Cultures,* edited by Tracey Skelton and Gill Valentine, 50–65. London: Routledge.

———. 1999a. "Contradictions of Community: Questions of Identity for Young British Muslim Women." *Environment and Planning A* 31: 53–68.

———. 1999b. "Veiled Meanings: Young British Women and the Negotiation of Differences." *Gender, Place, and Culture* 6: 5–26.

———. 2000. "Negotiating Diasporic Identities: Young British South Asian Muslim Women." *Women's Studies International Forum* 23: 475–86.

Dyck, Isabel, and Arlene T. McLaren. 2004. "Telling It Like It Is? Constructing Accounts of Settlement with Immigrant and Refugee Women in Canada." *Gender, Place, and Culture* 11: 513–34.

Eason, Andrew Mark. 2003. *Women in God's Army: Gender and Equality in the Early Salvation Army.* Waterloo: Wilfred Laurier Univ. Press.

Ebaugh, Helene Rose. 1993. "Patriarchal Bargains and Latent Avenues of Social Mobility: Nuns in the Roman Catholic Church." *Gender and Society* 7: 400–14.

ECHR (European Court of Human Rights). 2004. "Chamber Judgments in the Cases of Leyla Şahin v. Turkey and Zeynep Tekin v. Turkey." 29 June, http://www.echr.coe.int.

Eigler, Friederike. 1998. "Engendering German Nationalism: Gender and Race in Frieda von Bülow's Colonial Writings." In *The Imperialist Imagination: German Colonialism and Its Legacy,* edited by Sara Friedrichsmeyer, Sara Lennox, and Susanne Zantop, 69–85. Ann Arbor: Univ. of Michigan Press.

Eliade, Mircea. 1959. *The Sacred and the Profane: The Nature of Religion.* New York: Harcourt Brace Jovanovich.

Elphick, Richard. 1977. *Kraal and Castle, Khoikhoi and the Founding of White South Africa.* New Haven: Yale Univ. Press.

Elphick, Richard, and Hermann Giliomee. 1989a. "The Origins and Entrenchment of European Dominance at the Cape, 1652–1840." In *The Shaping of Southern African Society, 1652–1840,* edited by Richard Elphick and Hermann Giliomee, 521–66. Cape Town: Maskew Miller Longman.

———, eds. 1989b. *The Shaping of Southern African Society, 1652–1840.* Cape Town: Maskew Miller Longman.

Elphick, Richard, and V. C. Malherbe. 1989. "The Khoisan to 1828." In *The Shaping of Southern African Society, 1652–1840,* edited by Richard Elphick and Hermann Giliomee, 3–65. Cape Town: Maskew Miller Longman.

Elphick, Richard, and Robert Shell. 1989. "Intergroup Relations: Khoikhoi, Settlers, Slaves and Free Blacks." In *The Shaping of Southern African Society, 1652–1840,* edited by Richard Elphick and Hermann Giliomee, 184–239. Cape Town: Maskew Miller Longman.

Elster, Jon. 1983. *Sour Grapes: Studies in the Subversion of Rationality.* Cambridge: Cambridge Univ. Press.

England, Kim. 1994. "Getting Personal: Reflexivity, Positionality, and Feminist Research." *Professional Geographer* 46: 80–89.

Entwistle, Joanne. 2000. *The Fashioned Body: Fashion, Dress and Modern Social Theory.* Cambridge: Polity Press.

———. 2001. "The Dressed Body." In *Body Dressing,* edited by Joanne Entwistle and Elizabeth Wilson, 33–55. Oxford: Berg.

Entwistle, Joanne, and Elizabeth Wilson. 2001. Introduction to *Body Dressing,* edited by Joanne Entwistle and Elizabeth Wilson, 1–12. Oxford: Berg.

Evans, Richard. 1976. *The Feminist Movement in Germany: 1894–1933.* London: Sage Publications.

Fainstein, Susan. 1994. *The City Builders: Property, Politics, and Planning in London and New York.* Oxford: Blackwell.

Falah, Ghazi-Walid, and Caroline Nagel, eds. 2005. *Geographies of Muslim Women: Gender, Religion, and Space.* New York: Guilford Press.

Fast, Vera K., ed. 1999. *Companions of the Peace: Diaries and Letters of Monica Storrs, 1931–1939.* Toronto: Univ. of Toronto Press.

Fellman, Jerome, Arthur Getis, and Judith Getis, 2001. *Human Geography: Landscapes of Human Activities.* 6th ed. New York: McGraw-Hill.

Felmlee, Diane. 1984. "The Dynamics of Women's Job Mobility." *Work and Occupations* 11, no. 3: 259, 23.

Fenster, Tovi. 1999a. "Culture, Human Rights and Planning (as Control) for Minority Women in Israel." In *Gender, Planning and Human Rights,* edited by Tovi Fenster, 39–54. London: Routledge.

———. 1999b. "Space for Gender: Cultural Roles of the Forbidden and the Permitted." *Environment and Planning D: Society and Space* 17: 227–46.

———. 2000. "Ashkenazi Man–Ethiopian Woman: Between Centralistic and Social Planning." *Panim: Journal of Culture, Society and Education* 13: 54–60.

———. 2002. "Planning as Control: Cultural and Gendered Manipulation and Mis-use of Knowledge." *Hagar: International Social Science Review* 1: 67–84.

———. 2004. *The Global City and the Holy City: Narratives on Planning, Knowledge and Diversity.* London: Pearson.

———. 2005. "Identity Issues and Local Governance: Women's Everyday Life in the City." *Social Identities* 11, no. 1: 21–36.

Fessenden, Tracy. 2000. "The Convent, the Brothel, and the Protestant Woman's Sphere." *Signs* 25, no. 2: 451–78.

Fisk[e], Fidelia. 1866. *Recollections of Mary Lyon, with Selections from Her Instructions to the Pupils in Mt. Holyoke Female Seminary.* Boston: American Tract Society.

Forster, E. M. 1942. *A Passage to India.* London: J. M. Dent.

Foucault, Michel. 1977. *Language, Counter-Memory, Practice: Selected Essays and Interviews.* Oxford: Blackwell.

———. 1979. *Discipline and Punish: The Birth of the Prison.* New York: Vintage.

———. 1984. "Right of Death and Power Over Life." In *The Foucault Reader,* edited by Paul Rabinow. New York: Pantheon.

———. 1988. "Technologies of the Self." In *Technologies of the Self: A Seminar with Michel Foucault,* edited by L. Martin, H. Gutman, P. Hutton, eds. Amherst: Univ. of Massachusetts Press.

Frederiksen, Elke. 1981. Introduction to *Die Frauenfrage in Deutschland 1865–1915: Texte und Dokumente* [The women's question in Germany 1865–1915: Texts and documents], edited by Elke Frederiksen. Universal Bibliothek.

Fredrickson, George M. 1981. *White Supremacy: A Comparative Study in American and South African History.* New York: Oxford Univ. Press.

Friedrichsmeyer, Sara, Sara Lennox, and Susanne Zantop. 1998. Introduction to *The Imperialist Imagination: German Colonialism and Its Legacy,* edited by Sara Friedrichsmeyer, Sara Lennox, and Susanne Zantop, 1–29. Ann Arbor: Univ. Michigan Press.

Furnivall, J. S. 1944. *Netherlands India: A Study of Plural Economy.* Cambridge: Cambridge Univ. Press.

Garcia-Ramon, Maria-Dolores. 2003. "Gender and the Colonial Encounter in the Arab World: Examining Women's Experiences and Narratives." *Environment and Planning D: Society and Space* 21: 653–72.

Gerstner, Jonathan N. 1991. *The Thousand Generation Covenant: Dutch Reformed Covenant Theology and Group Identity in Colonial South Africa, 1652–1814.* Leiden: E. S. Brill.

———. 1997. "A Christian Monopoly: The Reformed Church and Colonial Society Under Dutch Rule." In *Christianity in South Africa: A Political, Cultural and Social History,* edited by Richard Elphick and Rodney Davenport. Oxford: James Curry.

Gilchrist, Beth Bradford. 1910. *The Life of Mary Lyon.* Boston: Houghton Mifflin Company.

Giliomee, Hermann. 2003. *The Afrikaners: Biography of a People.* Charlottesville: Univ. of Virginia Press.

Ginzberg, Lori D. 1990. *Women and the Work of Benevolence: Morality, Politics and Class in the Nineteenth Century United States.* New Haven: Yale Univ. Press.

Glaser, Barney G., and Anselm L. Strauss. 1967. *The Discovery of Grounded Theory: Strategies for Qualitative Research.* Chicago: Aldine Publishing Company.

Gökarıksel, Banu. 1998. "Consumption Sites in Globalizing Cities: The Case of Akmerkez in Istanbul." Masters thesis, Sociology, Boğaziçi Univ., Istanbul.

———. 2003. "Situated Modernities: Geographies of Identity, Urban Space and Globalization." Ph.D diss., Univ. of Washington.

Gökarıksel, Banu, and Katharyne Mitchell. 2005. "Veiling, Secularism and the Neoliberal Subject." *Global Networks* 5, no. 2: 147–65.

Göle, Nilüfer. 1996. *The Forbidden Modern: Civilization and Veiling.* Ann Arbor: Univ. Michigan Press.

———. 1997a. "The Gendered Nature of the Public Sphere." *Public Culture* 10, no. 1: 61–81.

———. 1997b. "The Quest for the Islamic Self Within the Context of Modernity." In *Rethinking Modernity and National Identity in Turkey,* edited by Sibel Bozdoğan and Reşat Kasaba, 81–94. Seattle: Univ. of Washington Press.

———. 1999. *Islamın Yeni Kamusal Yüzleri.* [The new public faces of Islam.] Istanbul: Metis.

———. 2000. "Snapshots of Islamic Modernities." *Daedalus,* Winter, 91–117.

———. 2002. "Islam in Public: New Visibilities and New Imaginaries." *Public Culture* 14, no. 1: 173–90.

Graham-Brown, Sarah. 2003. "The Seen, the Unseen and the Imagined: Private and Public Lives." In *Feminist Postcolonial Theory: A Reader,* edited by Reina Lewis and Sara Mills, 502–19. New York: Routledge.

Gratz, Katrin. 1998. "Walking on Women's Paths in Gilgit: Gendered Space, Boundaries and Boundary Crossing." In *Karakoram-Hindukush-Himalaya: Dynamics of Change,* edited by I. Stellrecht, 489–507. Koln: Culture Area Karakoram Scientific Studies, Rüdger Koppe Verlag.

Green, Elizabeth Alden. 1979. *Mary Lyon and Mount Holyoke: Opening the Gates.* Hanover: Univ. Press of New England.

Griffith, R. Marie. 1997. *God's Daughters: Evangelical Women and the Power of Submission.* Berkeley: Univ. of California Press.

Grimshaw, Patricia. 1989. *Paths of Duty: American Missionary Wives in Nineteenth-Century Hawaii.* Honolulu: Univ. of Hawaii Press.

Grosz, Elizabeth. 1997. "'Incriptions and Body Maps: Representations and the Corporeal." In *Space, Gender, Knowledge,* edited by Linda McDowell and Joanne Sharp, 236–47. London: Arnold.

Guelke, Jeanne Kay, and Karen M. Morin. 2001. "Gender, Nature, and Empire: Women Naturalists in Nineteenth Century British Travel Literature." *Transactions, Institute of British Geographers* 26: 306–26.

Guelke, Leonard. 1988. "The Anatomy of a Colonial Settler Population: Cape Colony 1657–1750." *International Journal of African Historical Studies* 21: 453–73.

———. 1989a. "The Origin of White Supremacy in South Africa: An Interpretation." *Social Dynamics* 20: 40–45.

———. 1989b. "White Farmers and Frontier Settlers, 1652." In *The Shaping of Southern African Society, 1652–1840,* edited by Richard Elphick and Hermann Giliomee, 66–108. Cape Town: Maskew Miller Longman.

Guelke, Leonard, and Robert Shell. 1983. "An Early Colonial Landed Gentry: Land and Wealth in the Cape Colony, 1682–1731." *Journal of Historical Geography* 9: 265–86.

———. 1992. "Landscape of Conquest: Frontier Water Alienation and Khoikhoi Strategies of Survival, 1652–1780." *Journal of Southern African Studies* 18: 801–24.

Guindi, Fadwa el. 2000. *Veil: Modesty, Privacy and Resistance.* Oxford: Berg.

Gülalp, Haldun. 2003. "Whatever Happened to Secularism? The Multiple Islams in Turkey." *South Atlantic Quarterly* 102, no. 2/3: 381–95.

Gupta, Akhil. 1995. "Blurred Boundaries: The Discourse of Corruption, the Culture of Politics and the Imagined State." *American Ethnologist* 22: 375–402.

Güzelaydın, Serdar. 1996. Editorial. *Galleria* 2.

Gwassa and John Iliffe, eds. 1967. *Records of the Maji Maji Rising.* Nairobi: East African Publishing House.

Hackett, David G. 1995. "Gender and Religion in American Culture, 1870–1930." *Religion and American Culture* 5, no. 2: 127–57.

Hagan, Jacqueline, and Helen R. Ebaugh. 2003. "Calling Upon the Sacred: Migrants' Use of Religion in the Migration Process." *International Migration Review* 37: 1145–62.

Hall, Timothy, and Phil Hubbard. 1996. "The Entrepreneurial City: New Urban Politics, New Geographies?" *Progress in Human Geography* 20, no. 2: 153–74.

Hanson, Susan, and Geraldine Pratt. 1991. "Job Search and the Occupational Segregation of Women." *Annals of the Association of American Geographers* 81, no. 2: 229–53.

Harvey, David. 1989. *The Condition of Postmodernity.* Oxford: Basil Blackwell.

Harvey, David L., and Michael H. Reed. 1996. "The Culture of Poverty: An Ideological Analysis." *Sociological Perspectives* 39, no. 4: 32.

Hassing, Per. 1970. "German Missionaries and the Maji Maji Rising." *African Historical Studies* 3: 2.

Hasson, Shlomo. 1996. *The Struggle of the Cultural Character of Jerusalem.* Jerusalem: Floersheimer Institute.

———. 2002. *The Struggle for Hegemony in Jerusalem: Secular and Ultra-Orthodox Urban Politics.* Jerusalem: Floersheimer Institute.

Hasson, Shlomo, and Amiram Gonen. 1997. *The Cultural Tension Within Jerusalem's Jewish Population.* Jerusalem: Floersheimer Institute.

Heaney, Jane Francis. 1993. *A Century of Pioneering: A History of the Ursuline Nuns in New Orleans, 1727–1827.* New Orleans: Ursuline Sisters of New Orleans.

Herod, Andrew. 2003. "Scale: The Local and the Global." In *Key Concepts in Geography,* edited by Sarah L. Holloway, Stephen P. Rice, and Gill Valentine, 229–47. London: Sage.

Herod, Andrew, and Melissa Wright, eds. 2002. *Geographies of Power: Placing Scale.* Malden, Mass: Blackwell.

Herrera, Linda. 2001. "Downveiling: Gender and the Contest Over Culture in Cairo." *Middle East Report* 219: 16–19.

Hervieu-Léger, Danièle. 2002. "Space and Religion: New Approaches to Religious Spatiality in Modernity." *International Journal of Urban and Regional Research* 26: 99–105.

Hiebert, Daniel, and David Ley. 2003. "Assimilation, Cultural Pluralism, and Social Exclusion Among Ethnic Groups in Vancouver." *Urban Geography* 24: 16–44.

Higham, C. L. 2001. "'A Hewer of Wood and a Drover of Water': Expectations of Protestant Missionary Women on the Western Frontiers of Canada and the United States, 1830–1900." *Canadian Review of American Studies* 31: 447–70.

Hill, Patricia Ruth 1985. *The World Their Household: The American Woman's Foreign Mission Movement and Cultural Transformation.* Ann Arbor: Univ. of Michigan Press.

Hitchcock, Edward (anon.) 1858. *The Power of Christian Benevolence Illustrated in the Life and Labors of Mary Lyon.* New York: American Tract Society.

Holland, Patrick, and Graham Huggan. 1998. *Tourists with Typewriters: Critical Reflections on Contemporary Travel Writing.* Ann Arbor: Univ. of Michigan Press.

Holloway, Julian, and Oliver Valins. 2002. "Editorial: Placing Religion and Spirituality in Geography." *Social and Cultural Geography* 3: 5–9.

Hondagneu-Sotelo, Pierrette. 1994. *Gendered Transitions: Mexican Experiences of Immigration.* Berkeley: Univ. of California Press.

Hopkins, Jeffrey. 1991. "West Edmonton Mall as a Centre for Social Interaction." *Canadian Geographer* 35, no. 3: 268–79.

Horowitz, Helen Lefkowitz. 1984. *Alma Mater: Design and Experience in the Women's Colleges from the Nineteenth-Century Beginnings to the 1930s.* Boston: Beacon Press.

Huber, Mary Taylor, and Nancy C. Lutkehaus, eds. 1999. *Gendered Missions: Women and Men in Missionary Discourse and Practice.* Ann Arbor: Univ. of Michigan Press.

Hume, Susan E. 2003. "Belgian Settlement and Society in the Indiana Rust Belt." *Geographical Review* 93: 30–50.

Hunter, Jane. 1984. *The Gospel of Gentility: American Women Missionaries in Turn-of-the-Century China.* New Haven: Yale Univ. Press.

Hurh, Won Moo, and Kwang Chung Kim. 1984. *Korean Immigrants in America: A Structural Analysis of Ethnic Confinement and Adhesive Adaptation.* Cranbury, N.J.: Associated Univ. Presses.

Iliffe, John. 1967. "The Organization of the Maji-maji Rebellion." *Journal of African History* 8: 3.

———. 1969. *Tanganyika under German Rule, 1905–1912.* London: Cambridge Univ. Press.

Ingersoll, Julie. 2003. *Evangelical Christian Women.* New York: New York Univ. Press.

Insel, Ahmet. 2003. "The AKP and Normalizing Democracy in Turkey." *South Atlantic Quarterly* 102, no. 2/3: 293–309.

Iversen, Joan S. 1997. *The Anti-Polygamy Controversy in U.S. Women's Movements, 1880–1925: A Debate on the American Home.* New York: Garland Publishing.

Jackson, Peter, and Nigel Thrift. 1995. "Geographies of Consumption." In *Acknowledging Consumption: A Review of New Studies,* edited by D. Miller, 204–37. London: Routledge.

Jackson, Robert. 1970. "Resistance to the German Invasion of the Tanganyikan Coast, 1888–1891." In *Protest and Power in Black Africa,* edited by Robert Rotberg and Ali Mazrui, 36–79. New York: Oxford Univ. Press.

Jenkins, Olivia. 2003. "Photography and Travel Brochures: The Circle of Representation." *Tourism Geographies* 5, no. 3: 305–28.

Kadıoğlu, Ayşe. 1998. "Cinselliğin Inkari: Büyük Toplumsal Projelerin Nesnesi Olarak Türk Kadınları." [Denial of sexuality: Turkish women as the object of social projects.] *75 Yılda Kadınlar ve Erkekler.* [Women and men in 75 years.] Istanbul: Tarih Vakfı [Historical Foundation], 89–100.

Kandiyoti, Deniz. 1988. "Bargaining with Patriarchy." *Gender and Society* 2: 274–90.

———. 1997. "Gendering the Modern: On Missing Dimensions in the Study of Turkish Modernity." In *Rethinking Modernity and National Identity in Turkey,* edited by Sibel Bozdoğan and Reşat Kasaba, 113–132. Seattle: Univ. of Washington Press.

———. 1998. "Afterword: Some Awkward Questions on Women and Modernity in Turkey." In *Remaking Women: Feminism and Modernity in the Middle East,* edited by L. Abu-Lughod, 270–87. Princeton: Princeton Univ. Press.

Kay, Jeanne. 1997. "Sweet Surrender but What's the Gender? Nature and the Body in the Writings of Mormon Women." In *Thresholds in Feminist Geography: Difference, Methodology, Representation,* edited by John Paul Jones III, Heidi J. Nast, and Susan M. Roberts, 361–82. Lanham, Md.: Rowman and Littlefield.

Kelly, Sr. Dominic, trans. 2000. *Marie of the Incarnation, 1599–1672.* Carrtron, Sligo: Irish Ursuline Union.

Kim, Ai Ra. 1996. *Women Struggling for a New Life: The Role of Religion in the Cultural Passage from Korea to America.* Albany: State Univ. of New York Press.

Kim, Illsoo. 1981. *New Urban Immigrants: The Korean Community in New York.* Princeton: Princeton Univ. Press.

Kim, Jung Ha. 1997. *Bridge-Makers and Cross-Bearers: Korean American Women and the Church.* Atlanta: Scholars Press.

King, John, and Bradley Mayhew. 1998. *Pakistan.* Australia: Lonely Planet Publications.

Kinnaird, Vivian, and D. Hall, eds. 1994. *Tourism: A Gender Analysis.* New York: John Wiley and Sons.

Kjekshus. 1977. *Ecology Control and Economic Development in East African History: The Case of Tanzania 1850–1950.* Berkeley: Univ. of California Press.

Kofman, Eleonore. 1995. "Citizenship for Some but Not for Others: Spaces of Citizenship in Contemporary Europe." *Political Geography* 14: 121–37.

Kofman, Eleonore, and E. Labas, eds. 1996. *Writings on Cities: Henri Lefebvre.* Cambridge: Blackwell.

Kong, Lily. 2001. "Mapping 'New' Geographies of Religion: Politics and Poetics in Modernity." *Progress in Human Geography* 25: 211–34.

Kopf, Jennifer. 2005. "Spatial Strategies of Resistance to Anti-Islamic Animus in German East African Transportation, Labor, Education, and Social Policies." Ph.D. diss., Univ. of Kentucky.

Koponen, J. 1994. *Development for Exploitation: German Colonial Policies in Mainland Tanzania, 1884–1914.* Hamburg: Lit Verlag.

Kowinski, William. 1985. *The Malling of America: An Insider Look at Great Consumer Paradise.* New York: William Morrow.

Kostovicova, Denisa, and Albert Prestreshi. 2003. "Education, Gender, and Religion: Identity Transformations Among Kosovo Albanians in London." *Journal of Ethnic and Migration Studies* 29: 1079–96.

Kuran, Timar. 1995. *Private Truths, Public Lies: The Social Consequences of Preference Falsification.* Cambridge, Mass: Harvard Univ. Press.

Kwamena-Poh, Michael, John Tosh, Richard Waller, and Michael Tidy. 1982. *African History in Maps.* New York: Longman.

Kwon, Okun. 2000. "Religious Beliefs and Socioeconomic Aspects of Life of Buddhist and Protestant Korean Immigrants." Ph.D. diss., City Univ. of New York.

Kymlicka, Will. 1998. "Multicultural Citizenship." In *The Citizenship Debate,* edited by G. Shafir, 167–88. Minneapolis: Univ. of Minnesota Press.

Larcom, Lucy. 1986. *A New England Girlhood Outlined from Memory.* Boston: Northeastern Univ. Press.

Lean, David, dir. 1984. *A Passage to India.* Columbia Pictures.

Lefebvre, Henri. 1991a. *Critique of Everyday Life.* London: Verso.

———. 1991b. *The Production of Space.* Oxford: Cambridge Univ. Press.

Legassick, Martin. 1980. "The Frontier Tradition in South African Historiography." In *Economy and Society in Pre-Industrial South Africa,* edited by Shula Marks and Anthony Atmore. London: Longman.

Lehr, John C., and Yossi Katz. 1995. "Crown, Corporation and Church: The Role of Institutions in the Stability of Pioneer Settlements in the Canadian West, 1870–1914." *Journal of Historical Geography* 21: 413–29.

Leiris, Michel. 1988. "The Sacred in Everyday Life." In *The College of Sociology 1937–39,* edited by Denis Hollier, 24–31. Minneapolis: Univ. of Minnesota Press.

Levin, Jeffrey S., Robert J. Taylor, and Linda M. Chatters. 1994. "Race and Gender Differences in Religiosity Among Older Adults: Findings from Four National Surveys." *Journal of Gerontology* 49, no. 3: S137–45.

Levin, Miriam R. 2005. *Defining Women's Scientific Enterprise: Mount Holyoke Faculty and the Rise of American Science.* Hanover: Univ. Press of New England.

Lewis, Oscar. 1966. *La Vida: A Puerto Rican Family in the Culture of Poverty—San Juan and New York.* New York: Random House.

———. 1968. "The Culture of Poverty." In *On Understanding Poverty: Perspectives from the Social Sciences,* edited by D. P. Moynihan, 187–200. New York: Basic Books.

Lewis, Reina. 1999. "On Veiling, Vision and Voyage: Cross-Cultural Dressing and Narratives of Identity." *Interventions* 1, no. 4: 500–20.

Lindley, Susan Hill. 1996. *"You Have Stept Out of Your Place": A History of Women and Religion in America.* Louisville: Westminster John Knox Press.

Lofland, Lyn. 1998. *The Public Realm: Exploring the City's Quintessential Social Territory.* Walter De Gruyter.

Lonely Planet. 1998. *Pakistan.* London: Pilot Film and Television Productions.

Longhurst, Robyn. 2005. "The Body." In *Critical Concepts in Cultural Geography,* edited by D. Atkinson, Peter Jackson, David Sibley, and N. Washbourne, 91–97. London: I. B. Tauris.

Lowe, L. 1991. *Critical Terrains: French and British Orientalisms.* Ithaca: Cornell Univ. Press.

Lurie, A. 1992. *The Language of Clothes.* London: Bloomsbury.

Lyon, Mary. 1839. *Female Education: Tendencies of the Principles Embraced and the System Adopted in the Mount Holyoke Female Seminary.* South Hadley, Mass.

MacCannell, Dean. 1999. *The Tourist: A New Theory of the Leisure Class.* Berkeley: Univ. of California Press.

MacCrone, I. D. 1965. *Race Attitudes in South Africa: Historical Experimental and Psychological Studies.* Johannesburg: Witwatersrand Univ. Press.

MacDonald, Kenneth. 1998. "Push and Shove: Spatial History and the Construction of a Portering Economy in Northern Pakistan." *Comparative Studies in Society and History* 40: 287–317.

MacDonald, Kenneth, and David Butz. 1998. "Investigating Portering Relations as a Locus for Transcultural Interaction in the Karakoram Region of Northern Pakistan." *Mountain Research and Development* 18, no. 4: 333–43.

Macey, Marie. 1999. "Religion, Male Violence and the Control of Women: Pakistani Muslim Men in Bradford, UK." *Gender and Development* 7: 48–55.

Madge, Clare. 1997. "Public Parks and the Geography of Fear." *Tijdschrift Voor Economisch en Sociale Geografie* 88, no. 3: 237–50.

Manji, Irshad. 2004. *The Trouble with Islam: A Muslim's Call for Reform in Her Faith.* New York: St. Martin's Press.

Margolis, Maxine L. 2000. *True to Her Nature: Changing Advice to American Women.* Prospect Heights, Ill.: Waveland Press.

Marshall, Thomas H. 1950. *Citizenship and Social Class and Other Essays.* Cambridge: Cambridge Univ. Press.

Marston, Sallie. 2000. "The Social Construction of Scale." *Progress in Human Geography* 24, no. 2: 219–42.

———. 2004. "A Long Way from Home: Domesticating the Social Production of Scale." In *Scale and Geographic Inquiry: Nature, Society, and Method,* edited by Eric Sheppard and Robert B. McMaster, 170–91. London: Blackwell.

Martin, B. G. 1969. "Muslim Politics and Resistance to Colonial Rule: Shaykh Uways B. Muhammad Al-Barawi and the Qadiriya Brotherhood in East Africa." *Journal of African History* 10, no. 3: 471–86.

Massey, Doreen. 1994. *Space, Place and Gender.* Minneapolis: Univ. of Minnesota Press.

Mazumdar, Sonjay, and S. Mazumdar. 2001. "Rethinking Public and Private Space: Religion and Women in Muslim Society." *Journal of Architectural and Planning Research* 18: 302–24.

McClintock, Anne. 1995. *Imperial Leather.* New York: Routledge.

McDannell, Colleen. 1994. *The Christian Home in Victorian America, 1840–1900.* Bloomington: Indiana Univ. Press.

McMichael, C. 2002. "'Everywhere is Allah's place': Islam and the Everyday Life of Somali Women in Melbourne, Australia." *Journal of Refugee Studies* 15: 171–88.

Mernissi, Fatima. 1975. *Beyond the Veil.* Cambridge, Mass.: Schenkman.

Middleton, John. 1994. *The World of the Swahili: An African Mercantile Civilization.* New Haven: Yale Univ. Press.

Mihesuah, Devon A. 1993. *Cultivating the Rosebuds: The Education of Women at the Cherokee Female Seminary, 1851–1909.* Urbana: Univ. of Illinois Press.

Mills, Albert J., and Catherine Ryan. 2001. "Contesting the Spiritual Space: Patriarchy, Bureaucracy, and the Gendering of Women's Religious Orders." *Journal of Critical Postmodern Organization Science* 1, no. 4: 60–79.

Mills, Sara. 1991. *Discourses of Difference: An Analysis of Women's Travel Writing and Colonialism.* London: Routledge.

———. 1994. "Knowledge, Gender, and Empire." In *Writing Women and Space: Colonial and Postcolonial Geographies,* edited by Alison Blunt and Gillian Rose, 29–50. New York: Guilford.

Min, Pyung Gap. 1990. "Korean Immigrants in Los Angeles." Paper presented at the Conference on California's Immigrants in World Perspectives, Univ. of California at Los Angeles, April.

———. 1992. "The Structure and Social Functions of Korean Immigrant Churches in the United States." *International Migration Review* 26: 1370–94.

Mintz, Jerome. R. 1994. *Hasidic People: A Place in the New World*. London: Harvard Univ. Press.

Mitchell, Don. 1995. "The End of Public Space? People's Park, Definitions of the Public, and Democracy." *Annals of the Association of American Geographers* 85, no. 1: 108–33.

———. 2000. *Cultural Geography: A Critical Introduction*. Oxford: Blackwell.

———. 2003. *The Right to the City: Social Justice and the Right for Public Space*. New York: Guilford.

Mitchell, Timothy. 1988. *Colonising Egypt*. Cambridge: Cambridge Univ. Press.

———. 2000. *Questions of Modernity*. Minneapolis: Univ. Minnesota Press.

———. 2002. *Rule of Experts: Egypt, Techno-Politics, Modernity*. Berkeley: Univ. of California Press.

Mock, John, and Kimberly O'Neil. 1996. *Trekking in the Karakoram and Hindukush*. Berkeley: Lonely Planet Publications.

Moghadam, V. M., ed. 1994. *Gender and National Identity*. London: Zed Books.

Moghissi, Haideh. 1999. *Feminism and Islamic Fundamentalism: The Limits of Postmodern Analysis*. London: Zed Books.

Mogull, R. J. 2000. "Estimating Poverty Rates in a Metropolis: The Example of Los Angeles/Long Beach." *Journal of Sociology and Social Welfare* 27, no. 4: 258–38.

Molotch, Harvey, and John Logan. 1987. *Urban Fortunes: The Political Economy of Place*. Berkeley: Univ. of California Press.

Moodie, Donald. 1960. *The Record*. Cape Town: Balkema.

Moore Milroy, Beth, and Susan Wismer. 1994. "Communities, Work and Public/Private Sphere Models." *Gender, Place, and Culture* 1: 71–90.

Morin, Karen M. 2000. "(Anti?) Colonial Women Writing War." *New Zealand Geographer* 56: 22–29.

Morin, Karen M., and Lawrence D. Berg. 2001. "Gendering Resistance: British Colonial Narratives of Wartime New Zealand." *Journal of Historical Geography* 27, no. 2: 196–222.

Morin, Karen M., and Jeanne Kay Guelke. 1998. "Strategies of Representation, Relationship, and Resistance: British Women Travelers and Mormon Plural Wives, c. 1870–1890." *Annals of the Association of American Geographers* 88, no. 3: 437–63.

Morin, Karen, Robyn Longhurst, and Lynda Johnston. 2001. "(Troubling) Spaces of Mountains and Men: New Zealand's Mount Cook and Hermitage Lodge." *Social and Cultural Geography* 2, no. 2: 117–39.

Morris, Meaghan. 1998. *Too Soon Too Late: History in Popular Culture*. Bloomington: Indiana Univ. Press.

Moss, Pamela, ed. 2001. *Placing Autobiography in Geography.* New York: Syracuse Univ. Press.

Mueller, Elizabeth J. 1992. "Latin American Women Immigrants in Los Angeles: Conflicts between Home and Work Roles and Poverty." Ph.D diss., Univ. of California, Berkeley.

Murphy, Dervla. 1995. *Where the Indus Is Young: A Winter in Baltistan.* London Transatlantic Arts.

Nagar, Richa, Victoria Lawson, Linda McDowell, Susan Hanson. 2002. "Locating Globalization: Feminist (Re)Readings of the Subjects and Spaces of Globalization." *Economic Geography* 78, no. 3: 257–85.

National Archives of Tanzania and Archivschule Marburg—Institut für Archivwissenschaft. 1973. *The United Republic of Tanzania National Archives of Tanzania: Guide to the Archives,* volume 1. Dar es Salaam, Marburg.

Navaro-Yashin, Yael. 2002a. *Faces of the State: Secularism and Public Life in Turkey.* Princeton: Princeton Univ. Press.

———. 2002b. "The Market for Identities: Secularism, Islamism, Commodities." In *Fragments of Culture: The Everyday of Modern Turkey,* edited by Deniz Kandiyoti and Ayşe Saktanber, 221–53. New Brunswick, N.J.: Rutgers Univ. Press.

Naylor, S. K., and J. R. Ryan. 1998. "Ethnicity and Cultural Landscapes: Mosques, Guradwaras, and Mandirs in England and Wales." Paper presented at the Religion and Locality Conference, Univ. of Leeds.

Newton-King, Susan. 1999. *Masters and Servants on the Cape Eastern Frontier 1760–1803.* Cambridge: Cambridge Univ. Press.

Norton, William. 1998. *Human Geography.* 3rd ed. Toronto: Oxford Univ. Press.

Nussbaum, Martha C. 2000. *Women and Human Development.* Cambridge: Cambridge Univ. Press.

O'Reilly, Bernard. 1894. *The Mirror of True Womanhood; a Book of Instruction for Women in the World.* New York: P. J. Kennedy and Sons.

Öktem, Binnur. 2003. "Using the Global City Discourse in the Formation of the Central Business District of Istanbul." Ph.D. diss., Cardiff Univ.

Olsen, D. H., and Jeanne Kay Guelke. 2004. "Spatial Transgression and the BYU Jerusalem Centre Controversy." *Professional Geographer* 56: 503–15.

Öncü, Ayşe. 1995. "Packaging Islam: Cultural Politics on the Landscape of Turkish Commercial Television." *Public Culture* 8: 51–71.

———. 1999. "Istanbulites and Others: The Cultural Cosmology of Being Middle Class in the Era of Globalism." In *Istanbul: Between the Global and the Local,* edited by Çağlar Keyder, 95–119. Oxford: Rowman and Littlefield.

——. 2002. "Global Consumerism, Sexuality as Public Spectacle and the Cultural Re-mapping of Istanbul in the 1990s." *In Fragments of Culture: The Everyday of Modern Turkey,* edited by Deniz Kandiyoti and Ayşe Saktanber, 171–90. London: I. B. Tauris.

Ong, Aihwa. 1997. "Chinese Modernities: Narratives of Nation and Capitalism." In *Ungrounded Empires: The Cultural Politics of Modern Chinese Transnationalism,* edited by Aihwa Ong and Donald Nonini, 171–202. New York: Routledge.

Orange, Claudia. 1996. "The Maori People and the British Crown (1769–1840)." In *The Oxford Illustrated History of New Zealand,* edited by Keith Sinclair. Auckland: Oxford Univ. Press.

Ortner, Sherry. 1999. *Life and Death on Mt. Everest: Sherpas and Himalayan Mountain-eering.* Princeton: Princeton Univ. Press.

Özdalga, Elisabeth. 1998. *The Veiling Issue, Official Secularism and Popular Islam in Modern Turkey.* Surrey: Curzon Press.

Özdemir, Ayşe. 1999. "Socio-Morphological Transformations of Urban Space After the 1980s: A Study of Istanbul City Core In a Comparative Perspective." Ph.D diss., Middle East Technical Univ., Ankara.

Pain, Rachel. 1991. "Space, Sexual Violence and Social Control." *Progress in Human Geography* 15, no. 4: 415–31.

Park, Chris. 1994. *Sacred Worlds: An Introduction to Geography and Religion.* London: Routledge.

Pascoe, Peggy. 1990. *Relations of Rescue: The Search for Female Moral Authority in the American West, 1874–1939.* New York: Oxford Univ. Press.

Peleman, Kathleen. 2003. "Power and Territoriality: A Study of Moroccan Women in Antwerp." *Tijdschrift voor Economische en Sociale Geografie* 94: 151–63.

Pessar, Patricia R. 1999. "The Role of Gender, Households, and Social Networks in the Migration Process: A Review and Appraisal." In *The Handbook of International Migration: The American Experience,* edited by C. Hirschman, J. De Wind, and P. Kasinitz, 54–70. New York: Russell Sage Foundation.

Pieterse, Jan Nederveen. 1992. *White on Black: Images of Africa and Blacks in Western Popular Culture.* New Haven: Yale Univ. Press.

Porterfield, Amanda. 1997. *Mary Lyon and the Mount Holyoke Missionaries.* New York: Oxford Univ. Press.

Pratt, Mary Louise. 1992. *Imperial Eyes: Travel Writing and Transculturation.* New York: Routledge.

Purcell, Mark. 2003a. "Citizenship and the Right to the Global City: Reimagining the Capitalist World Order." *International Journal of Urban and Regional Studies* 27, no. 3: 564–90.

———. 2003b. "Islands of Practice and the Marston-Brenner Debate: Toward a More Synthetic Critical Human Geography." *Progress in Human Geography* 27: 317–32.

Radikal. 2004. "Teziç'ten Kamusal Örnek." [An example of "public" from Teziç.] *Radikal* (Istanbul) 1: 6.

Ramusack, Barbara. 1990. "Cultural Missionaries, Maternal Imperialists, Feminist Allies: British Women Activists in India, 1865–1945." *Women's Studies International Forum* 13, no. 4: 309–21.

Redmond, Patrick. 1975. "Maji Maji in Ungoni: A Reappraisal of Existing Historiography." *International Journal of African Historical Studies* 8.

Rigby, Cynthia L. 2000. "Exploring Our Hesitation: Feminist Theologies and the Nurture of Children." *Theology Today* 56, 4: 540–54.

Riggs, Maida Leonard, ed. 1996. *A Small Bit of Bread and Butter: Letters from the Dakota Territory, 1832–1869.* South Deerfield, Mass: Ash Grove Press.

Robert, Dana Lee. 1993. "Evangelist or Homemaker? Mission Strategies of Nineteenth-Century Missionary Wives in Burma and Hawaii." *International Bulletin of Missionary Research* 17: 4–12.

———. 1996. *American Women in Mission: A Social History of Their Thought and Practice Macon.* Mercer Univ. Press.

———. 2002. "The Influence of American Missionary Women on the World Back Home." *Religion and American Culture* 12: 59–89.

Rose, Nikolas. 1999. *Powers of Freedom: Reframing Political Thought.* Cambridge: Cambridge Univ. Press.

Rose, Gillian. 1997. "Situating Knowledges: Positionality, Reflexivities and Other Tactics." *Progress in Human Geography* 21: 305–20.

Ross, Robert. 1983. *Cape of Torments: Slavery and Resistance in South Africa.* London: Routledge.

———. 1993. *Beyond the Pale: Essays on the History of Colonial South Africa.* Hanover: Univ. Press of New England.

Rowbotham, Sheila. 1998. "'Hear an Indian Sister's Plea': Reporting the Work of 19th-Century British Female Missionaries." *Women's Studies International Forum* 21, no. 3: 247–61.

Ruddick, Susan. 1996. "Constructing Difference in Public Spaces: Race, Class, and Gender as Interlocking Systems." *Urban Geography* 17: 132–51.

Said, Edward. 1978. *Orientalism.* New York: Vintage Books.

Saktanber, Ayşe. 1997. "Formation of a Middle-Class Ethos and Its Quotidian: Revitalizing Islam in Urban Turkey." In *Space, Culture and Power: New Identities in Globalizing Cities,* edited by Peter Weyland and Ayşe Öncü. London: Zed Books.

———. 2002. "'We Pray Like You Have Fun': New Islamic Youth in Turkey Between Intellectualism and Popular Culture." In *Fragments of Culture: The Everyday of Modern Turkey,* edited by Deniz Kandiyoti and Ayşe Saktanber, 254–76. London: I. B. Tauris.

Sayyid, Bobby S. 1997. *A Fundamental Fear: Eurocentrism and the Emergence of Islam.* London: Zed Books.

Scammel, G. V. 1980. *The World Encompassed: The First European Maritime Empires c. 800–1650.* Berkeley: Univ. of California Press.

Schecher, Solomon, and Michael Friedlander. n.d. Erub. *Jewish Encyclopedia.com.* http://www.jewishencyclopedia.com.

Scheyvens, Regina. 2002. "Backpacker Tourism and Third World Development." *Annals of Tourism Research* 29, no. 1: 144–64.

Scott, James. 1998. *Seeing Like a State: How Certain Schemes to Improve Human Condition Have Failed.* New Haven: Yale Univ. Press.

Scott, Paul. 1966. *The Jewel in the Crown.* London: Heinemann.

Secor, Anna. 2002. "The Veil and Urban Space in Istanbul: Women's Dress, Mobility and Islamic Knowledge." *Gender, Place and Culture* 9, no. 1: 5–22.

———. 2003. "Citizenship in the City: Identity, Community, and Rights Among Women Migrants to Istanbul." *Urban Geography* 24: 147–68.

———. 2004. "'There Is an Istanbul that Belongs to Me': Citizenship, Space and Identity in the City." *Annals of Association of American Geographers* 94, no. 2: 352–68.

———. 2005. "Islamism, Democracy and the Political Production of the Headscarf Issue in Turkey." In *Geographies of Muslim Women: Gender, Religion and Space,* edited by Ghazi-Walid Falah and Caroline Nagel, 203–25. New York: Guilford.

Segale, Blandina. 1990. "If You Are Not Afraid, Neither Am I." In *So Much To Be Done: Women Settlers on the Mining and Ranching Frontier,* edited by Ruth B. Moynihan, Susan Armitage, and Christiane Fischer Dichamp, 237–67. Lincoln: Univ. Nebraska Press.

Sen, Amartya K. 1992. *Inequality Reexamined.* New York: Russell Sage Foundation.

———. 1997. "Individual Preference as the Basis of Social Choice: Social Choice Re-Examined." In *Proceedings of the International Economic Association Conference* held at Schoss Hernstein, Berndorf, Austria, vol. 1, edited by K. J. Arrow, A. K. Sen, K. Suzumura. New York: Macmillan Press.

———. 1999. *Development as Freedom.* New York: Anchor Books.

Sharpe, Jenny. 1993. *Allegories of Empire: The Figure of Woman in the Colonial Text.* Minneapolis: Univ. of Minnesota Press.

Shell, Robert. 1994. *Children of Bondage: A Social History of the Slave Society at the Cape of Good Hope, 1652–1838.* Hanover: Univ. Press of New England.

Sheppard, Eric, and Robert B. McMaster. 2004. *Scale and Geographic Inquiry: Nature, Society, and Method.* London: Blackwell.

Shilav, Yosef. 1997. *Governance in an Ultra Orthodox City.* Jerusalem: Floersheimer Institute.

Shiva, Vandana. 1988. *Staying Alive: Women, Ecology, and Development in India.* London: Zed Books.

Sibley, David. 1995. *Geographies of Exclusion: Society and Difference in the West.* London: Routledge.

———. 1998. "Problematizing Exclusion: Reflections on Space, Difference and Knowledge." *International Planning Studies* 3, no. 1: 93–100.

Singh, Sarina, Lindsey Brown, Owen Bennett Jones, John Mock, Kimberly O'Neil, and Samina Yasmeen. 2004. *Pakistan and the Karakoram Highway.* China: Lonely Planet Publications.

Sklar, Katharine Kish. 1973. *Catherine Beecher: A Study in American Domesticity.* New Haven: Yale Univ. Press.

———. 1979. "The Founding of Mount Holyoke College." In *Women of America: A History,* edited by Carol Ruth Berkin and Mary Beth Norton, 177–201. Boston: Houghton Mifflin Co.

Small, Mario L., and Katherine Newman. 2001. "Urban Poverty After the Truly Disadvantaged: The Rediscovery of the Family, the Neighborhood, and Culture." *Annual Review of Sociology* 27: 23–45.

Smith, Helmut Walser. 1998. "The Talk of Genocide, the Rhetoric of Miscegenation: Notes on Debates in the German Reichstag Concerning Southwest Africa, 1904–1914." In *Complicating Categories: Gender, Class, Race and Ethnicity,* edited by Eileen Boris and Angelique Janssens. Cambridge: Cambridge Univ. Press.

Smith, Neil. 1992. "Geography, Difference and the Politics of Scale." In *Postmodernism and the Social Sciences,* edited by Joe Doherty, Elspeth Graham, and Mo Mallek, 57–79. London: Macmillan.

Sorensen, Anders. 2003. "Backpacker Ethnography." *Annals of Tourism Research* 30, no. 4: 847–67.

Sorkin, Michael, ed. 1992. *Variations on a Theme Park: The New American City and the End of Public Space.* New York: Hill and Wang.

Spain, Daphne. 1992. *Gendered Spaces.* Chapel Hill: Univ. of North Carolina Press.

———. 2001. *How Women Saved the City.* Minneapolis: Univ. Minnesota Press.

Staeheli, Lynn. 1994. "Empowering Political Struggle: Spaces and Scales of Resistance." *Political Geography* 13: 387–91.

Sterling, Dorothy, ed. 1984. *We Are Your Sisters: Black Women in the Nineteenth Century.* New York: W. W. Norton.

Stitziel, Judd. 1996. "God, the Devil, Medicine, and the Word: A Controversy Over Ecstatic Women in Protestant Middle Germany 1691–1693." *Central European History* 29: 309–38.

Stollowsy, Otto. 1988. "On the Background to the Rebellion in German East Africa 1905–1906." *International Journal of African Historical Studies* 21: 4.

Stowe, Sarah D. Locke. 1887. *History of Mount Holyoke Seminary During Its First Half Century, 1837–1887.* South Hadley, Mass.: Mount Holyoke Seminary.

Strasser, Ulrike. 2001. "Bones of Contention: Catholic Nuns Resist Their Enclosure." In *Unspoken Worlds: Women's Religious Lives,* edited by Nancy Auer Falk and Rita Gross. 3rd ed. Wadsworth.

Stump, Roger. 2000. *Boundaries of Faith: Geographical Perspectives on Religious Fundamentalism.* Lanham: Rowman and Littlefield.

Sunseri, Thaddeus. 1997. "Famine and Wild Pigs: Gender Struggles and the Outbreak of the Maji Maji War in Uzaramo (Tanzania)." *Journal of African History* 38.

Swain, M. B., and Janet Momsen, eds. 2002. *Gender/Tourism/Fun(?)/.* Elmsford, N.Y.: Cognizant Communication Corp.

Sweeney, Megan M. 2002. "Two Decades of Family Change: The Shifting Economic Foundations of Marriage." *American Sociological Review* 67, no. 1: 132–47.

Sweet, Leonard I. 1985. "The Female Seminary Movement and Woman's Mission in Antebellum America." *Church History* 54: 41–55.

Sweetman, Paul. 2001. "Shop-Window Dummies? Fashion, the Body, and Emergent Socialities." In *Body Dressing,* edited by Joanne Entwistle and Elizabeth Wilson, 59–78. Oxford: Berg.

Swidler, Ann. 1986. "Culture in Action: Symbols and Strategies." *American Sociological Review* 51: 273–86.

Tanzanian National Archives, Dar es Salaam, German Records Division, Records of the German Colonial Government, Section 9. Kirchen—und Schulwesen [church and school matters]; B. Sonstige Kirchensachen, Islam [other church affairs, Islam]. "Ergreifung von Maßnahmen gegen die Ausbreitung unerwünschter islamischer Bewegungen insbesondere gegen die angeblichen antieuropäischen Hetzereien der im Juli 1908 in Lindi aufgetauchten Mekkabriefe sowie Lageberichete verschiedener Bezirksämter über den Islam." [Actions taken against the spread of undesired Islamic movements, in particular against the supposedly anti-European excitement of the Mecca letter which appeared in Lindi in July 1908 as well as reports by various district officers on the situation regarding Islam.] Volume 1, G 9/46; volume 2, G 9/47; volume 3, G 9/48.

Taylor, Robert J., Jacqueline Mattis, and Linda M. Chatters. 1999. "Subjective Religiosity Among African Americans: A Synthesis of Findings from Five National Samples." *Journal of Black Psychology* 25, no. 4: 524–43.

TCSCR. 1999. "Geleceği Gören Kazanır." [The winners are those who can forecast.] *ARASTA*, 28–32.

Templin, J. Alton. 1984. *Ideology on a Frontier: The Theological Foundation of Afrikaner Nationalism.* Westport, Conn.: Greenwood.

Thom, H. B., ed. 1954. *Journal of Jan van Riebeeck, 1651–1662.* Cape Town: Balkema.

Thomas, Louise Porter. 1937. *Seminary Militant: An Account of the Missionary Movement at Mount Holyoke Seminary and College.* South Hadley, Mass: Department of English.

Thompson, Leonard. 1969. "Co-operation and Conflict: The High Veld." In *The Oxford History of South Africa,* edited by Monica Wilson and Leonard Thompson. Oxford: Oxford Univ. Press.

Tonkovich, Nicole. 1997. *Domesticity with a Difference: The Nonfiction of Catharine Beecher,* Sarah J. Hale, Fanny Fern, and Margaret Fuller. Jackson: Univ. of Mississippi.

Turner, L., and J. Ash. 1975. *The Golden Hordes: International Tourism on the Pleasure Periphery.* London: Constable.

Urry, John. 2002. *The Tourist Gaze.* 2nd ed. London: Sage.

Valentine, Gill. 1989. "The Geography of Women's Fear." *Area* 21, no. 4: 385–90.

———. 1996. "(Re)Negotiating the 'Heterosexual' Street: Lesbian Productions of Space." In *BodySpace: Destabilising Geographies of Gender and Sexuality,* edited by Nancy Duncan, 146–55. London: Routledge.

———. 2001. *Social Geographies: Space and Society.* Harlow, England: Pearson Education.

———. 2002. "People Like Us: Negotiating Sameness and Difference in the Research Process." In *Feminist Geography in Practice,* edited by Pamela Moss, 116–26. Cambridge, Mass.: Blackwell.

Valins, Oliver. 2000. "Institutionalised Religion: Sacred Texts and Jewish Spatial Practice." *Geoforum* 31: 575–86.

———. 2003. "Stubborn Identities and the Construction of Socio-Spatial Boundaries: Ultra-Orthodox Jews Living in Contemporary Britain." *Transactions of the Institute of British Geographers* 28: 158–75.

Veijola, Soila, and Eeva Jokinen. 1994. "The Body in Tourism." *Theory, Culture and Society* 11: 125–51.

Viljoen, Russell. 1995. "Till Murder Do Us Part: The Story of Griet and Henrik Eksteen." *South African Historical Journal* 33: 13–32.

———. 2001. "Aboriginal Khoikhoi Servants and Their Masters in Colonial Swellendam, South Africa, 1745–1795." *Agricultural History* 75: 28–51.

Webster, A. R. 1995. *Found Wanting: Women, Christianity, and Sexuality.* London: Cassell.

Weiss, Robert S. 1994. *Learning from Strangers: The Art and Method of Qualitative Interview Studies.* New York: Maxwell Macmillan International.

Werkerle, Gerda. 2000. "Women's Rights to the City." In *Democracy, Citizenship and the Global City,* edited by E. Isin, 203–17. London: Routledge.

White, Jenny. 1999. "Islamic Chic." In *Istanbul Between the Global and the Local,* edited by Çağlar Keyder, 77–91. Lanham, Md.: Rowman and Littlefield.

———. 2002. *Islamist Mobilization in Turkey: Studies in Modernity and National Identity.* Seattle: Univ. of Washington Press.

———. 2002. "The Islamist Paradox." In *Fragments of Culture: The Everyday of Modern Turkey,* edited by Deniz Kandiyoti and A. Saktanber, 191–217. New Brunswick, N.J.: Rutgers Univ. Press.

Wiesner-Hanks, Merry E. 2000. *Christianity and Sexuality in the Early Modern World: Regulating Desire, Reforming Practice.* New York: Routledge.

Wildenthal, Lora. 2001. *German Women for Empire: 1884–1945.* Durham: Duke Univ. Press.

Wills, Anne Blue. 1997. "'Memorial Stones': The Geography of Womanhood in *Heathen Woman's Friend,* 1869–1879." *Religion and American Culture* 7: 247–69.

Wright, Marcia. 1968. "Local Roots of Policy in German East Africa." *Journal of African History* 9: 4.

Wuthnow, Robert. 1992. *Rediscovering the Sacred: An Essay on Public Religion.* Chicago: Univ. of Illinois Press.

Yacobi, Haim. 2003. "Everyday Life in Lod: On Power, Identity and Spatial Protest." *Jamaa* 10: 69–109.

Yalçınkaya, Mahfuz. 2004. "Kamusal Alan Dersi." [A lesson in public space.] *Vakit* (Istanbul) 12.

Yavuz, Hakan. 2003. *Islamic Political Identity in Turkey.* Oxford: Oxford Univ. Press.

Yavuz, Hakan, and John Esposito. 2003. "Islam in Turkey: Retreat from the Secular Path?" In *Turkish Islam and the Secular State,* edited by Hakan Yavuz and John Esposito, xiii–xxiii. New York: Syracuse Univ. Press.

Yeğnoğlu, Meyda. 1998. "Veiled Fantasies: Cultural and Sexual Difference." In *Postcolonial Feminist Reader,* edited by Reina Lewis and Sara Mills, 542–65. London: Routledge.

Yohn, Susan M. 1995. *Contest of Faiths: Missionary Women and Pluralism in the American Southwest.* Ithaca: Cornell Univ. Press.

Young, Iris Marion. 1998. "Polity and Group Difference: A Critique of the Ideal of Universal Citizenship." In *The Citizenship Debate,* edited by G. Shafir, 263–90. Minneapolis: Univ. of Minnesota Press.

Yuval-Davis, Nira. 2000. "Citizenship, Territoriality and Gendered Construction of Difference." In *Democracy, Citizenship and the Global City,* edited by E. Isin, 171–87. London: Routledge.

———. 2001. "Women, Citizenship and Difference." *Feminist Review* 57: 4–27.

Yuval-Davis, Nira, and F. Anthias, eds. 1989. *Women-Nation-State.* New York: St. Martin's Press.

Zamen. 2004. "Kamusal Alan Özgürlüğü Tanımlar Yasağı Değil." [Public space defines freedom, not prohibition).] *Zaman* (Istanbul) 1.

Zepp, Ira. 1997. *The New Religious Image of Urban America: The Shopping Mall as Ceremonial Center.* Boulder: Univ. Press of Colorado.

Zimmerman, Andrew. 2001. *Anthropology and Antihumanism in Imperial Germany.* Chicago: Univ. of Chicago Press.

Zührer, Erik. 1993. *Turkey: A Modern History.* London: I. B. Tauris.

Zwiep, Mary. 1991. *Pilgrim Path: The First Company of Women Missionaries to Hawaii.* Madison: Univ. of Wisconsin Press.

Index

Page numbers in *italic* type indicate photographs. Entries followed by (pseud.) indicate pseudonyms for interviewees.

dress (*cont.*)
158; semiotic approach to, 151–54; state
regulation of, xxv, 61, 154; as technology
of self, 154–55; of travelers in Pakistan,
81–97, 170n. 5, 170n. 13; western women
expatriates in Pakistan and, 96. *See also*
head coverings; *shalwar kameez;* veiling
dupatta, 95, 96–97, 100, 171n. 15
Dutch East India Company: colonization
in Indonesia, 24; control of Cape Town
society, 22, 38; racial policies of, 22–31,
37; relations with Khoikhoi, 25, 26–27
Dutch Reformed Church: apartheid and,
xxviii, 22–24; conversion of women of
color to Christianity, xxvii–xxviii, 22,
24, 25–26, 27; as denomination in South
African colony, 31; education of slaves
in South Africa, 27; Khoikhoi and, 26,
28–29, 32–33; racism and, 32–38; tenets
of, 24; unequal status of non-Europeans
in, 28–34
Dutch South Africa: conversion of women of
color to Christianity, xxvii–xxviii, 22, 24,
25–26, 27; division of colony from Cape
Town, 31; emergence of Afrikaner identity, 36; emergence of class-race-based
society, 31; establishment of colony, 25;
European settlement of, 29–34; racial policies in, 22–31; relations between Dutch
and Khoikhoi, 25, 26–27, 34–35; religion
as basis of racial domination, 33–34
Du Toit, André, 37
Dwyer, Claire, 128
Dyck, Isabel, 128

economic realm, 54, 129
education: of Dutch slave children, 25–26,
27; for female Korean immigrants, 134;
of Korean children, 172n. 4; missionar-

ies and, xxx, 125–26; Mount Holyoke
Female Seminary and, 120–21; in ultra-
orthodox Jewish communities, 47–48;
Ursuline nuns and, 116, 117
Eksteen, Hendrik, 35
election 2004 (U.S.), xiii–xv, xxxi
Elphick, Richard, 37
Elster, Jon, 129, 137
Entwistle, Joanne, 153
Erdoğan, Recep Tayyip, 72
eruv (erub), 52–53, 58–59, 164n. 9
Esposito, John, 167n. 15
Esra (veiled woman), 76, 77–78
ethnic churches, 127, 133–36, 144. *See also*
Christianity; Korean Presbyterianism
European Court of Human Rights (ECHR),
61
Europeans: black women in art of, 5;
colonialism (*see* Dutch South Africa;
German East Africa); culture wars, 5;
migration to South Africa, xxvii, 27, 31;
racism of, xxvii–xxviii, 24–25, 32–38;
ultraorthodox Judaism and, xxix, 44,
58; view of Africans, 7, 8, 10, 17; view of
religion, xv; view of 2004 U.S. election,
xiv. *See also* Germany
Eva (converted Khoikhoi), 26, 27–29
Evangelical feminists, 141
Evren, Kenan, 168n. 24

Falah, Ghazi-Walid, xxii, xxiii
family: husband as head of, 140–44; industrialization in Germany and, 7; Korean
ideology and mobility, 138–40; religious
unification of, 144–46
Felicity Party (Turkey), 72
female-only residences: convents, xx,
109–10, 112, 116, 118–19, 125; seminaries, xxx, 105, 110, 120–23, 125

female seminaries, xxx, 105, 110, 120–23, 125

Fenster, Tovi, xxviii, 41–60, 149, 152, 153, 156

Fessenden, Tracy, xxi

fez, 70

Forster, E. M., 89

Foucault, Michel: on bio-power, 19, 69; on power functions on bodies, 46, 49, 50; on seeing and being seen, 76

France, xxv

Fredrickson, Elke, 29

free burghers, 25, 27

freedom, 155

Galleria mall, 66–67, 76, 167nn. 16–17

gender beliefs, 130

gendered rights to the city, 56, 57–60

gendered spatial practices: cosmopolitan female travelers and, 97–100; creation/regulation of religious subjectivities, 158; as critical to creation/enactment of religious subjectivities, 151; dress and, 83, 85; driving in Los Angeles and, 139; of female Korean immigrants, 137–40; modesty walls and, 152; multiplicity of understandings of, 148–49; in Pakistan, 171n. 21; production of, 151; religion and, xxv–xxvi

gender roles: changes in for women, 4, 6–9, 11; Christianity and, 138; communal labor projects and, 11; in Korean families, 138–44

gender segregation: cosmopolitan female travelers and, 83, 97–100; in Mea Shearim, 50–52; at Muslim modern facilities, 73; in Pakistan, xxx, 82–83; in religious practice, xix–xx; in Turkish public spaces, 70, 168n. 27

gender socialization process, 130

General German Women's Association, 7

genocide, 10, 34, 106, 119

geography: developed by American female missionaries, 107–8, 122–23, 125; Mount Holyoke Female Seminary instruction, 122–23, 125; religious expressions and, xix; religious tensions and, xii–xvi, xvi; studies of gender, religion, and, xxi–xxiv

geopolitical scale, 113

German East Africa: anti-Arab prejudices in, 161n. 4; change in gender roles in, 6–9; Dervish circles in, xxvii, 3–4, 6, 10, 17–20, 21; establishment of colony, 5–6; geographic location and time of, 5; Maji-Maji rebellion, 10–12; Mecca letter, 12–16; mobility of women in, 4–5, 20–21, 162n. 9; Nama and Herero Wars, 10; response to Mecca letter, xxvii, 3, 6, 10, 12–16, 20–21, 162n. 6; suppression of Muslim women's organizations in, xxvii, 3–21; tribal government in, 162n. 7, 163n. 9

Germany: colonial tendencies of, 161n. 3; colonial wars of, 10–12; culture wars in, 5; gender roles in, 6–7; restriction of women's movements in, 162n. 7; search for national identity, 5; suppression of Muslim women's organizations by, xxvii, 3–21

Gerstner, Jonathan, 23, 28, 37–38

Giliomee, Hermann, 37–38

Ginzberg, Lori D., 109, 119

God's plan, 134–36

Gökarıksel, Banu, xxix, 61–80, 149, 151, 152, 153

Göle, Nilüfer, 70, 71

Gonen, Amiram, 45

government. *See* municipal government; state

Great Britain, 58

differences in dress of women, xxix; German repression of women and, 3–21; laicism in Turkey and, 65–66; Mecca letter and, 12–16; military coup in Turkey and, 71; multiple forms of, 148, 157; perceptions of modernity and, 86; political power in Turkey, 72–73; Rechenberg's division of groups of, 18; secularism in Istanbul and, xxix, 63; suppression of Muslim women's movements, xxvii, 3–21; whirling Dervishes of, 17–20, 21. *See also* gender segregation; *hijab;* seclusion; *tesettür;* veiling

Islamic fundamentalism, 65, 68, 168n. 25

Islamists: middle-class identity, 77–78, 79–80; objection to representations of Islam, xvi; rise of, 72, 167n. 14, 168n. 24

Islamist Welfare Party (Turkey), 67, 72, 168n. 25

Israel, 44, 46–47, 50, 57–58, 163n. 5. *See also* Jerusalem; Mea Shearim

Istanbul: class divisions in, 71, 74–76; construction of middle-class identity in, 76–78; reemergence of Islamic lifestyles, 72–73; secularism vs. traditional Islam in, xxix, 63; shopping malls in, 66–68, *68,* 152; understanding of rights in, 156; veiling practices in, 73–76, 165n. 3

Jackson, Robert, 13

Jang Un Lee (pseud.), 133

JDP (Justice and Development Party), 72, 168n. 26

Jerusalem: comfort of women in, 42, 44; conflicts in social, cultural, and political identity, 45; dress restrictions in sacred places, xxix, 48–53; gendered signs in, 48–53, *49, 51,* 57, 163n. 5; Mea Shearim community, 42, 44, 45, 46–53, *49, 51,*

152, 164n. 7; municipal government of, 47, 57; view of youth in, 164n. 8; views of public spaces in, 46–53

Jewel in the Crown (Scott), 89

Judaism: challenge to municipal authorities, 57; development of theology and practices of, xix; establishment of Mea Shearim, 46; gender segregation, 51; Hasidism, 163n. 4; multiplicity of understandings of, 149; municipal government and, 57–60; political power of, 163n. 3; primary arena of women in, xx; proper attire for women and, xxix, 42; Sabbath of, 45, 52–53, 164n. 9; separation of worshipers, xix–xx, xxv; tolerance toward secular groups, 164n. 6. *See also* Orthodox Judaism; ultraorthodox Judaism

Justice and Development Party (JDP), 72, 168n. 26

Kaahumanu (queen of Hawaii), xxiii–xxiv, xxv, xxvi

Kalden, Reverend Petros, 32–33

Karaduman, Mustafa, 169n. 28

Kemalism, 65–71, 167n. 14

Khoikhoi: disintegration of society of, 28, 34–35; Dutch Reformed Church and, 26, 28–29, 32–33; Dutch view of, 28–30; European settlement of lands of, 29–30, 33, 36; relationship with Dutch East India Company, 25, 26–27

Khoisan, 25, 33. *See also* Khoikhoi

Kim, Ai Ra, 128

Kim, Jung Ha, 130

King, John, 92

Kiryat Joel, New York, 47, 58

Kong, Lily, 63

Kopf, Jennifer, xxvii, 3–21, 149, 151–52

municipal government, 42–43, 55, 57–60

Murphy, Dervla, 89

Muslim Swahili culture, 5, 6

Muslim women: constructing as middle-
class subjects, 76–78; Dervish circles
and, xxvii, 3–4, 6, 10, 17, 19–20, 21;
Mecca letter and, xxvii, 3, 6, 10, 12–16,
20–21, 162n. 6; Orientalist representations of, 82–83; repression of movements in Tanzania, 3–21; Turkish
modernization and, 61, 64–65, 70–71,
73–78, 79, 165n. 3, 168n. 22, 168n. 25,
169n. 29; Westernization of, 7. See also
gender segregation; seclusion; veiling

Nagel, Caroline, xxii, xxiii

Nama War, 10

Nam-Hee Choi (pseud.), 135

nationalism, 172n. 1

national space, 153

nation-state building: American expansionism and, 107, 110–11, 123; formation of
Tanzania, 3–21; formation South Africa,
22–38; modernization of Turkey, 61–80

Native Americans, 107, 110–11, 117, 123

neocolonialism, xxx

neoliberalism, 78–79

New York, xxix, 58

9/11 terrorist attacks, xv, 44

nongovernmental organizations, 79, 169n. 29

nonreligious women, dress codes and, xxx,
81–101

Northern Areas (Pakistan), 87, 93, 96

nuns: administrative influence of, 119–20,
126; community work of, 118; convents
of, 109–10, 112, 116, 118–19, 126; dress
of, 106, 153; production of space, xxv; upscaling by, 119; Ursuline order, 116, 117

Nyerere, Julius, 10–12

Omari, Kadi, 16

Ong, Aihwa, 63–64

Orange Free State, 36

O'Reilly, Monsignor Bernard, 115

Orientalism (Said), 169n. 3, 170n. 4

Orientalist worldview: guidebooks and,
85–86, 100; organization of hierarchy,
87; representation of men, 88–90, 170n.
11; representation of women, 82–83;
veiling and, 94

Orthodox Judaism: political power of, 163n.
3; Sabbath of, 164n. 9; separation of
worshipers, xix–xx, xxv; women's dress
requirements, xxix, 42. See also Judaism;
ultraorthodox Judaism

Özal, Turgut, 66, 168n. 24

Özgür-Der, 169n. 29

Pakistan: appropriate dress/practices of
female travelers in, 81–101; diversity of
Muslim practices in, 82, 95, 96; dress
and mobility in, 81–97, 152; gender-
appropriate conduct in, xxx, 82–83,
170n. 13, 171n. 21; spatial practices
and travelers in, 97–100; view of
Lonely Planet guidebooks in, 170n.
12; view of western women's dress in,
171n. 19

Pakistan (King and Mayhew), 84–85, 88–89,
92, 98–99

Pakistan and the Karakoram Highway
(Singh et al.), 92

Passage to India (Forster and Lean), 89

patriarchy: of Bedouin culture, 56; challenges to, 130–31; female creation of
politics of scale and, xx, xxi, 114, 124–
25; in German East Africa, 8–9; Korean
immigrants and, 130–31, 140–44; of
Mea Shearim, xxix, 52; mission work

212 / Index

religion (*cont.*)
mobility and, 138–41; impact on mobility of female travelers, 83, 97–101; influence on lifestyle, 130; Kemalism and, 65;
limitation of capabilities and, 128–29; as
mode of subjection, 151, 152, 154–55;
modernization and, 70; multiplicity of
understandings of, 148–49; populism
in Turkey and, 71–73; production of
scale, 109–13; racism and, 29, 32–38; the
state and, 150–52; study of gender and
geography and, xxi–xxiv; unification of
the family, 144–46; as way of holding
oneself in the world, 148, 150, 151, 156,
157; women's spaces and, xxvi–xxvii;
women's sphere of activities and, xxvi.
See also Christianity; Confucianism;
Hinduism; Islam; Judaism
Religion, Dress, and Body (Arthur), 153
religious organizations, 119
religious space, 62
religious women's geography, 107–8,
122–23, 125
reorientation, 54
Republican Party (U.S.), xiii
rescaling, xxvi–xxvii, 54, 113, 119
research sources: on Istanbul malls, 166nn.
8–9; on Jerusalem and London residents, 41–42; on Korean immigrants
in United States, 128–29, 131–33; on
modernity in Turkey, 64; on travelers in
Pakistan, 84, 90, 170n. 7
reterritorialization, 54
Retief, Piet, 36
Riggs, Mary Ann, 107, 109
rights: of citizenship and consumerism,
77–78; concept of, 155–57; dress and
citizenship rights, 43, 79; of individual
vs. group right to difference, 54–55,
172n. 4; right to difference, 44–46,

52–60, 95; of U.S. First Amendment, xvi;
of widows in South Africa, xxviii, 32, 35;
of women to own property, xx–xxi, xxiv,
xxv, xxvi, 32, 35, 109–10, 117, 119. *See
also* right to the city
right to difference, 44, 52–56, 57–60, 95
right to the city: components of, 43–44,
54; definition of in Mea Shearim, 42;
individual rights vs. group differences,
44–45; for Muslim women in France,
xxv; politics of the body and, 42–46;
right to difference and, 52–60
Roman Catholic Church: community
work of, 109; convents of, xx, xxv, 110,
112, 116, 118–19, 126; culture wars in
Germany and, 5; gender separation
of orders, xix; home shrines and, 115;
lifestyle of nuns, xxiii, 109–10; Ursuline
nuns, 116, 117
Rose, Nikolas, 155
Ross, Robert, 37, 38

Sabbath, 45, 52–53, 58–59, 164n. 9
sacralization of public spaces, 42, 46–53,
55–56, 57–60
sacred places: Christian home as, 115–16;
Mea Shearim as, 42, 46–53, 57; right to
the city and, 44
Said, Edward W., 83, 169n. 3
Saktanber, Ayşe, 168n. 22
Salvation Army, 115
Sami, Şemesettin, 167n. 19
San, 25, 33, 34, 36
Satmar, 47, 163n. 4
Sayyid, Bobby, 157
scale: production of, xxvi–xxvii, 109–13,
120–23; of secular spaces, 62; women's
negotiation of, 105–6
Scott, Paul, 89

xiii–xiv; limitations on right to the city in, 44; missionary women in, 105–26; response to 9/11 attacks, xv, 44; shopping mall development in, 166n. 11; treatment of Native Americans, 107, 110–11, 117, 123; ultraorthodox Jewish communities in, xxix, 47, 58; view of religion in, xv

upscaling, xxvi–xxvii, 113, 119

urbanization (Germany), 5

urban management, 42–43, 55–59

urban space: definitions of, xxviii–xxix; geographic differences in dress of women, xxix–xxx, 42–60; right to the city and, 43–46; sacralization of, 42, 44, 46–53, 57–60

Ursuline nuns, 116, 117

Utah, xxvi, 44, 171n. 2

Vakko scarves, 77, 169n. 28

Valentine, Gill, xxix

Valins, Oliver, 59

Van Gogh, Theo, xvi

Van Reede, Adrian, 30–31

Van Riebeeck, Jan, 25, 26

veiling: access to public areas and, xv–xvi; ban in France, xxv; ban in Turkey, 61, 71; contestation of public space and, 61–80, 83, 85, 93, 97–101; cosmopolitan female travelers in Pakistan and, 94–97; diversity of practices, 94–95; lack of fashion stores in Turkish malls, 68–69; modernization in Turkey and, 64–65, 70–71, 165n. 3, 168n. 25; motivations for, 170n. 5; NGO's focusing on, 79, 169n. 29; perceptions of in Turkey, 73–78; restriction of behaviors and spaces by, 74, 168n. 22; *tesettür,* 68–69, 75, 76–77, 79, 167n. 19; *türban,* 65,

73–74; Vakko scarves and, 77, 169n. 28; various readings of, 151; Western debates over, xxiv. *See also dupatta;* head coverings; *hijab*

vernacular modernity, 167n. 15

Versailles Treaty, 5

Viljoen, Russell, 35

Voortrekkers, 36, 37

voting patterns: of ultraorthodox Jews, 47, 163n. 3; of women in the United States, xiv–xv, xxxi

Welfare Party, 72

Wendt (district officer), 12, 14–15, 16

Westernization, 7, 64–70

whirling Dervishes. *See* Dervish circles

Wildenthal, Lora, 9, 13–14

women: affirmation of identity, 96; "bikini bourka" and, xvi; as central to construction of spaces, 61; changing roles in Germany, 7; conversion of in Dutch South Africa, 22, 25–26; Dervish influences and, 3–4, 17, 19–20; dress requirements in Mea Shearim, 42; empowerment in margins, 105–26, 127–47; enlargement of religious sphere, xx–xxi; evangelical work of, xxiii–xxiv, xxvi–xxvii, xxx–xxxi, 105–11; geography and appropriate dress, xxix–xxx; German concepts of sexuality, 7–8; Mecca letter and, 3, 13–14, 20–21; memsahibs, 88; migration into South Africa, 27, 30; as missionaries, xxiii, xxx–xxxi, 106–11; mobility and religion, xxiii–xxiv; new Muslim woman, 73; in Pakistan, 171n. 17; prescribed dress for Jewish women, 48, 50; production of scale by, 109–13; production of space by, xxxi; religious experiences of, xix–xx; religious influences on voting of,